D0190001

TELL
TO
WIN

ALSO BY PETER GUBER

Shoot Out: Surviving Fame and
(Mis) Fortune in Hollywood

Inside the Deep

BRISTOL CITY COUNCIL	
1803118193	
Bertrams	23/05/2011
650.1	£12.99
BSAR	

TELL
TO
WIN

Connect, Persuade, and Triumph
with the Hidden Power of Story

PETER GUBER

P

PROFILE BOOKS

First published in Great Britain in 2011 by
PROFILE BOOKS LTD
3A Exmouth House
Pine Street
London EC1R 0JH
www.profilebooks.com

First published in the United States of America in 2011 by
Crown Publishing Group, a division of Random House, Inc.

Copyright © Peter Guber, 2011

1 3 5 7 9 10 8 6 4 2

Printed and bound in Great Britain by
Clays, Bungay, Suffolk

Book design by Maria Elias
Jacket design by David Tran

The moral right of the author has been asserted.

All rights reserved. Without limiting the rights under copyright reserved above, no part of this publication may be reproduced, stored or introduced into a retrieval system, or transmitted, in any form or by any means (electronic, mechanical, photocopying, recording or otherwise), without the prior written permission of both the copyright owner and the publisher of this book.

A CIP catalogue record for this book is available from the British Library.

ISBN 978 1 84668 556 9
eISBN 978 1 84765 776 3

The paper this book is printed on is certified by the © 1996 Forest Stewardship Council A.C. (FSC). It is ancient-forest friendly. The printer holds FSC chain of custody SGS-COC-2061

FSC
Mixed Sources
Product group from well-managed
forests and other controlled sources
Cert no. SGS-COC-2061
www.fsc.org
© 1996 Forest Stewardship Council

CONTENTS

CONTENTS

THE END . . .

LET ME GIVE AWAY THE ENDING OF THIS BOOK . . .

There's treasure to be discovered, and it's inside you. Built into your DNA is humanity's ten-thousand-plus years of telling and listening to oral stories. This veneration of story is a force so powerful and enduring that it has shaped cultures, religions, whole civilizations. Now, through telling to win, you can harness this force to achieve your most cherished goals.

It was by telling *many* purposeful stories, face-to-face, over the course of a long career—sometimes unconsciously—that I discovered this secret to success. In this book my mission is to be your catalyst, coach, and champion, passing along tools and techniques gleaned not just from my own experiences, but from soliciting the wisdom of people I consider master tellers. I will take you backward and forward through my career and demonstrate how, properly used, these skills have the potential to *immediately* change your life.

For too long the business world has ignored or belittled the power of oral narrative, preferring soulless PowerPoint slides, facts, figures, and data. But as the noise level of modern life has become a cacophony, the ability to tell a purposeful story that can truly be *heard* is increasingly in demand. Moreover, in this age of acute economic uncertainty and rapid technological change, it's not the 0's and 1's of the digital revolution, but rather the oohs and aahs of telling to win that offer the best chance of overcoming fear or compelling listeners to act on behalf of a worthy goal.

As I look back on my four decades in business, I see that persuading customers, employees, shareholders, media, and partners through telling to win has been my single biggest competitive advantage. And I dedicate this book to making it yours.

VOICES

Oscar Goodman, mayor of Las Vegas

Richard Bangs, founding member of the executive team of Expedia.com

Robert Rosen, professor and former dean, UCLA School of Theater, Film and Television

Dr. Dan Siegel, neuroscientist, codirector of UCLA's Mindsight Institute

Susan Feniger, restaurateur, Border Grill, Ciudad, and Street, and costar of the Food Network's *Too Hot Tamales*

Stacey Snider, cochairman and CEO, DreamWorks Studios

Michael Jackson, iconic entertainer

Charles Collier, president and general manager AMC Network

Steve Denning, consultant, former director of knowledge management at the World Bank, and author of *The Leader's Guide to Storytelling*

Magic Johnson, NBA all-star, chairman and CEO of Magic Johnson Enterprises

Ken Lombard, president and partner, Capri Capital Partners; formerly cofounder and partner/president, Johnson Development Corp., and past president of Starbucks Entertainment

Chad Hurley, CEO and cofounder, YouTube

Chris Anderson, editor in chief, *Wired* magazine, and author of *Free* and *The Long Tail*

Gentry Lee, chief engineer, solar system exploration, Jet Propulsion Laboratory

Dr. Marco Iacobani, professor, Department of Psychiatry and Biobehavioral Sciences, and director, Transcranial Magnetic Stimulation Lab, Ahmanson-Lovelace Brain Mapping Center, David Geffen School of Medicine, UCLA

Michael Wesch, associate professor of cultural anthropology, Kansas State University; U.S. professor of the year 2008; and *National Geographic* emerging explorer 2009

Richard Rosenblatt, chairman, CEO, and cofounder, Demand Media, and former chairman, MySpace.com

Wolfgang Puck, restaurateur, Spago, Cut, and Chinois; entrepreneur; and chef

Norma Kamali, president, owner, and designer, OMO (On My Own)

King Bhumibol Adulyadej, king of Thailand

Norio Ohga, former CEO, Sony Corporation

Deepak Chopra, MD, best-selling author, endocrinologist, and founder of the Chopra Center for Wellbeing

John Paul Dejoria, cofounder, chairman, and CEO, John Paul Mitchell Systems; cofounder and chairman, Patrón Spirits Company; and cofounder and chairman, John Paul Pet

Gene Simmons, rock legend, KISS

Alice Walker, Pulitzer Prize–winning author, *The Color Purple*

Scott Sanders, president and CEO, Scott Sanders Productions, and coproducer, Tony Award–winning musical *The Color Purple*

Larry King, host, *Larry King Live*

David Begelman, former chairman, Columbia Pictures

William D. Simon (Bill), global managing partner, media and entertainment, Korn/Ferry International

Teri Schwartz, dean, UCLA School of Theater, Film and Television

Lynda Resnick, vice chairman, Roll International, and co-owner and marketing entrepreneur behind Teleflora, POM Wonderful, FIJI Water, Wonderful Pistachios, and Cuties

Pat Riley, NBA Championship coach and president, Miami Heat

Rob Pardo, executive vice president of game design, Blizzard Entertainment

Wally Amos, founder, Famous Amos Cookies

Nelson Mandela, former president of South Africa

Jodi Guber, entrepreneur, designer, and founder, i am BEYOND

Dr. Robert Maloney, famed LASIK surgeon, Maloney Vision Institute

Gareb Shamus, chairman and CEO, Wizard Entertainment Group, and cofounder, geekchicdaily.com

Tim Burton, film director, *Alice in Wonderland, Batman, Beetle Juice*

Michael Milken, financier, philanthropist, and chairman, the Milken Institute

Jason Binn, CEO and founder, Niche Media

Bill Clinton, forty-second President of the United States

Bob Dickman, coauthor, *The Elements of Persuasion: Use Storytelling to Pitch Better, Sell Faster & Win More Business,* and founder, FIRSTVOICE

Barry Levinson, Academy Award–winning director, *Rain Man*

Tom Cruise, actor and producer, United Artists

The 14th Dalai Lama, Tibetan spiritual leader

Bill Haber, founder, CAA; president, Save the Children and Ostar

Kevin Plank, founder and CEO, Under Armour

Peter Lowy, managing director, Westfield Group

Tina Sinatra, board of directors, Frank Sinatra Enterprises

George Lopez, actor, comedian, and producer

Arne Glimcher, founder of the Pace Gallery, filmmaker, and author

Jack Warner, founder, Warner Bros.

Dan Rosensweig, former CEO and president, Activision Blizzard's Guitar Hero franchise, and president and CEO, Chegg.com

Will Wright, creator and game designer of *The Sims* and *Spore* and CEO, Stupid Fun Club

Shirley Pomponi, PhD, executive director of Harbor Branch Oceanographic Institute at Florida Atlantic University

Nora Roberts, best-selling author and owner of Inn BoonsBoro

Bethany Hamilton, champion surfer

Kirk Kerkorian, entrepreneur and former owner of MGM

Anderson Cooper, veteran news journalist, CNN

Al Giddings, award-winning cinematographer, *The Deep, Titanic*

Mark Shapiro, former president and CEO, Six Flags, Inc., and former executive vice president, programming and production, ESPN, Inc.

Terry Semel, former chairman and CEO, Yahoo! and Warner Bros., and chairman and CEO, Windsor Media

Dr. George E. Marcus, professor of political science, Williams College

Jerry Weissman, founder, Power Presentations, Ltd.

Dr. Warren Bennis, distinguished professor of business administration, University of Southern California

Mark Burnett, Emmy Award–winning producer, *Survivor, The Apprentice, Are You Smarter Than a 5th Grader?, The MTV Awards*

Keith Ferrazzi, professional relationship expert, author of *Never Eat Alone* and *Who's Got Your Back,* and CEO and founder, Ferrazzi Greenlight

Steve Tisch, co-owner, New York Giants; winner of the Vince Lombardi Trophy; Academy Award–winning producer, *Forrest Gump;* and partner, Escape Artists

Mark Victor Hansen, coauthor, *Chicken Soup for the Soul* series

Ned Tanen, former president, Universal Pictures

David Copperfield, renowned magician

Carl Sagan, astrophysicist, Pulitzer Prize–winning author, and advisor to NASA

Muhammad Ali, world heavyweight champion boxer

Susan R. Estrich, professor, USC Gould School of Law; first woman to manage a presidential campaign; lawyer; and commentator for Fox News

Tony Robbins, renowned life strategist, author, and turnaround expert

Fidel Castro, former president of Cuba

Curtis Hanson, Academy Award–winning writer-director, *L.A. Confidential*

Rob Quish, COO, JWT North America, and CEO, JWT inside

Steven Spielberg, renowned filmmaker and co-chair, DreamWorks Studios; Academy Award–winning director and producer

Sidney Poitier, director and Academy Award–winning actor

Nancy Traversy, owner and CEO, Barefoot Books

Bert Jacobs and **John Jacobs,** cofounders, Life is good product line

Tom Werner, chairman, Boston Red Sox; cofounder, Carsey-Werner Company; and owner, Good Humor TV

Bran Ferren, cofounder, Applied Minds, and former president, research and development, Walt Disney Imagineering

Brian Solis, digital analyst, sociologist, and futurist publisher at BrianSolis.com.

Chris Kemp, chief technology officer, NASA

Arianna Huffington, cofounder and editor in chief, The Huffington Post

Phil McKinney, VP and chief technology officer, Hewlett-Packard Company

PART ONE

THERE'S NO BUSINESS WITHOUT STORY BUSINESS

WHY TELLING TO WIN IS YOUR ULTIMATE SUCCESS TOOL

CHAPTER ONE

It's the Story, Stupid

The boom in Vegas was our golden ticket. This thought propelled me up the Strip to meet with the city's political gatekeeper, Mayor Oscar Goodman. As chairman of Mandalay Entertainment Group, I was determined to ride the momentum that had turned Sin City family-friendly. So many new residents had been drawn to Las Vegas in the early 2000s that the construction crane was laughingly referred to as the city's official bird, and all this wholesome expansion virtually guaranteed the business home run that I was about to deliver for my company's professional baseball division.

Our proposition: to build the ultimate state-of-the-art ballpark in the entertainment capital of the world. Our agenda: to elevate our sports entertainment business onto the national stage. Our success hinged on my ability to persuade Las Vegas's chief politician to lead the campaign for a municipal bond to fund this multimillion-dollar civic project. But since this huge, iconic city currently had *no* quality professional stadium, let alone the kind of cutting-edge venue that was Mandalay's specialty, my proposal had to be a no-brainer for the mayor. Or so I thought.

Mandalay Baseball at the time owned five professional minor-league franchises across the country, including Single-A, Double-A, and Triple-A teams, and our partners included basketball superstar Magic Johnson; Heisman Trophy–winner Archie Griffin; and Tom Hicks, owner of the Texas Rangers. There's nothing minor about the business of the minor leagues, which attract more than 40 million fans each year, and our profits validated that. We had an established track record of attracting public money, winning local support, and building top-of-the-line stadiums. Recently we'd acquired the Las Vegas Triple-A franchise of the legendary LA Dodgers. Now we wanted to elevate this franchise by moving its location from Cashman Field, the outdated university ballpark where it currently played, and building the twenty-first-century world-class stadium that Las Vegas's home team so richly deserved. As I arrived at the mayor's headquarters, I thought, *OK, let's play ball!*

Even though I was late, the mayor made me wait. Goodman was a shrewd wielder of power. The decor of his anteroom let you know you were dealing with somebody in show business—he showed you his business wherever you looked, from the replica of the iconic Las Vegas sign that read, WELCOME TO FABULOUS MAYOR GOODMAN'S OFFICE, to the glass display cases crammed with more awards and tchotchkes than I could count. There were photos of Goodman with everyone from President Bill Clinton to Michael Jackson and actors Tony Curtis and Steven Seagal. I even noticed a pair of Muhammad Ali's boxing gloves.

Every detail of that office screamed, *Major League!* If only I'd paid attention.

Finally the mayor was ready for me. But before I could get a word out, he peppered me with talk about the movies I'd produced, executive produced, or supervised, especially the two—*Rain Man* and *Bugsy*—that were made in Vegas. He asked if I had any plans to make another film in his fair city. Then he quoted the box office numbers that had lifted *Batman* into the stratosphere. I took all this foreplay as proof that Goodman was the perfect audience for my perfect pitch.

I told him I'd come to deliver box office success for Vegas—this time not through movies but through baseball. As proof, I reeled off the data that I was sure would mesmerize him: figures proving Mandalay kept design and construction costs down, quality up, and completion on schedule. Our most recent stadium, built for our Single-A Cincinnati Reds team in Dayton, Ohio, featured amenities such as upper-deck seating and luxury suites, making it unique among minor-league ballparks at the time.

I gestured toward the window view of cranes marching across the desert. "All those new hometown fans in Las Vegas deserve a legacy team and ballpark of their own."

The mayor considered this statement. Then he asked, "Can you deliver a major-league team here?"

Had someone dubbed the word "major" into his mouth? He'd stopped listening the instant I said "minor-league," but I was so caught up in my facts and figures that I thought he was just confused. "This is professional baseball, all major-league affiliates," I assured him. "You'll be able to ride on the back of the most storied team in pro history—the Los Angeles Dodgers."

He shook his head. "We're overdue for something really, really big."

"What I'm proposing is huge," I insisted. "In the years since our stadium opened in Dayton, we've sold out *every single game*. That's an unprecedented phenomenon. And we intend to surpass it here."

Goodman shot me a cold squint. "This ain't Dayton, kiddo."

Even though I met with the mayor several more times, bringing him to my home in Los Angeles and presenting him with several more decks of killer data, my efforts only proved that you never get a second chance to make a first impression. And I never even made it to first base with my "guaranteed" home run.

This failure haunted me. How had I managed so decisively to turn our winning odds to a loss in Vegas? The metrics certainly weren't to blame. Not long after striking out with Goodman, a car dealer out of Detroit named Derek Stevens attended a game at Cashman Field and was excited by exactly the same vision we'd had, that of building Las

Vegas a professional ballpark. Good luck! We sold him our Las Vegas Triple-A franchise for a then record price, making a handsome profit for Mandalay. But my business goal had been to turn Vegas into the engine that would lift our company to the next level. The economic windfall was little consolation. I'd lost the game I came to play.

Failure, however, is an inevitable cul de sac on the road to success. As we began crafting a new strategy, one of my Mandalay colleagues remarked, "We'll have to change our story."

And that's when the lightbulb turned on: *Ahha! You forgot to tell a story, stupid!*

I'd thrown a powerful barrage of raw facts at Goodman—data, statistics, records, forecasts—but I didn't organize them in any way to engage his *emotions*. No wonder he hadn't swung at my offering!

"Stupid" was right. I'm in the entertainment business! If anybody should know the strategic difference between a data dump and a winning story, I should. I'd produced dozens of films and television programs. Before starting Mandalay, I'd been studio chief at Columbia Pictures, co-chairman of Casablanca Record and Filmworks, CEO of Polygram Pictures, and chairman and CEO of Sony Pictures Entertainment. My core business was telling stories to move people! Furthermore, as a full professor in the UCLA School of Theater, Film and Television, I'd taught just about every possible aspect of this business to graduate students of film, business, and law, and the number one lesson was to distinguish a data dump from a well-told story. How many times had I pounded into them all the things that stories are *not*? Stories are *not* lists, decks, Power-Points, flip charts, lectures, pleas, instructions, regulations, manifestos, calculations, lesson plans, threats, statistics, evidence, orders, or raw facts. While virtually every form of human communication can *contain* stories, most conversations and speeches are not, in and of themselves, stories.

What's the essential difference? Non-stories may provide information, but stories have a unique power to move people's hearts, minds, feet, and wallets in the story teller's intended direction. Come to think of it, if it hadn't been for the *story* I told to move my listeners in Dayton, I wouldn't even have had all those metrics to prove Mandalay's process to Goodman!

Initially, Dayton had seemed as much of a long shot as Vegas had seemed a sure bet. Ohio's media had suggested that the rundown city center was an irredeemable blight on the landscape and not worth a dime of investment. Few of Dayton's officials thought suburban fans would venture downtown after dark, and the urban dwellers supposedly couldn't afford the luxury of a ball game. Besides, the press insinuated, those two cultures would never mix. But we shaped the perfect story to turn those attitudes around.

We told them the core tale of *Field of Dreams,* in which Kevin Costner's character, Ray Kinsella, was perceived as out of his mind for building a ballpark in the middle of a cornfield. Instantly, I had their attention. Then I ignited their imagination by portraying our new stadium as the catalyst for a rebirth of the city's center. "If we build it," I told them, "they will come."

Our story had even the naysayers believing that our stadium really might bring commerce back into the downtown area. Together we really could create the kind of wholesome family entertainment experience that was Mandalay's specialty. And if we succeeded, this would give the city a unique new story and brand.

We told the same story—that we were building a real-life Field of Dreams—to persuade Magic Johnson and Archie Griffin to invest in the project. Then we kept telling the story together until Dayton's civic leaders sponsored a municipal bond just like the one I'd needed in Vegas.

It would have taken a totally different story, of course, to drive home our Vegas proposition to Oscar Goodman. Although I failed to realize it at the time, Vegas was beginning to shift its brand from a family-friendly city, for which family-friendly baseball was a perfect fit, to "what happens in Vegas stays in Vegas." So even if I'd realized my story could be a game-changer, I'd have had to tell Goodman a tale that delivered the majors with an R rating! Sadly, I never told him *any* story, let alone the right one! Of all people, I should have known better, and yet I still defaulted to the standard operating procedure of American business, relying solely on talking points and financial models. The numbers were so good, how could Mayor Goodman fail to be wowed?

He didn't fail. I did—several times over. I failed to grasp my audience's interests. I failed to listen to my audience. And I failed to tell him a story. How could I have been so clueless?

I wondered . . . Could the reason be that I'd aimed for Goodman's head and wallet instead of his heart? In the movie business this would be strategic suicide. Miss the audience's heart as a filmmaker, and the only wallet that gets hit will be your own. That's because the heart is *always* the first target in story telling. But my Vegas strikeout suggested that this rule went beyond show business. What if reaching the audience's heart was critical to winning in *every* business?

COULD TELLING TO WIN BE *YOUR* GAME-CHANGER?

In my life I've experienced tremendous success across diverse ventures and industries, but I've also had a boatload of professional tip-overs, economic mishaps, managerial disasters, and creative flops. I've backed products that left my bank account empty and my garage full of unsold inventory. I've started music companies that were off-tune and bought the Las Vegas Thunder, a pro hockey team that then went on to a five-year profit-losing streak with an audience that didn't give a puck. My movies weren't all boffo, either. Folks tried to walk out on *The Bonfire of the Vanities* even when it was shown on planes, and I certainly had my ups and downs at Sony. These losses were financially and emotionally painful— and often highly public. And my many successes only made the failures that much more confounding. For years I wondered, was I ruled by dumb luck? Or was there a game-changer that would enlarge my target, sharpen my trajectory, accelerate my momentum, and shorten the distance to my goal? Wouldn't it be terrific if this game-changer also increased the joy of the enterprise? If somebody invented a technology that accomplished all this, they'd make a fortune!

After my loss in Vegas, it occurred to me that everybody in business shares one universal problem: To succeed, you have to persuade others to support your vision, dream, or cause. Whether you want to motivate your executives, organize your shareholders, shape your media, engage your customers, win over investors, or land a job, you have to deliver a clarion call that will get your listeners' attention, emotionalize your goal as theirs, and move them to act in your favor. You have to reach their hearts as well as their minds—and this is just what story telling does!

What if purposeful story telling was the game-changer I'd been looking for all along?

I'd taught for more than thirty years that stories teach, model, unite, and motivate by transporting audiences emotionally. Many of my films, including *Rain Man, Gorillas in the Mist,* and *Midnight Express,* delivered purposeful calls to action that went far beyond entertainment. Because audience members were emotionally moved by each film's central message, they passed that message on to others by telling and retelling the story of their own experience of the film. And that word of mouth moved millions more as the story traveled orally around the globe. Each of these retellings extended the reach and impact of the original story, but each new teller also turned that story into something new and different by adding his or her own emotion to it—proof that you don't have to be a professional to tell a moving story. Anyone can do it, and everyone does do it!

I got more and more excited as I began to see telling to win as the secret sauce for success. You don't need a special degree to tell the story of your company, brand, or offering and make it a powerful call to action. You don't need money or privilege. This really is a vital skill that's freely available to anyone! Moreover, telling stories is a source of joy as well as success. It's like a guilty pleasure that's also lucrative. What could be better?

But if this was so, how could I possibly have failed to see the strategic importance of telling to win before in my career? Or had I? Was it possible I'd benefited from this art without even realizing it? Suddenly I felt as if lightning had struck.

IT WAS THE EARLY 1990s. I'd been named CEO of Sony's then-recent acquisition, Columbia Pictures Entertainment. This multibillion-dollar global media conglomerate was a later incarnation of Columbia Pictures, where I'd served as studio chief twenty years earlier, so at first this new job felt like a homecoming. But it wasn't long before I realized the company had lost its center.

For years before Sony came along, Columbia had been in the going-out-of-business business, with all divisions greased and oiled for sale to the highest bidder. Although the biggest revenue generator in the film industry at the time was video, Columbia and TriStar's video distribution had been sold to RCA, which was then acquired by General Electric before my arrival. The loss of that asset was a drag on company morale and productivity. And there was no unified direction or vision connecting the various surviving divisions. The assets of Sony's acquisition included two film studios (TriStar and Columbia Pictures), global television operations, and the Loews theater circuit. Its executives were spread among rental facilities from coast to coast, with the studio's production and management teams occupying the once-great but now dilapidated MGM lot. The lion on the sign at an adjacent building MGM still owned seemed to be pondering our future.

Not only were our new Japanese owners 7,000 miles and a major culture gap away, but recent history had shown that any time a foreign corporation such as Sony bought an American entertainment enterprise, the For Sale sign was bound to go up again before long. With our revenues in free fall, many of Columbia's veteran executives had taken their profits as shareholders from the sale to Sony and were now looking for more robust opportunities elsewhere. Since Columbia was no longer public, we couldn't even offer stock to incentivize them to stay. My only prayer of succeeding was to find some other, more creative way to persuade *both* Sony and the disparate, disgruntled but talented band of executives I'd inherited to unite and play for the future. But how?

This was the question consuming me when I was summoned to the phone late one afternoon from a financial PowerPoint presentation in the bowels of the historic Thalberg Building (named, of course, for Irving Thalberg, the hugely successful MGM studio chief of the 1920s and '30s). These were pre–cell phone days, and the nearest telephone was in a basement storage room, but since the call was from my Japanese colleagues, I settled in for the duration. Unable to concentrate on the halting Japanese-English discussion, I was flipping distractedly through some framed movie stills stacked against the wall when suddenly a photograph of Peter O'Toole in a flowing white robe caught my attention. I recognized the image from one of Columbia Pictures' most cherished films, *Lawrence of Arabia*. In the scene, Lawrence was pondering an eerily familiar challenge: *How do you unite a disparate group to fight for their future when none believe they can or should work together?*

O'Toole's character, T. E. Lawrence, was a British military officer and expert in Arab affairs during the early 1900s, when Britain's rival, the Turkish Ottoman Empire, ruled Arabia. Lawrence realized that the only way to expel the Turks from the region was by uniting the Arab tribes against them. But the tribes all had different values, beliefs, and rules. And Lawrence, as the representative of another foreign empire, was considered suspect. The Brits in Arabia at the time were the equivalent of the Japanese in Culver City—tolerated but hardly understood. Nevertheless, Lawrence believed that if he could convince the tribes of their own power to achieve the impossible by acting together, they would unite as one. His epiphany: *"Aqaba!"*

Aqaba, the heavily fortified port city at the tip of the Arabian Peninsula, was protected on the north by the seemingly impassable Nefud Desert. Certain that they could never be attacked from the desert side, the Turks had fixed all their gun emplacements to face the Red Sea. But Lawrence's plan was to do the impossible: march across the desert to surprise the Turks from the rear. "I'll do it if you will," he challenged the tribal leaders.

And they did. By charging Aqaba's undefended back, they crushed the Turks and shared the gold and glory. The story of that miracle was then told and retold across Arabia and around the world, turning an obscure battle into an immortal legend. This magical tale of accomplishing the impossible became the catalyst for a new world order.

Could this be the answer I was searching for? I quickly concluded my phone call and screened the whole film. Yes! This story might be perfect to inspire the people of this company to reclaim its storied heritage and profitability.

I began by telling the Aqaba story to our employees at our huge annual Christmas party. I showed them that seminal picture of Lawrence and gave Lucite-framed copies of the photograph to selected executives as a reminder of our mission.

"This is who we are," I told them. "We're a disparate group of businesses but we're one tribe. We need to believe we can make the impossible possible."

As Columbia's new mantra, the story of Aqaba traveled virally among the employees. It helped reverse the organization's mind-set, reshape attitudes, and frame our collective state of the heart. Lawrence's story prompted our tribe to envision an integrated future that would engage Japanese resources and prevent their retreat.

Now I had to spur my audience to action, aligning hearts with feet and wallets. Story was the call to action, the game-changer, but this was just the beginning. We had to take this story and run with it—*on to Aqaba!*

Our first order of business was to establish a base of operations as tangibly significant as Aqaba had been for Lawrence's tribes. In keeping with Sony's mission to build a state-of-the-art entertainment and technology empire, we invested $100 million to convert and expand our dilapidated Culver City lot into a cutting-edge headquarters that would showcase Sony's full technological prowess and accommodate our entire tribe at a single location.

Then we raised the flag of unity. We bought that adjacent building, took down its leering MGM lion, and replaced it with Sony's insignia. This announced to all comers that Columbia and Sony were one. And since Sony's highly protective Japanese board never would include us under their globally renowned brand unless they considered us part of *their* tribe, the display of this logo also secured our new owners' commitment to our employees. The executive exodus reversed. Soon we'd persuaded Sony to rename the company Sony Pictures Entertainment. We bought back the video library from Jack Welch's GE and placed the Sony trademark as a unifying imprimatur on each video—and everything else we owned or produced. And by integrating Sony's cutting-edge SDDS sound and IMAX systems into gleaming new multiplexes in New York City, Chicago, and San Francisco, we gave our fading Loews exhibition circuit a radically successful makeover as Sony Theaters.

With the tribe now pulling together, our studios began to accomplish the impossible, releasing a string of hits that included *Philadelphia, Sleepless in Seattle, Terminator 2, Groundhog Day, A Few Good Men, A League of Their Own, Boyz n the Hood,* and *Awakenings*. Columbia and TriStar's films received more than one hundred Oscar nominations, the highest four-year total for a studio in film history at that time, and in 1991 earned an industry best domestic box office market share.

The net result of all these changes is that, while Sony's rival Matsushita controlled our Hollywood competitor Universal Pictures for only five years before pulling out, Sony has stayed the course. Though I left in 1995, having faced both success and failure, Sony Pictures Entertainment today has morphed into an American company with its world headquarters still in New York City and a non-Japanese CEO, Howard Stringer. It generates annual sales of more than $7 billion, and its motion picture library of more than 3,500 films continues to grow.

As we made our incredible journey, I would check in regularly with the executives who'd come together to achieve our Aqaba-like victory. There in their offices, among the pictures of their families, sat the photo of O'Toole as Lawrence of Arabia. There was no doubt that this story shaped the direction of our company. How? By moving every member of our tribe to *feel*—and therefore believe—that by pulling together we all could gain in security, opportunity, achievement, and pride.

I REALIZED IN RETROSPECT that my experience at Sony demonstrated that the face-to-face telling of the right story in the right room at the right time and in the right way can galvanize listeners to action and reset the teller's success trajectory. That should have made me an apostle for the art of purposeful story telling twenty years ago! Yet throughout the first two acts of my career I'd generally succumbed to our culture's dominant assumption that hard business decisions are governed exclusively by numbers, tactics, concepts, raw data—"hard stuff." Only now, in my third act—as I considered Aqaba in light of the role that purposeful oral story telling had played in Dayton, and in Vegas by its absence—had I gained the perspective to become a believer.

Still, I needed more evidence than these few experiences. Had my friends and colleagues also found telling to win to be a game-changer? Was this tool of person-to-person story telling equally powerful across all industries? Were there perils to beware of? My mission was not to conduct a scientific study or write a linear account of my career. My interest was in discovery, not chronology. But I did want to see if the evidence supported my view of the power of oral story. And I wanted to decode the seminal elements of this power. Then other business professionals could benefit in their Acts I and II from what I was only learning in Act III.

I began by traveling backward and forward in time, searching for other stories I'd told in the course of my own career, and scrutinizing the reasons and ways they had or hadn't worked to leverage success. I also reviewed the stories that others had told to instruct, persuade, or motivate me. How and why had they been effective? What had given these stories their power? What could I learn from these recollections?

I was stunned to discover how clearly I still remembered these stories, in some cases after forty or more years! The precise dates and circumstantial details may have blurred in my memory, but the stories themselves remain resonant, clear, and actionable. That alone is a tribute to telling to win!

Next I turned to other business leaders—especially those *outside* the entertainment business—to find out how my epiphany resonated with them. My personal and professional network spans a wide variety of industries and academic fields, and includes many of the most successful people in America. So I began, like a detective, engaging friends and colleagues in conversation about the stories they'd personally told—or personally been told by others—that influenced their careers. I listened to their tales, asked what they thought had made these tellings resonant and actionable, and informally gathered their insights. I also hosted a series of conclaves at which experts in psychology, narrative medicine, and organizational story telling shared their research and perspectives. I invited these and other experts to my UCLA classes to speak to the following questions: Was purposeful story telling a vital success tool that many in business mistakenly ignored? If so, what were the keys to telling to win, and how were they best employed? Where exactly did the desire to tell and listen to stories come from anyway? And could telling to win help anyone to succeed, or did it take special talent?

If the answers to these questions showed I was right about the strategic power of oral narrative, then this game-changer was bound to make business a lot more fun, interesting, and rewarding—and a whole lot less painful. But there was one burning question that needed to be answered before any of the others . . . What exactly *is* a story?

aHHa!

- Move your listeners' hearts, and their feet and wallet will follow.
- Data dumps are not stories—dump them, don't tell them!
- Story isn't the icing on the cake, it *is* the cake.
- Don't leave home without it . . . your story, that is.

CHAPTER TWO

Got Story?

I had a problem: liability through death. Deep in the Grand Canyon, I was hosting a five-day river running trip for ten friends on the rapid-rich and ever-thrilling Colorado River, and the guys had become rambunctious on my watch. Among our all-male crew were type A powerhouses NFL Network president and CEO Steve Bornstein, Bear Stearns managing director Dennis Miller, Onex chairman and CEO Gerry Schwartz, Pierce Brosnan (aka James Bond), ESPN programming topper Mark Shapiro, New Line president Toby Emmerich, life strategist and author Tony Robbins, and rambunctious Joe Francis, who'd steered his career through the rapids of Girls Gone Wild. The entire group had spent the first two days throwing water bottles at one another, leaping from boat to boat, and generally ignoring our expedition guides. Five thousand feet below the rim of one of the world's seven natural wonders, they were having the time of their lives on the Big Wild Red, but I'd run the Red before. I knew what was coming, and the prospect of losing some of these lives was starting to feel like a clear and present danger.

Richard Bangs, one of the guests on the expedition, also had been eyeing the rowdier members of our group. Unlike all the neophytes in our boat, Richard was a serious adventurer. He'd led first descents of thirty-five rivers around the globe, including the Yangtze in China and the Zambezi in Southern Africa. He founded Sobek Expeditions, one of America's premier adventure travel companies, and in 1980 provided expert supervision during the highly dangerous river chase scenes in a movie we were producing called *The Pursuit of D. B. Cooper,* about the real-life hijacker who jumped out of a 727 with $200,000 in ransom money, never to be seen again. The chase through a river filled with rapids in that film put the actors Robert Duvall and Treat Williams, as well as their doubles, in serious risk, but Richard got everybody through safe. Now he told me, "We've got to get these guys to wise up. And soon."

Then, as we came ashore on the third day, Dennis cocked his ear to a muffled roar in the distance. "Listen," he said. "I didn't know trains ran through here!"

This was just the opening Richard had been looking for. "Let me show you this train." He led us up the side of the canyon to a precipice overlooking the infamous Lava Falls, a class 10 rapid and the source of the thunderous roar. The river here dropped thirty-seven feet in just a few hundred yards, making this the fiercest white water in the canyon. The locomotive roar made the group go dead silent, and then Steve Bornstein said, "I sorta wanna go home now"—only half joking.

"There's no way out but through," Richard said, and with that he had our full and sober attention. "Risk can be transformative, but only if you survive it."

Yes, that was just the thought that had been running loops in my own head. I was grateful when Richard volunteered, "I'm in the risk management business."

He continued, "The reason I named my adventure company after Sobek, the ancient deity that protects boats crossing the Nile, was this story. Listen!

"Three thousand years ago, the first king of Egypt—a notorious asshole—was screwing around during a hunting party and so pissed off his dogs that they turned on him. The pack chased him all the way to the

Nile, which was infested with crocodiles. One of these huge reptiles lay sunning itself on the bank. It offered to ferry the king across the river, and he was so desperate he agreed. To his surprise, the croc actually did take him safely across, but then his savior revealed that he was Sobek, the crocodile spirit. In return for saving the king's life, Sobek demanded some serious change. The king had to wise up and lead his people to treat the river and all its creatures with due respect. As long as the humans paid homage, their boats would be granted safe passage."

At this point in the story Richard glanced down at Lava Falls and grimly raised his voice. "Only once, about two thousand years later, did a military flotilla forget to appease Sobek. During that crossing the river claimed a thousand lives."

"So now there are crocs in the Colorado?" Pierce asked, attempting levity.

"No. But these falls will tear you to pieces just like the crocodiles if you don't respect them." Encoded in these words was the message that nature can be ferocious. To survive and advance, you need to honor the environment.

A hush fell over the group as we trudged back to camp. Bangs had delivered his message where it counted, and for the first time we worked together to plan the next day's strategy. We got to sleep early, and the next morning everyone was quiet and focused as we loaded in and began the slow drift toward the precipice.

Soon, with the increasing volume of the falls, our adrenaline began pumping. As we neared the edge, Gerry Schwartz yelled out, "OK, crocs, here we come!" And with that the rapids gripped us, yanking our three boats forward and down. We rowed in frantic unison to avoid the razor-sharp rocks to the right. The boats tipped up, nearly vertical, then slammed on their sides into a quiet eddy before plunging into the river-wide trough that shot us back out like a slingshot. An extra inch to the right would spell disaster, but we paddled and leaned together as if our lives depended on it—which we knew from Sobek they did!

Richard was absolutely right. The exhilaration was so intense that afterward, we all felt transformed. So it made sense when he told me the next afternoon that Mountain Travel, which merged with Richard's company in 1991, decided not only to keep Richard as a partner but also to keep the name Sobek. "The legend of Sobek was the game-changer in the deal," Richard said. "I wanted them to understand, I wasn't in the people transportation business, I was in the human transformation business. Telling them his story was the best possible way to get that across."

WHY IS *THAT* A PURPOSEFUL STORY?

Thinking back on that river trip five years later, I can still recall every beat of Richard's Sobek legend. I remember the way we all had to lean in to hear Richard over the noise of the falls, the way we hung on his words to find out what happened next. In retrospect, I realize our transformation actually began the moment he said "story." That word was like a bell that compelled us to listen up. We'd all been conditioned since childhood to expect that a story would deliver a mental reward, and this expectation held us captive.

But what exactly made the Sobek legend a "story"? Would it have qualified if Richard hadn't mentioned the king? If he'd delivered an hour-long discourse on crocodiles and Egyptian belief in deities or dissected Sobek's strategy for changing the king's behavior? Would it still have been a story if Sobek had been an ordinary croc that ate the king?

For answers, I turned to Robert Rosen, former dean of UCLA's School of Theater, Film and Television, who co-taught the course Navigating a Narrative World with me. "Stories put all the key facts into an emotional context," Rosen said. "The information in a story doesn't just sit there as it would in a logical proposition. Instead, it's built to create suspense." And the building blocks of all compelling stories, whether they're told in person, in the pages of a book, or via actors on a screen or monitor, are *challenge, struggle,* and *resolution.*

Here, then, is how you build a story:

- First . . . get your listeners' attention with an unexpected challenge or question.
- Next . . . give your listeners an emotional experience by narrating the struggle to overcome that challenge or to find the answer to the opening question.
- Finally . . . galvanize your listeners' response with an eye-opening resolution that calls *them* to action.

Applying this concept to the legend of Sobek, I realized that the story began with the challenge to the king's life that sent him in search of safety. The middle of the story forced him to struggle with three seemingly impossible choices—trusting a crocodile, throwing himself without any protection into the river, or facing his own bloodthirsty dogs. And the ending resolved the king's struggle by transforming him from the kind of guy who could piss off his own dogs, into an upstanding keeper of the river code, which his descendants would follow from that day forward.

Would the story have worked if the beginning, middle, and end had been rearranged? Filmmakers and writers often play around with the order in which information is revealed, sometimes to great effect. But I knew from my years in the movie business that they're skunked if they don't deliver the three-part *story-listening experience* that audiences seem instinctively to expect. Listeners are rarely hooked if they don't sense some compelling challenge in the beginning. They won't stay engaged if they're not excited by the struggle of the middle. And they won't remember or act on the story unless they feel galvanized by its final resolution.

The way Richard Bangs told us the legend of Sobek showed that stories don't have to be long or involved. But they do have to surprise us. The Sobek story first set us up to expect the king to fight his dogs, but instead he met up with a crocodile! Logically we'd expect the crocodile to eat him, but instead it offered protection! Then we'd expect either the king or the croc to trick the other, but instead, the spirit of man-eating crocodiles became man's new best friend—as long as due homage was paid!

Anybody who's ever read a novel or watched a movie knows that a story that fails to deliver surprise is dead on arrival. The same rule holds for stories told in person to business audiences. The shock value may be as subtle as a shrug or a pang of regret. Not every story needs thrills and chills, but without *some* surprise, you'll lose your listener's attention. Why? Figuring there had to be something in our brains that craves this jolt, I turned to my UCLA friend and colleague neuroscientist Dan Siegel for answers.

Siegel, who codirects UCLA's Mindsight Institute and is author of the scientifically acclaimed books *The Developing Mind* and *The Mindful Brain,* broke down the essential sequence of surprise as *expectation + violation of expectation.* He quoted Jerome Bruner, one of the fathers of cognitive psychology, who said "narrative emerges from violations to expectations." Then Siegel gave me an example. "You have expectations in your head; I have expectations in my head. We sit down to breakfast. I tell you, 'I got up this morning, I went into the bathroom and picked up my toothbrush and put toothpaste on it, blah, blah, blah.' Our expectations are totally in sync. There's no violation of them. It's boring. It's not memorable." It's not surprising, so it's not a story!

Why didn't Bangs just lecture us on river safety? Given our slaphappy condition and attitude, we probably would have thrown *him* in the river. Lectures are as boring as dog-bites-man stories! Instead, Bangs grabbed our attention with a totally unpredictable man-befriends-croc story. This surprising tale got through to us just the way he needed it to—not like a barking dog or a threatening croc, but like a Trojan horse.

According to the myth of the Trojan Horse, the ancient Greeks were fed up with their ten-year siege of Troy, so they built a huge hollow wooden horse, which they left outside the Trojans' city gates. Then they pretended to sail away. Thinking the horse was a victory trophy, the Trojans pulled it inside the city. That night a troop of Greek soldiers crept out from their hiding place inside the horse and unlocked the gates. The full Greek army then swarmed into the city, surprising the Trojans and winning the war.

The Trojan Horse was a delivery vehicle in disguise. So, too, are purposeful stories. They cleverly contain information, ideas, emotional prompts, and value propositions that the teller wants to sneak inside the listener's heart and mind. Thanks to their magical construction and appeal, stories emotionally transport the audience so they don't even realize they're receiving a hidden message. They only know after the story is told that they've heard and felt the teller's call to action.

There are innumerable calls to action that a purposeful story can deliver. If you're a salesperson, your goal might be to persuade your customer to buy more products. An HR manager's goal may be to get employees to embrace his company's culture. A creative director may want to inspire creativity in her staff, a lawyer to persuade a jury to convict or acquit her client. A politician's goal is to win votes, a comedian's to win laughs, a nonprofit's to win donors. In every case, your success will ride on your ability to get your intention inside your listeners in a way that moves them to action. What better tool to accomplish that than storytelling!

Several years ago I was eating dinner for the first time at a restaurant near my home called the Border Grill. The Grill's owners, Susan Feniger and Mary Sue Milliken, had their own Food Network television shows, a line of prepared foods under their Border Girls brand, and had written five cookbooks together. And they had multiple restaurants in Los Angeles, as well as one in Vegas. Curious to know how they had distinguished their culinary empire, I ordered a fish taco. The taste blew me away. Seeing the excitement on my face, the waiter came over for a chat.

"You know," he said, "there is an adventure inside that taco." He went on to tell me how Mary Sue and Susan had found themselves stranded at four in the morning twenty years earlier, in a seaside village in the Yucatan. The only thing open was this tiny taco stand, where Milliken and Feniger were impressed by the array of fresh ingredients—lobster and salmon and shredded cucumber, a bottle of olive oil. "The man, he made these little corn tortillas with his huge hands." The waiter gestured with his own palms. He described how Susan and Mary Sue stood there for an hour with a notebook, trying to figure out what this taco man was doing, what the ingredients were, and what created that brilliant taste? Then the man came out and brought them a couple beers and two more tacos. They ended up eating every single thing he was making, and he invited them back the next day.

By now I was hooked. "It was Sunday," the waiter continued. "The stand was closed, but just for them he made this amazing stew of red beans and salsa." He pointed to the item on the Border Grill menu and I immediately nodded for him to bring it. "They spent the whole afternoon with this family in Mexico!"

I felt as if I'd just had my own global culinary adventure without even leaving the table. I consumed the story and the food with equal gusto. The experience so impressed me that I later approached Susan Feniger to visit our UCLA course and share how she encourages the waiters to tell purposeful stories like this.

She said that story telling is an essential part of her staff's training. She and Milliken traveled the world to find the authentic flavors and cultures, colors, foods, music, and architecture that distinguish the Border Grill, as well as their later restaurant Ciudad. So they use the stories of their adventures just like Trojan horses to plant their passion inside their staff. "If they're excited about what we're doing, then they want customers to know the story of where we got that dish and how we were influenced." Those customers then go out and tell the stories to their friends. In this way, Feniger and Milliken's stories turn both staff and customers into viral marketers.

Feniger stressed that the Border Grill brand is not just about the taste, quality, or quantity of food, or even the atmosphere or clientele of their restaurants. There are hundreds of restaurants in LA that boast superior cooking and high style. What Feniger and her partner have always emphasized is the passion they invest in their restaurants. Their call to action is for customers not just to come and eat, but also to share their *emotional experience.* Oral stories are uniquely suited to deliver this call because people actually want to be moved when listening to a story.

WHAT *FUELS* EMOTIONAL TRANSPORTATION?

It was Stacey Snider, the former chair of Universal Pictures and now co-chair of DreamWorks Studios, who first said to me, when she was president of my company more than twenty years ago, "The best stories lead from the heart, not the mind." I was immediately impressed by this insight. Of course! In the entertainment business, there's a perpetual push to ramp up state-of-the-art technology, but without emotional propulsion, no amount of digital effects or gadgetry will get audiences truly excited.

What do I mean by "emotional transportation"? I'm talking about the complex system of action and reaction that operates within stories to move listeners. Stories that "work" transport audiences emotionally. They move us to laugh, cry, gasp, sigh, or yell in sympathetic rage, and every listener intuitively demands this emotional propulsion. It's important to remember that this is true even in a business context. Businesspeople are human beings who grew up listening to stories, just like everybody else. So in any business, as in show business, if you fail to transport your listener emotionally, you will lose your audience. Lose your audience, and your Trojan horse can't possibly deliver your intended call to action.

But the three-part structure of challenge, struggle, and resolution only gives a story its shape. What is the fuel that propels this vehicle? As I reflected on the purposeful business stories that had moved me most in the course of my career I realized that emotional transportation depends on four critical elements.

1.
TRUE HEROES ARE SYMPATHETIC AND RECOGNIZABLE CHARACTERS

Try to imagine a story without at least one character. It's impossible. Who would you root for? Who acts out the story? Who makes things change? And why should we care what happens if it doesn't happen *to* a character with whom we can identify or empathize? Whether man, woman, animal, company, tribe, product, or Jolly Green Giant, that character is our hero.

If story is emotional transportation, the hero is our conductor. The more sympathetic this character, the more we feel bound to the story, but this doesn't mean the character has to be cute and cuddly, or even necessarily nice. And don't confuse sympathetic with pathetic! Sympathy can best be summed up by the phrase "I feel your pain." Audiences feel sympathy for characters whose struggles and concerns make them seem authentic and vulnerable. Emotions like hope, love, determination, and longing make for much more compelling heroes than do intelligence, good looks, brawn, or cool. If you doubt me, just consider how you respond to the true stories that are being played out by real characters around you every day. These observed events not only teach us at a visceral level how emotional transportation works, but they often become powerful stories that we will tell and retell to serve a variety of purposes throughout our lives.

Case in point: One of the most heroic characters I've ever encountered was a young boy with a crippling degenerative disease, who lived near me when I was growing up in Boston. His speech was garbled. He couldn't walk, and he wasn't able to go to school with the rest of us in the neighborhood. But I could see him at his window every day watching us bicycle up and down the block.

One day his father appeared on the sidewalk hauling a bicycle with training wheels on the front and back. This six-wheeler looked as if an elephant could ride it without falling. As I watched from my window, the boy's father carried him out and put him on the contraption. Then the father went back inside.

The kid started to pedal and in a minute the bike tipped over. I could see the father in his window watching. So could the boy. His dad watched him lying there and did nothing. Finally the boy pulled himself up. Then he went about three feet and fell to the other side. Again the father just stood there watching. For weeks, that kid kept trying and falling, and the father didn't lift a finger. I complained to my mother, but she told me to mind my own business. I couldn't. The drama was too seductive.

One Saturday morning, the boy crashed off the curb. I had to go down. But when I reached the sidewalk, the kid waved me off. Then his father tapped on the window glass and shook his finger at me to go away. Convinced he must be some kind of monster, I left the boy trying to pull himself up and ran back home.

Then, a couple of days later, the kid was out there again. Over he went; up he went. Again.

But then, suddenly, he was rolling! He made it about sixty feet . . . then he turned around. And he rode all the way back without falling!

I looked up and there was the father grinning down at his son. I looked back to the boy, and he was beaming up at his father. Then they both started laughing and waving like crazy. And I started to cry.

Finally I got it! They both knew the boy *needed* to face the challenge and struggle through it on his own. He needed to be his own agent of change, to be active in his own rescue. If his father did it for him, the boy wouldn't feel like a hero. And only if he was the hero would this seminal victory empower him to face the other inevitable and monumental challenges that lay in this boy's future. The only thing better than being the hero of his own story was being the hero in his own life—and I learned that day just how closely the two are intertwined.

The joy I felt at that kid's little sixty-foot bike ride was overwhelming. My experience of his unique challenge, struggle, and triumph became an archetypal tale of persistence that I told myself every time my grades fell in school, or bullies beat me up, or I failed at some enterprise. The story of the boy on the bike taught me that failure really is just a speed bump on the road to success. Heroes don't quit, so the only true failure is the failure to get up. This story's call to action was to keep getting up.

I paid that story forward through many knockdowns in my career, especially early on. When I was barely thirty years old, Columbia Pictures promoted me to run the studio. I was terrified not only by the responsibility but also by the resentment of older, more experienced men who wanted and had expected my job. One of these men was John Veitch, Columbia's chief of physical production at the time. A bona fide war hero, John had been injured fighting in the Pacific in World War II. He could smell fear a mile away, and he knew it was not a good quality in a leader. Needless to say, he could smell my anxiety and dread after the disappointing release of *Lost Horizon*. As a more junior executive, I unfortunately had supported at its inception this musical embarrassment for then superstars Burt Bacharach and Hal David. Knowing that this could be his opportunity to climb over me to the top of the company, Veitch approached me as everyone was walking out on this fiasco's premiere. "So," he asked, "are you afraid of what comes next?"

I knew John was tough, but I also knew he appreciated toughness. I gathered my thoughts and then answered, "Absolutely." And I told him my story of the boy on the bike. "I may get knocked down," I concluded, "but as long as I'm breathing and still have the strength to keep trying, I will get up. That boy's story taught me, it's what I focus on that grows and determines where I'll end up, not what gets in my way."

That story helped convert John from a competitor to a collaborator. It proved to him that I appreciated the qualities necessary for success. And it proves to me now that compelling heroes and purposeful stories lurk in every corner of our lives, ready for the telling.

2.
DRAMA GETS YOUR STORY MOVING

Once you've got your hero, what gets the emotion moving? What holds us spellbound, begging for more? Michael Jackson taught me in no uncertain terms, the answer is drama.

Back in 1991, Jackson already was a force to be reckoned with. After renewing his contract with Sony for a record-setting $65 million, he released his eighth album, *Dangerous,* with the singles "Black or White" and "Remember the Time," both of which dominated the pop charts. As CEO of Sony Pictures, I'd sat in on the studio production of that album and was overwhelmed by Michael's creative intensity and perfectionism. His ambition knew no bounds. But when Sony's most important musical asset invited me to his home in Encino to discuss his plans to get into movies and television, I was taken aback. Michael had proven he knew everything there was to know about pop music, but movies were a different animal. He wanted to produce as well as act. That meant telling stories. Could he do it?

I didn't even have to ask the question. "In both films and music," Michael said, "you have to know where the drama is and how to present it." He gave me a long, intense stare and abruptly stood up. "Let me show you."

He led me upstairs to the hallway outside his bedroom, where we stopped in front of a huge glass terrarium. "This," he said, "is Muscles."

Inside, a massive snake was coiled around a tree branch. His head was tracking something in the opposite corner of the terrarium.

Michael pointed with his finger at the object of Muscles' obsession. A little white mouse was trying to hide behind a pile of wood shavings.

I said hopefully, "Are they friends?"

"Do they look it?"

"No. The mouse is trembling."

Michael said, "We have to feed Muscles live mice, otherwise he won't eat. Dead ones don't get his attention."

"So why doesn't he just go ahead and eat it?"

He said, "Because he enjoys the game. First he uses fear to get the mouse's attention, then he waits, building tension. Finally, when the mouse is so terrified it can't move, Muscles will close in."

That snake had the attention of that mouse, and that mouse had the attention of that snake—and Michael Jackson had my attention.

"That's drama," he said.

"It sure is!" I said. "This story has everything—stakes, suspense, power, death, good and evil, innocence and danger. I can't stand it. And I can't stop watching."

"Exactly," he said. "What's going to happen next? Even if you know what it is, you don't know how or when."

"Maybe the mouse will escape."

Michael let out one of his high, strange laughs. "Maybe."

If I'd had the slightest doubt about Jackson's command as a teller of stories, it evaporated that day. His telling to win profoundly and clearly taught me that nothing grabs our attention faster than the need to know *what happens next?*

Back at UCLA, I asked Dan Siegel to help me understand from his perspective as a neuroscientist why people are so enthralled by drama. Siegel pointed out that emotions don't occur spontaneously. Nor, as any actor knows, can they be summoned at will. Emotions have to be aroused. "And arousal gets heightened," Siegel said, "when you realize, *I don't know if the mountain lion's still there; I don't know if the spaceship is going to get back; I'm not sure he's going to win the race.* You have to have tension between expectation and uncertainty. Emotional tension drives you to think it might go this way, but it might go that way, and that makes you wonder, what will happen next?" The more you wonder what will happen next, the more you pay attention. And the more attention you pay, the more you hear, notice, and retain.

One reason I was so helplessly enthralled as I watched Michael Jackson's mouse and snake was that they were enacting a story of primal desire and dread. Somewhere deep in our DNA, we all have this story lurking because, at some stage of our evolution, if not in our more immediate existence, we *lived* this story. We were the weaker prey that hid trembling inside the cave from the saber-tooth lurking outside.

Of course, most business story tellers don't need to set dramatic stakes as high as death or survival. But even business stories are told best if they trigger the conflict between dread and desire. Desire is a core human need which in business may translate as landing a job, motivating employees, keeping an account, impressing a boss, successfully launching a product, or securing a brand. The more we desire something, the greater our fear of not achieving it. And that emotional tension engages your audience because it makes them feel "what's in it for them."

It's not the volume of words that creates this impact. Even a quick story can produce dramatic tension. For example, Charles Collier recently told me the story he used to motivate his employees when he became president of AMC, the movie classics network that distributed the long-running television series *Shootout,* which I cohosted with Peter Bart. Collier wanted to take the cable network in a new direction that would include edgy original shows like *Mad Men,* as well as its established slate of old movies, but he had a problem. Many of his employees had a disengaged punching-the-clock approach toward work. If he didn't change the autopilot attitude of his people, he'd never change the aptitude of the organization. So he told them a very simple story about how he used to just punch in and out as a kid when his parents made him take piano lessons. Hours passed as he doodled with his fingers. He was there, but he wasn't *there*—he never showed up mentally. Years later he realized how much that cost him in experience and time. He wasted that chance to become skilled enough to really *enjoy* playing music, and he never got those hours back. But he could still learn from that loss. He could change. Now he made it a point to show up—not just physically but also emotionally. If he didn't, he told his employees, he knew he'd be the loser. And if his employees didn't change their ways, Collier's story implied, both their jobs and AMC's survival would be up for grabs. Collier understood that "story matters." In fact, that phrase became the core brand of his cable network.

Collier's story illustrates one of the key advantages of story telling that Steve Denning has identified since he's been on the trail of organizational story telling. Denning is former director of knowledge management at the World Bank, author of the award-winning books *The Secret*

Language of Leadership and *The Leader's Guide to Storytelling,* and a noted authority on leadership strategy. I invited Steve to participate in one of the story conclaves I hosted in 2008, where he pointed out that the brevity of stories can give leaders a telling edge in organizational settings. "You may have no more than minutes, even seconds," he said, "but an oral story can get the job done in that short time frame." Moreover, Denning has found, when listeners hear a story—as opposed to a data dump—is coming, they usually welcome it. They relax, come to attention quickly, and focus on the teller. They don't squirm and busy themselves with text messaging as I've seen so many employees and students do when a strategy lecture or PowerPoint presentation begins.

In this engaged state, listeners also are more receptive to the emotional and human truth within the teller's story. Business audiences actually will trust a teller like Collier who acknowledges his own human frailty more than they would if he'd pretended to be some sort of executive god who could do no wrong. Tales of perfection fail dramatically because they never ring true. But when a leader uses authentic drama to reveal the hidden truth about a problem his business is facing, he guides the audience to feel as if they're uncovering the truth themselves. Compelling drama convinces listeners that the teller has heart.

3.
YOU HAD ME AT AHHA!

Your story's moment of truth is the galvanic climax when your "ah" meets your listener's "ha!" to form that magically unifying "ahha!" In this eureka moment your Trojan horse delivers its payload. Your listener experiences the same thrilling charge of emotion, purpose, and meaning that you felt when you experienced your original epiphany. Your call to action hits home with a resounding "I got it!"

I was on the receiving end of just such a call back in the early 1990s when basketball superstar Magic Johnson and his business partner Ken Lombard came to my office at Sony at the request of my COO, to discuss a business proposition. How could I turn down Magic Johnson? This was one of the perks of my job.

The first thing Ken said was "Close your eyes. I'm going to tell you a story about a foreign country."

This seemed a little unorthodox, but I went along with him and shut my eyes. "Now," he continued, "this is a land with a strong customer base, great location, and qualified investors. You know how to build theaters in Europe and Asia and South America, right?"

Of course I did. As CEO of Sony, I had the ultimate responsibility for the enormous Loews theater circuit.

"You know how to invest in foreign countries that have different languages, different cultures, different problems. What you do, Peter, is you find a partner in that country who speaks the language, knows the culture, and can handle the local problems. Right?"

I nodded, eyes still shut. Sony had such outposts all over the world.

"Well," Ken continued, "what if I told you a promised land exists that already speaks English, craves movies, has plenty of available real estate, and no competition? This promised land is about six miles from here."

I opened my eyes, wide. We all knew that Loews was always looking for new sites and expansion opportunities.

Ken looked over at Magic, who shot me his famous million-dollar smile. Ken went on. "I grew up in that land, in a family of small-business people. We did not make a lot of money, but we were always in the neighborhoods, dry cleaners—you know, my great-grandfather had this crazy ice truck. There was some serious entrepreneurial spirit."

His face, he was saying, was the same face as the audience I coveted. You know, he told me, a quarter of all the moviegoing audience is African-American. And this audience—Magic's and Ken's—had its own thriving community, which I, as a wealthy white businessman, could not access.

"Ahha!" I cried. I got it! This promised land was right in the middle of Los Angeles, and Ken and Magic's story revealed that they would be the perfect local heroes to build theaters for us there. "But wait a minute,"

I said, flashing back on Columbia's *Boyz n the Hood,* the John Singleton drama aimed at black males under twenty-five, which had been a big winner for Sony. "In those urban locations, theaters became the lightning rod for the gangs and frightened the mall owners as well as other theatergoers."

Most of the anger that we all witnessed in the black communities, Magic explained, had to do with the fact that those neighborhoods were owned by outsiders. A cornerstone of the Magic Johnson brand story was his belief in local proprietorship. Everything he and Ken were building would be of the people, by the people, and for the people of their community. "You protect your own," Magic said, "because that's your team." And if anybody knew about teamwork, it was NBA all-star Magic Johnson. He was telling me that these two guys would stand in the fire and say to the Crips and the Bloods, or anyone else who might try to hijack us in this promised land, "Not on my watch."

We made the deal.

The coda to this story is that, fortunately, Ken and Magic really were prepared to protect their—and now our—promised land, because as soon as construction started, the gangs showed up.

"I tried to be polite," Ken recalled when telling this story to my UCLA class years later. "I said to the leader, 'You know what, you and I should talk.' He said, 'Get the f—— out of my face, I got things to do.' Well, one of my security guys used to be Mike Tyson's bodyguard. So he gets up and says, 'Look, you need to talk to my guy. Because, you know, he's running it.' Well, the leader takes this as a challenge. Those two are going at it, and the thirty-five guys flank us. At that point, I said, 'Look, if it's jobs you want, then let's talk about jobs. But if it's a shakedown, you got your thirty-five, I got my six; I guarantee you, half of you are going to the hospital.'"

They got it!

"Once they saw we were going to defend our land, the guys came back and said, 'OK, if you're going to give us jobs, then that's what we're here for.'" Ken hired about two dozen of the gang members, and half of them stayed on with the construction company even after the theater complex was completed.

In its first four weeks this Magic Johnson Theater was one of the top five highest grossing theaters in the Sony chain.

Lombard ultimately paid this story forward. Ken and Magic had told Howard Schultz, the founder of Starbucks, the same story they told me. They wanted Starbucks to enjoy the same success that Sony had by thinking globally, acting locally, and entrusting Ken and Magic with the role of local hero. Schultz agreed to let them open the only dually owned Starbucks in his chain. Then they went on to leverage the same story into fifty-fifty partnerships with T.G.I. Friday's and Washington Mutual, adding restaurants and home loan centers to underserved areas. The results were so successful that Howard Schultz in 2004 hired Ken Lombard to become CEO of Starbucks Entertainment.

4.
THE ME-TO-WE FACTOR

The most propulsive business stories shine the light on an interest, goal, or problem that both the teller and the audience share. The power of these stories stems from the strong me-to-we connection that forms as soon as it registers that the teller is talking about a feeling or situation that the listener personally has experienced. That connection ignites the audience's empathy, secures their trust in the teller, and guarantees their interest in the call to action.

One story that's spawned a multibillion-dollar company thanks to its me-to-we factor is the story of YouTube. At one of our narrative conclaves, YouTube founder Chad Hurley shared this story, which he and his partner Steve Chen told to prospective backers, customers, and the media as they were struggling to launch their venture in 2005—just one year before they sold the company to Google for $1.6 billion. "We were having a party in San Francisco during the pre-YouTube era. We'd shot a lot of great videos of our guests, which we wanted to load onto the Internet to share with other friends and family. Our problem was, we wanted to get them out right away. But uploading was time-consuming and complicated, and the net result looked like garbage. It shot our enthusiasm, and the fun of the moment was lost."

They realized that anyone in this situation would feel the same way, since the impulse to share positive experiences immediately is universal. This realization told them their problem contained an opportunity. If they could figure out a way to upload videos freely with speed, ease, and quality, everyone would want to use it.

Accepting the challenge, they got busy and created an efficient, fast, and simple-to-use vehicle that everyone everywhere could share, even if they all uploaded their videos at the same time. The story's happy resolution was the successful creation of YouTube.

When the me-to-we factor is strong in a story, the primary benefit for the teller is empathy. Hurley and Chen's story told their listeners, in essence, "I'm you. I have the same problems and frustrations as you do." Their first audience of investors trusted that Hurley and Chen were "regular" people who understood the frustration that they themselves had experienced and that these guys really would make sure their YouTube solution was easy for anyone to use. When YouTube was released, the partners continued to tell their story, reducing customers' possible resistance to the novel technology and ramping up their audience's eagerness to try their new solution. By 2006, 100 million video clips were viewed daily on YouTube, and 65,000 new videos were being uploaded every twenty-four hours.

The second benefit of the me-to-we factor is that it makes stories more digestible and accessible. The faster your story establishes common ground between you and your listener, the more of your story your listener will absorb, both emotionally and intellectually. If your audience can't identify with your problem, they likely will not care to hear the resolution of your story. On the other hand, once they feel the experience of your story as their own, their attention becomes automatic. Response to the YouTube story was virtually instantaneous, and because the story was so universal, it was repeated over and over among users and in almost all media coverage of the company.

THE BEAUTY OF THE me-to-we factor is that it highlights the essence of telling to win as a shared experience. Telling a story is a two-way process that engages and, ideally, benefits both the teller and the listener. But does that also imply that listeners and tellers are equally capable of telling stories? If so, that would mean that telling to win truly is a tool that anyone can use, and not just an advantage for the lucky few.

Now that I had a better grasp on what defines a *story,* I decided to explore this practice of *telling* more deeply. I wanted to find out where the skill of the tell originates, who's really got it, and why.

aHHa!

- A purposeful story is a call to action—be sure to make your call.
- A story without structure leaves your goal unfulfilled. . . .
  - ➤ Craft the beginning to shine the light on your challenge or problem.
  - ➤ Shape the middle around the struggle to meet that challenge.
  - ➤ End with a resolution that ignites in the listener your call to action.
- Get your audience to step into your hero's shoes.
- Lead from the heart, not the head.
- Employ the element of surprise.
- Successful stories turn "me" to "we"—align your interests!
- Be sure your story tells what's in it for them.
- You're not done till they say, "Ahha! I got it!"

CHAPTER THREE

You've Got It!

P apua, New Guinea, held the missing link. More than 80 percent of the population there still lived as tribal hunters and gatherers, just as their Stone Age ancestors had. Even in 2005, some had never laid eyes on a white person. And in spite of the fact that their eight hundred indigenous languages represented one fifth of all the languages spoken on earth, most of these tribes had no written language. All this meant that New Guinea would take me as close to the origins of oral story telling as I was likely to get in the twenty-first century. I packed my bags and headed for the far side of the world.

What I found was beyond far out. Papuan native dress included bones through the nose and wigs the size of Chicago. Some tribes harvested spiders as a delicacy. Others slathered themselves in mud. Just a few decades earlier, I'd have had to consider the threat of cannibalism, not a comforting feeling. But I found that old-fashioned Polaroids were a great tool for making friends. I handed the locals the self-developing snapshots, and they were so awed by the slowly appearing images of themselves that they stuck them in their headbands to show one another who they were. I got the feeling they'd be telling the story of those pictures for generations to come.

Telling stories turned out to be a way of life in New Guinea. Each tribe had distinctive costumes, habitats, food and hunting rituals, and spiritual beliefs, and all of these were bound to the culture through story. This meant that each tribe's survival depended on the younger generations learning and living by these stories, the most important of which were passed down during initiation rites. In the village of the Crocodile Men, who lived along the Blackwater River, I was invited into a long thatched lodge called the Spirit House, to witness one of these rites.

Male initiation in this tribe involved a gruesome ordeal of razor cuts that left scars in the pattern of crocodile skin. As the boys bled and healed, the elders told them the stories that gave meaning to those scars. Most of these tales connected to the tribe's origin myth, which reminded me of Richard Bangs's legend about the Egyptian crocodile spirit. But the Crocodile Men called their spirit Nashut.

My guide translated the tribal leader's telling of the story that gave the ritual its significance. The hero of his story was a tribal ancestor who'd dropped his spear in the river. Diving down after it, he discovered a magic house on the bottom of the lake. When he entered the house, the crocodile spirit trapped him. For a month Nashut held the man captive, teaching him everything he needed to know about warfare, head-hunting, farming, and building. The spirit also said that if the man cut himself to look like the crocodile—in effect, if he adopted Nashut's brand—he would absorb Nashut's power and become the strongest and most ferocious warrior on the river. Then he let the man go on condition that he tell his people everything Nashut had taught him.

This myth, I realized, was the Crocodile Men's Trojan horse. It held not only the tribe's history but also, through its hundreds of sequels and spin-offs, all the skills the group needed to survive. These people used mythology as information technology. They thought in stories. They remembered through stories. They communicated through stories. And they related through stories. Even their word for "talk" literally meant "to story." Every member of the tribe was both a story listener and a natural teller of tales.

Even though I couldn't understand the story tellers' exact words in the Spirit House, I could feel that the person-to-person interaction heightened the magic. The tellers' vocal sounds of surprise and pain and longing, their lunging gestures and wide-armed stances, and their direct eye-to-eye contact enthralled their audience. Tellers and listeners swayed together. They swooned. They gasped—"Ahha!" One-to-many, each teller delivered his story through his whole body and spirit, straight to the hearts of his listeners. This fundamental full-body, real-time experience, I realized with a shock, is what gives *all* oral stories their persuasive advantage over written, filmed, or otherwise mediated stories.

Even in a modern business context, when you tell a story directly in the room with your listeners, you naturally tune your whole body to them, and they pick up on you just as instinctively. It's a natural reflex! So even though the story you tell in a negotiation, interview, or sales conference might not require quite the same level of theatrics as the Crocodile tales, every oral story is by definition interactive. Physical immediacy forces both teller and audience to perceive each other as active, not passive, participants in the tell. And this engagement remains active even during silent pauses, even through an exchange as subtle as a meeting of the eyes. It's like a game of pitch and catch, with the ball of story constantly traveling back and forth between teller and listener.

By the time I left New Guinea, I was convinced that the skills of story listening and story telling are coded deep in our DNA. Oral narrative— stories told face-to-face and in the room—is the seminal information technology, and we've all got it!

BUT COULD OUR CONNECTION to stories be *too* deeply wired? This was the contention of Chris Anderson, editor in chief of *Wired* magazine and author of the best-selling books *Free* and *The Long Tail,* when he visited one of my UCLA courses.

Our conversation began to heat up when Chris said, "Our hunger, our appetite for stories—for beginning, middle, and end—is a bug in our brain." He explained that stories assume certain patterns of logic that evolution—since the Stone Age!—has trained the human brain to anticipate. Over the course of a story, we expect something to happen to or change for a character or characters we can empathize with. We assume the outcome will be the result of whatever happens in the course of the plot. We not only want the story to make sense, but we assume the events within the story will make *more* sense to us after the story's conclusion. "It's our wiring," he acknowledged, "an evolutionary skill set that's allowed us to teach each other and grow, to establish social networks and culture, but it's a distortion of the truth."

But if story telling were a liability, I challenged Chris, evolution surely would have weeded it out of our systems long ago. "Instead the research proves that we're hardwired for story. Children as young as age two are able to tell and follow a story!"

Stories are accessible, Chris pointed out, because they're concrete, active, visual—in other words, easily digestible.

"Exactly!" I said. "Stories take bits of reality and, through the magic of emotional transportation, leverage them into the illusion of a much larger truth than facts alone could ever provide. This is what accounts for the certainty we feel after we hear an effective story. It also accounts for the danger that troubles you, Chris. As soon as we suspend judgment, a gap opens that the story listener can fill with hope or hatred, compassion or vengeance, and energy that is either constructive or destructive, according to the teller's designs. The paradox is that, as a technology, story telling is agnostic about the messages, values, and beliefs conveyed within the stories. Like a car or a bicycle, it's an equal opportunity vehicle that doesn't care who rides it or what cargo it delivers."

Chris surprised me by validating my points. "My contention is not that narrative isn't important," he clarified. "It's that we're so intrinsically drawn to story telling that we often miss the statistical randomness of life—because it doesn't fit into our sense of how the story should go.

The tragedy of our species is that we're wired for narrative, yet live in a world that's random."

"But"—I now was unable to contain myself—"the evolutionary process is a lot slower than technology, so if human beings are wired this way, then to be effective you *have to* narrate the facts and figures! Especially in business, you've got to provide an emotionally propelled vehicle to communicate data to people." Furthermore, I pointed out, "Nobody knows this better than you do, Chris. You write books and run a magazine filled with stories!"

He shrugged. "The marketplace wants stories. I give them stories that package complicated ideas in terms that will resonate with people. Narrative is an imperfect tool, but incredibly powerful."

My exchange with Chris energized me to pursue my detective work in new directions. How exactly did story telling become such a powerful evolutionary instrument? Where did it originate? I began reaching out not only to my business connections, but also to scientists, psychologists, and experts in organizational story telling who could help me answer these questions.

FROM CELLULAR PILLOW TALK TO TELLING TO WIN

I started by asking my friend Gentry Lee to help me understand how human beings first became story telling machines. Gentry is that unique master scientist who can translate the complexities of the cosmos into language that anyone can understand and get excited about. I had the privilege years ago of introducing Gentry to the great science fiction maestro Arthur C. Clarke. Subsequently Gentry became Clarke's coauthor. Now, as chief engineer for the Solar System Exploration Directorate at the Jet Propulsion Laboratory (JPL), he's responsible for the engineering integrity of robotic planetary missions that include the Phoenix mission, which landed in the Martian arctic in May 2008; the twin rover missions to Mars that landed in January 2004; and NASA's Deep Impact and Stardust missions. I figured if Gentry could land a robot on Mars, he probably knew where stories come from. Predictably, he explained the science by telling me a story.

"For three billion years," Gentry said, "everything that was alive on planet Earth was a single cell. And one of the great mysteries that all of us should wonder about—because we wouldn't be here otherwise—is what caused these cells to suddenly combine and share functions, do different jobs, and communicate. If you're a single cell, to reproduce you simply split yourself apart and off you go. If you're two cells trying to reproduce together, it's much more difficult. But early cells did somehow manage to talk to each other, and suddenly they became more successful. The multicellular creatures survived because they shared their functionality and rose to a higher level."

That reproductive persuasion and sharing of functionality, Gentry said, was the metaphoric equivalent of story telling. "We share ideas. We break our functions into parts and assign them. The net result is that by exchanging stories, we do better as a group."

But how did story telling and story listening make the evolutionary leap from cellular pillow talk to human narrative? Marco Iacoboni, professor of psychiatry and biobehavioral sciences at UCLA, offered my graduate students one likely answer when he came to my class to describe his pioneering research into mirror neurons. These brain cells are the modern descendants of Gentry Lee's original interactive cells. They allow us to read one another's actions and feelings *as if* we are entering and living one another's experience.

Mirror neurons make it possible for us to imitate, learn, and intuit one another's goals through feelings of empathy and connection. "Without them," Iacoboni explained, "we would likely be blind to the actions, intentions, and emotions of other people." We also would be blind to the meaning of stories, since stories work by turning on and tuning in both the teller's and the listener's mirror neurons. "Evolution shaped our brains to learn through narrative," Iacoboni said.

The impact of a story is intensified during oral telling because these cells are also turned on by the physical sounds, expressions, smells, and movements of the people in the room. *Both* teller and listener feel this mirror effect. "Our gestures, facial expressions, and body postures are so-cial signals," Iacoboni said. "When I see you smiling, my mirror neurons for smiling fire up too, initiating a cascade of neural activity. I experience immediately and effortlessly what you are experiencing."

This two-way attunement of mirror neurons creates the optimal state for telling a story. If a story is well told, both teller and audience will re-main in this state right through to their shared "ahha!" when the teller's original epiphany is experienced by the listener as his or her *own* eureka. The value added by attunement suggests a major advantage that business people lose when they communicate through documents and media pre-sentations instead of oral narrative.

THE MISSING LINK IN BUSINESS

At one of the narrative gatherings I hosted in 2009, our guest speaker was Michael Wesch, a cultural anthropologist at Kansas State University and expert on information technology, from indigenous cultures to new media. It was Wesch who clinched my suspicion that telling to win actu-ally is the missing link in business.

In addition to sparking mirror neurons, Wesch said, telling and listen-ing to stories ignites the regions of the brain that process meaning. Why is this important? "Because humans are meaning-seeking creatures. It's not just about taking in information. We can't remember anything with-out giving meaning to it."

Wesch described the significance of story in a verbal equation: *meaning + memory = knowledge-ability.* Meaning, he said, emerges when we make connections between bits of information. Why did we lose $200,000 in the last quarter? How does the new CEO differ from the last one? How come we made $12 million more on this product than on that one? Those sorts of connections are the cargo hidden inside purposeful narratives. Stories package these connections and, when told, propel them to listeners through state-of-the-heart technology. The emotional reward of the story makes the connections easy to remember, and every time we do remember, we also experience why the information tucked inside the story matters. By contrast, what's the meaning you attach to a list of numbers in a PowerPoint? Zilch! And that's why lists of numbers or facts are not memorable. "If you're going to pass on ideas and influence people," Wesch concluded, "you have to be able to tell a story."

But is a story told orally person-to-person any more persuasive within organizations than its print or screen equivalent? At another of our conclaves, Steve Denning recalled how he'd asked that same question back when he was knowledge director at the World Bank. To find the answer, he had his team deliver twenty-five well-crafted stories of innovation to staffers at the World Bank, through a variety of media. The people who read the stories in booklets or newsletters or watched them on video hardly mentioned them to their colleagues. They said they didn't trust these packaged presentations from "the system" because the presentations didn't feel genuine or authentic. However, when the same stories were told person-to-person, audiences listened closely and repeated them to others. The more the audience trusted the speaker, the more they trusted the authenticity of the telling and the greater its power to influence them. "It wasn't the *story* that was having the impact," Steve realized, "but oral story *telling*."

Denning's finding reminded me of a comment that famed financier Mike Milken once told me about his success on Wall Street. "I used to team up the data guys with good story tellers," he said. "That's how we got many things done."

Milken's success with this strategy reflected the fact that when someone tells us a story with data tucked inside, our brains cleverly lock the data onto the feelings we experience while listening to that story. Then, when the information is recalled, so is our feeling of that tell. The more rewarding our experience of the tell, the more positive our view of the data is likely to be. So a teller who can render a positive emotional experience—by putting the audience at ease and making them laugh, gasp, sing, dance, or even get a little teary-eyed—provides an added incentive for the audience to embrace the information within his story.

Why, then, I asked Steve Denning, do so many businesspeople discount or completely ignore this potent organizational tool? Denning pointed out that our educational system puts a premium on intellectual reasoning at the expense of emotion. Learning becomes increasingly conceptual and impersonal as you move into graduate degrees. And because the professional world is dominated by university graduates, businesspeople now take it for granted that theoretical and statistical models are *worth more* than stories.

But that does not mean that stories go away! "Whenever we relax with our friends outside of school or the office," Steve said, "we lapse right back into story telling. We are at home with it. So why not communicate with people in their native language?"

Denning's comments reminded me of an incident in one of my UCLA classes that stunningly proved his point. That semester I was teaching production management to a group filled with what I call "multi-threats"—aspiring writer-director-producers and MBA students enrolled in UCLA's highly competitive Producer and Director Program. Before class one day I found myself eavesdropping on one such student, a young woman who had her heart and mind set on a career in the business of filmmaking. She was telling a friend that she'd chosen this profession because her father couldn't read.

The friend looked at her incredulously. "Why not?"

My student's voice got very tender. She didn't exactly answer the question. Instead she said that her father, a farmer, was visually literate—he could make out Stop signs because of the shape of the sign. "In restaurants when I was a kid, I'd watch my dad hold the menu, and it would shake a little when the waitress came over. He never told us what was going on. He never asked for help. Instead he would run his finger down the column that had the picture of a hamburger at the top, and midway down he'd stop at another visual symbol and point to show the waitress. My mom said he was too proud to go back to school, and maybe he was afraid. But he was *not* dumb, and he was ferocious when it came to my education."

The pain and love this young woman felt for her father had motivated her to study visual literacy so that she could tell her father's story and help others like him. She'd let nothing get in the way of that goal.

What a story! It had pain, struggle, love, desire, as well as an element of suspense. I wanted this young woman to succeed. I wanted to see what that kind of genuine passion was going to produce.

At the end of the semester students had to do a presentation highlighting their professional qualifications, artistic goals, and personal motivations. To make this more than just a dress rehearsal, I invited a couple of executives from New Line and Paramount to sit in the audience. They were always looking for new talent, and this was a way to jump-start the more promising students' entry into the creative marketplace. I was sure the farmer's daughter would blow us all away.

But when it was her turn, she stood up and delivered her résumé. She listed her degrees and the schools she'd attended, announced her grade-point average, and summarized a couple of articles she'd published. She showed video clips from her student films. And she sat down.

I was dumbstruck and heartsick. I wanted to grab her by the shoulders and shout, "Is *that* the story you're telling to make me want to hire you, to send me out of here singing your praises, to insist that my friends give you a job?"

What happened? Here was a girl who could tell a story in a way that was deeply persuasive and resonant. Yet when she presented herself to the very audience that could help her realize her dreams, all she did was regurgitate her minimal credits and credentials.

It was as if she forgot that people in business are human too. Oops! No matter how common this mistake may be, it doesn't change the fact that relationships are the foundation stones of every career. And relationships are fundamentally emotional and intuitive connections forged through the two-way exchange of empathy. No empathy, no relationship. Do résumés and bullet points ignite empathy? No! Does telling to win? You bet!

So if a born story teller fails to tell purposeful stories in business, it's an egregious mistake. But what about people who are not natural born tellers? Many people will insist they couldn't tell a story if their lives depended on it. And many of those people live and work in the business world. Some rise to the very top of their industries. Is it true that they succeed without telling stories? To find out, I approached a few of the most successful confirmed *non*-story tellers I know.

NOT FOR STORY TELLERS ONLY

RICHARD ROSENBLATT

A couple of years ago new media wunderkind Richard Rosenblatt and I jointly taught a graduate course at UCLA called the Convergence of the Poet and the Engineer, with the guiding idea that technology and creativity could be elegant and fortuitous partners. Richard, famous for selling iMall to Excite@Home for $565 million at the ripe old age of thirty, and for building Intermix Media, the parent of MySpace.com, before selling that to Rupert Murdoch's News Corp. when he was thirty-seven, was a huge draw among our film, business, and law students. Yet for all his achievements, Richard was an intuitive entrepreneur who did not spend a lot of time analyzing his success. He readily admitted that he was learning as much from our course as the students were.

One night as we walked across campus after teaching, I was thinking about Richard's statement in class that he'd pulled off his $580 million Intermix sale to Murdoch in just twenty minutes. I asked him how he'd done it.

"I was extremely nervous," Richard remembered. Murdoch, with a vast global media empire that included the Fox TV network, Britain's Sky TV, and legions of major newspapers, was one of the most powerful men in the world, and Richard had never met him before. Moreover, Murdoch could not have been a less likely buyer for Richard's company. Having dabbled in the Internet in the nineties before pulling completely out and staying out for the past six years, Murdoch had become the Scrooge of new media. To make the Intermix deal, Richard had to completely transform him, changing his mind about the Web and propelling him back into the game of Internet technology.

Richard didn't even realize it as he was telling me what he'd done, but I soon realized he'd told Murdoch a classic vision story in the mold of Charles Dickens's *A Christmas Carol*. Instinctively, he had cast Murdoch himself as the wayward hero who needed to redeem his honor—before it was too late.

"I said, 'Mr. Murdoch, with all due respect, you are the biggest guy in media on the entire planet. It doesn't make any sense that you've been completely forward-thinking in everything, whether it was DirecTV or newspapers, and you're nowhere when it comes to the Internet.'"

Richard gave me a sheepish look. "I remember thinking how bold that was, but I said it in a very humble way."

Next, he described the struggle that Murdoch had been trying to avoid by staying off the Web—the expense of new forms of content creation, the need for perpetual innovation, and the complexity of online distribution. But Richard held out the process that promised to turn this problem into profit—if Murdoch would dare to take the risk. "I said, 'Mr. Murdoch, Intermix is the perfect media company. You don't have to spend $1 million an episode; you spend nothing because the users create all the content. You don't have to pay for distribution because the users invite their friends and drive traffic. All you have to do is sell ads.'" Selling ads, of course, was what Murdoch did best and feared least.

So the middle of the story called for Murdoch to take the plunge and buy Intermix, harnessing the power of happy users who would voluntarily function as his creative and distribution force. Then, having aligned his listener's head and wallet, Richard promised a transformative resolution that would capture his heart. "One year from today," Richard predicted, "you will be on the cover of *Wired* magazine."

I shook my head. "And you say you can't tell a story."

Suddenly Richard grinned at me in amazement. "You're right. It was all a story! He would be the hero because he was bold and understood what this would do for his company. When I think about talking like that, it seems insane. But you know what? I have a signed autograph from him on the cover of *Wired* magazine exactly one year later."

Richard's story of Murdoch as the hero who overcomes his misguided past provided the leverage that won Richard a $580 million sale. Not bad for a guy who "couldn't" tell a story!

WOLFGANG PUCK

"When I started at Ma Maison, I was new to Los Angeles and felt so lucky to be chef at this premier restaurant," Wolfgang Puck said. We were talking over his signature smoked-salmon-and-caviar pizza at his flagship Beverly Hills restaurant, Spago, in 2009, but I remembered Wolfgang back in the seventies, when Ma Maison was the watering hole of choice for every major celebrity in film, TV, and music, as well as all the looky-loos. "I was so nervous when the owner pushed me out to stand in front of the customers and talk," Wolfgang said. "I wanted to hide in the kitchen, but he said, 'People will eat it up!' I wish somebody had told me, 'Wolfgang, just tell your story; it's easy.' I thought, I'm not a story teller! What am I going to tell them? My focus was on the food and its creation."

Not only does Wolfgang today own and operate four award-winning fine dining restaurants, each with multiple locations, but his companies also include two other brands: Wolfgang Puck Catering and Wolfgang Puck Worldwide, which operates and franchises the Wolfgang Puck Bistros, Wolfgang Puck Expresses, and Wolfgang Puck Cultural Center

Cafés and also licenses Chef Puck's name for consumer goods such as kitchenware, cookbooks, and food products. Especially when I'm traveling, I feel as if Wolfgang is omnipresent, in airports, malls, entertainment venues. You name it, he's there—so often in person! And every one of these enterprises reflects his reputation for freshness, quality, and superior taste. I wanted to know what he told employees, product purveyors, and franchisees to maintain his standard of excellence across so many different types of restaurants in so many different geographic locations when he couldn't physically be in each location himself.

"Well," he admitted, "ironically I learned what to say to anyone managing my brand through my experience with the franchise guys, because they're in it only for the money. See, I'm in because I love it and it's my passion, but the franchise guy says, 'We'll put Wolfgang's name on it and then screw the customer. Because it's a Wolfgang Puck restaurant, they all will just line up.' But what they forget, it's like a two-sided sword. Because it has my name on it, the customer's expectation is much higher.

"Those expectations are based on my personal standards of excellence," Wolfgang said. And those standards are summed up in the acronym WELL, which stands for Wolfgang, Eat, Love, Live. "It came from a radio show I did once. They asked me 'What is your motto in life?' and I said, 'Live, love, eat, and drink good wine.' That's my standard and that is the passion that is now represented in our commitment to provide food made with only the freshest and most natural and organic ingredients, to celebrate local farmers and seasonal ingredients, and to use only humanely raised animal products."

"So what did you tell your franchisees that had to meet this standard, to bring them into line?" I prompted. "When you opened a new place did you sit them down and tell them what you expected of them?"

"I did. I told them"—he looked at me with surprise—"a story!"

Then he told me that story, about one of his early franchised restaurants, in Atlanta. "I was there maybe for the first week when it opened to make sure everyone involved was properly trained and followed the standard and that everything went smoothly. In the beginning there was a line out the door and they almost doubled the amount of money we had expected. So I said 'OK. They are doing very well.' And I left them alone. But six months later I was in for a surprise, when I came back to Atlanta on other business, to bid on the catering contract for the Georgia Aquarium.

"I was doing my presentation. And this feisty older guy says, 'That franchise café of yours downtown. You should close it down. Take the key, throw it out the door, lock it up. It's not you.' So the next morning at six a.m. I went to check on the café, unannounced. And the sandwich bread was old and dry. The romaine had brown spots on the side. You have the simplest thing, a Caesar salad, but it's terrible because the ends are brown. It's not that we bought worst quality; it's just that instead of prepping every day, they did it every three days because that's cheaper and easier. The chicken came from an unexpected and unreliable source. It wasn't me; I really wanted just to close that franchise down immediately.

"I realized I needed to galvanize everyone involved with my brand in a different way, so I told them, 'It always makes me nervous opening a new restaurant, because I think, *What if it doesn't work out? What will people think? Why did I do another restaurant? What if nobody shows up?* It's very, very difficult and it makes me feel very insecure. But that anxiety is a good thing, too, because it keeps me on my toes. And that's the story here, too. You know how everyone is on their toes opening night. The attitude of the staff has to shine. The food has to be top quality and the service premium because the critics will notice every detail. On opening night everyone is on best behavior, making sure everything is just right.'"

Wolfgang's definition of opening night included an attitude toward employees and customers that makes them all feel like part of the Wolfgang Puck family. He was talking about energy and excitement that the staff would transmit to customers who, on any given night, are as important to the restaurant's future as the critics who come on the real opening night. And not just to one particular restaurant's future, either, Wolfgang added, but to the whole enterprise. "People might come to Atlanta from Michigan," he explained. "So you engage with them as if it was opening night and they could be a major critic. You say, 'Oh, you're from Michigan. You know that we have a restaurant in Detroit at the MGM.' Then they are happy because they found out about our restaurant and it's good business for us in both locations."

And then, Wolfgang would tell his employees, "Every night must be opening night in every one of my restaurants. We should always be up to our standard—WELL—and making sure everything is just so. To do less is to fail."

Opening night? Ahha! His staff might not be all that enthusiastic about changing their ways, but they suddenly got exactly the call to action embedded in Wolfgang's Atlanta/opening night story.

Wolfgang realized that the ultimate beneficiary of this story was the customer, who on any night consumes not just food, but the entire experience of a Wolfgang Puck opening night. More than a standard, this story reflects what's necessary for his customers to carry forth when the critic is long gone. They experience opening night, savor it, and retell it.

"A lot of people spend money on advertising," Wolfgang said. "Instead, we advertise to the people we know by following this story every night, and treating them so well that they come back. They bring their friends. They tell their friends."

"And they all tell your story," I said, "because you've made them feel as if they were there on opening night."

He nodded. "As I said, I wish somebody had told me, 'Wolfgang, just tell a story; it's easy!'"

NORMA KAMALI

Of all the people I know in business, one of the most unpredictable is the high fashion designer Norma Kamali, whose boutique creations ordinarily retail for thousands—if not tens of thousands—of dollars apiece. In 2008 I was astonished by an announcement that Kamali would be doing a clothing line for Walmart, with price points of $20 and under. Somebody had to have told somebody a story to pull this one off, I thought.

I'd known Norma since the mid-1970s when she had a small store in upper Manhattan and I was producing *The Deep*. I brought our star, the gorgeous Jacqueline Bisset, to Norma for some help with the wardrobe, which included bathing suits for our underwater scenes. Unfortunately for us, Norma's swimsuit creations tended toward gold lamé with strategic cutouts and leopard-spotted bikinis with rhinestones. Jackie's character was a scuba diver, not a beach bunny, and even though she was an established sex symbol, she wanted to be known as a serious actress. The bikinis were too risqué.

Norma wasn't thinking story when she said, "Oh, just throw a T-shirt on over it." But the "it" shone through, and the rest was pinup history. Jackie Bisset's wet T-shirt gave birth to wet T-shirt contests and propelled our movie into the national consciousness. Norma went on to become a giant in the fashion world, winning Coty and CFDA honors and expanding her brand to include everything from cosmetics to sleeping bag coats.

Nothing Norma had ever done, though, was as unexpected as her joint venture with Walmart. It only made sense in the context of Norma's own backstory. "I never felt that I was pretty or attractive," she told me. But through fashion, she discovered, she could play up her naturally quirky style and feel different but equal to more conventionally pretty girls. This skill became the basis of her brand. "I use fashion to help women gain self-esteem." So when Walmart approached her about designing a line for lower-income women, she got excited about helping a less advantaged segment of the population feel good.

But the problems were legion. How could she design for this price point without alienating her high-end customers and retailers? How could she explain this move to the media? Norma thought back through her own story and decided that the same discovery she'd made as a kid could guide her now. *Different but equal* became her credo for this new enterprise.

The clothes she designed for Walmart would be entirely different from her elite designs. They'd be styled more flexibly and use less expensive materials in order to meet the radically reduced price point. Nevertheless, her goal was to make them look so good that even the high-end customers would admire and want to own them.

But how could she possibly get this different-but-equal concept across to Walmart suppliers—the people who actually cut and sewed the garments? These workers were used to producing clothes as cheaply and quickly as possible. She needed to persuade them that by applying more care and attention, without cutting corners, they could make a low-cost product of high-end quality. But they were the incumbents here, and incumbents rarely want to change. To sway them, Norma needed to reach their hearts. How to do that?

She looked into her own heart. What specifically in her own experience had motivated her to jump at this opportunity to design for Walmart? What she remembered was the stories she had been told by low-income mothers at a public high school in Manhattan where she was organizing students to form their own creative businesses. Those mothers were so ashamed of their clothes that they never came in for school conferences or even met their kids' teachers. That memory resonated with Norma's own story and convinced her that her new line of different-but-equal designs could meaningfully change women's lives. By telling this story of need and opportunity to the suppliers who made these new fashions, Norma showed them how they could be heroes to these women. Her story engaged them in her true purpose, and like proud champions, they overcame their reluctance to change.

Norma told the same story to the vendors, sales force, and media, and everyone who supported this new brand felt like a hero. At the opening of the line in her local Walmart, employees of all different ages, shapes, and sizes volunteered to be human mannequins, standing on platforms in her display area. "They were so proud to sell it," Norma told me. "I was in tears." Now, that is the power of telling a purposeful story!

Norma Kamali's story shows how narratives you have lived or experienced can give rise to powerful, purposeful stories you later may tell in business. But not all the stories that arise from personal experience are helpful. Some are downright paralyzing. Those who master telling to win know how to confront and overcome these negative stories. Better yet, they know how to turn potentially damaging backstories to purposeful advantage.

aHHa!

- You're prewired for story, but you must turn it on!
- The marketplace wants stories, so give them what they want.
- Stories make facts and figures memorable, resonant, and actionable.
- Ignite empathy in the room and face-to-face, and your audience won't just hear you, they'll feel you!
- Purposeful story telling isn't show business, it's *good* business.

CHAPTER FOUR

The Story That Runs Your Story

T he king and I needed to dance. Thai pirates were plundering a wide array of Sony products, and only King Bhumibol Adulyadej could help us stop this theft. So as chairman of Sony Entertainment in the early 1990s I flew to Bangkok with Sony Corporation's top brass, Norio Ohga and Mickey Schulhof, to entreat the king to join our cause. Thailand would be a litmus test for a new Sony strategy to combat the global menace of commercial piracy.

Because entertainment products produced on my watch were among the Sony assets most frequently pirated, I knew I'd need to present my case. I spent most of the flight working with Schulhof on my approach. Mickey was Ohga's confidant and right-hand man in America, and since spearheading Sony's purchase of Columbia Records a few years earlier, he'd been passionately interested in the issue of piracy as it affected Sony's music interests. The king himself was a musician, so I was sure I could present the issue in a way that would resonate with him.

I decided I'd tell the king about an experience I'd had in Chiang Mai just a couple of years earlier, after noticing a local theater displaying a handmade copy of the original poster for my movie *Rain Man,* with Dustin Hoffman and Tom Cruise. I was naturally curious to see how a Thai audience would respond to the movie. I bought a ticket and found a seat in the teeming theater. The dubious projection, I would tell the king, made me feel for the film's director Barry Levinson, who'd labored so hard for perfection. Still, I hoped the Thai audience could appreciate the quality of the drama and superb acting.

The climax of my tale would come just a few minutes after *Rain Man's* opening credits, when someone stood up in front of the projector. Then I realized the person obscuring the screen was not in front of the projector but *inside* it! We were watching a pirated copy of the film, which someone had surreptitiously videotaped in a U.S. theater, then duplicated and distributed for his own profit. This pirate was stealing the economic benefit from all the artists and producers, including myself, who'd devoted years to creating this film. Yet when I complained to the Chiang Mai theater manager, he just shrugged and said, "Everyone does it."

Having told that story, I'd appeal to the king's heart. As a musician himself he had to understand that if artists can't support themselves through their art, they'll be forced to abandon their dreams. And yet all was not yet lost! If His Majesty would help enforce the international anti-piracy laws already on the books, together we could thwart the pirates, defend the creative dream, and protect the rights of artists and producers so they could continue to make great films, music, and technological innovations.

I arrived in Bangkok secure in the knowledge that I'd prepared the best possible story for this royal audience. But my confidence took a hit at first sight of the king's ornate palace. It was like a stage set on steroids. As we were led back to His Majesty's enormous reception chambers, I half expected to see Yul Brynner step around the corner. Instead I found myself face to face with a towering figure in a starched white uniform covered with multicolored badges.

A cold sweat broke out all over my body. The last time I'd seen a grown man wearing that many badges, I was a kid. I'd been hauled into the headmaster's office after my fourth fight in just two weeks at a new school. For half an hour I'd sat in the hallway listening to the headmaster tell my parents his story of what happened—casting me as the villain. "He's no good. He's had three fights with these other students. He has a bad attitude. He's not even trying to fit in." *Fit in?* I was being tormented and assaulted! The headmaster's story didn't mention the older kids who kept beating me up for my lunch money. It didn't mention that all I'd done was hold up my metal lunch tray—the bigger kid swung and broke his own hand, and I never even touched him! Finally I couldn't take it anymore. I charged in to tell *my* side of my story. But the sight of the headmaster made me choke on my words. He was wearing a scoutmaster's uniform with what seemed like a thousand merit badges emblazoned on a sash across his chest. The authority implied by those emblems rendered me mute and defenseless. I just stood there with my mouth hanging open as he acted on his story and threw me out of his school.

That story had lodged in the weeds of my unconscious for more than thirty years, making special appearances any time a figure drenched in authority confronted me. Now in Thailand it roared back with such ferocity that it was all I could do not to make a run for it. But somehow I knew what was happening and sucked it up. I told myself, *Not this time, buddy.*

At full throttle I raced into my prepared story. Every so often I'd come up for air and check for audience reactions. The king seemed almost beatifically empathetic as he listened, nodding and smiling. I noticed Chairman Ohga tweaking his head at something across the room, but since the king was the only audience that mattered, I kept going.

Then Ohga tugged on my sleeve. I whispered sideways, "Just a moment. I've nearly convinced the king!"

"Guber *san*," Ohga said under his breath, "this man is not the king. He is the guard." He nodded to a figure in a rumpled gray suit, talking animatedly to Schulhof on the other side of the room. "That is the king."

Oh my God! In one horrifying instant I realized I'd been sabotaged. Like matches to kindling, those badges had ignited my childhood backstory and sent my attention, intention, and basic common sense up in one disastrous conflagration. I'd been so bamboozled by my own backstory, I'd told the perfect face-to-face front story to the wrong face!

Fortunately, I recovered from my gaffe and later confessed my mistake to the real king. He chuckled, then listened to an abbreviated version of my piracy story. His Majesty sighed and told a story of his own about a ruler who had performed the music of his country and sold 65,000 CDs of his proud work. "Unfortunately, fifty-five thousand of them were pirated," he said. "And I was that ruler. If I can't protect my own music in my own country, how can I help you?"

OOOPS! I thought. Maybe my perfect front story wasn't so perfect, either. But stories work in mysterious ways. Apparently this one was slow-acting. Months later the king did order his government to enforce some of the antipiracy laws. So my story served my purpose after all. But on a personal level it also taught me a sobering lesson about the hidden power of backstories to blur focus, trigger insecurities, deflate enthusiasm, and derail success.

THE HIDDEN POWER OF BACKSTORIES: TIME BOMBS OR BURIED TREASURE?

Reviewing my misadventure in Thailand in light of my present exploration of telling to win, I couldn't help but wonder what was really happening inside my head that day. How could an event so deeply buried in my past have sabotaged me all those decades later? Wasn't there something I could have done to expel or defuse that memory? I wondered, does everyone carry around these hidden time bombs the way I do? If so, was there a way to employ backstory instead of submitting to it, as I had?

For help in decoding these mysteries, I invited my friend Deepak

Chopra to discuss the phenomenon of backstory at my UCLA course Navigating a Narrative World. In addition to being a best-selling author, an endocrinologist, and the founder of the Chopra Center for Wellbeing, Deepak is a practitioner of narrative medicine. This approach to treatment, now gaining ground throughout mainstream medicine, is based on scientific evidence that backstories affect and afflict everyone's life. For better or worse, Deepak told us, they're always there. And because of that, story tellers need to pay close attention not only to their own backstories, but also to their listeners'.

Backstories, he explained, emerge out of our memories of past experiences, imagination, and desire. "You create stories around these thoughts. Then you live out those stories and you call it life." Backstories actually can define a person's future, he said, "because we're conditioned by experience to repeat our stories." Depending on the nature of those stories, this repetition can produce positive or negative results.

As a positive example of backstory, Deepak told the tale his mother used to tell him when he was a child. " 'There's this goddess of wisdom. And there's a goddess of wealth. If you pursue the goddess of wisdom, then the goddess of wealth will become jealous and pursue you.' I started having relationships with these imaginary gods and goddesses and enacting my own stories with them." Those relationships became a core part of his lived backstory.

Having known Deepak for years, I can attest that he's never stopped pursuing the goddess of wisdom, and the goddess of wealth has filled his wallet many times over. But if childhood myths have so much power, why doesn't every kid who listens to fairy tales grow up to be as successful as Deepak Chopra?

Because, he answered, negative memories like my meltdown in front of the headmaster can overwhelm the power of imagination and even the desire for a happy ending. "What makes a person extraordinary," he said, "is that he or she finds a way to tell a *new* story." This doesn't mean changing the experience on which the story is based. It means mentally creating a new context and a new meaning that breaks the pattern and hold of the backstory. The new story then serves as "a bridge from what is to what could be."

To illustrate how all this works, Deepak pointed to the *placebo* and *nocebo* effects observed in medicine. Placebo treatments, or dummy sugar pills, have a proven success rate of about 30 percent in treating a wide variety of ailments, from chronic pain to cancer. And the placebo *effect* accounts for about a third of the benefit of clinically proven drugs. In other words, having confidence in a drug measurably increases its effectiveness, regardless of the drug's proven value. By contrast, the nocebo effect, caused by a belief that the drug will *not* work, measurably reduces the drug's actual effectiveness. "It's not the sugar pill that helps or fails patients," Deepak explained, "but the story about the sugar pill. It's the *story* rather than the pill that's determining the result." Pharmaceutical companies, Deepak pointed out, are mindful of these dueling effects when developing TV ads. To encourage a placebo response, they weave strong emotional story lines around a drug's potential benefits, but deliver the FDA-mandated list of negative side effects in a clipped, emotionless manner that's easy to ignore.

To illustrate the power of personal narratives on the body, Deepak told our class about a soldier that his father, also a physician, had treated during his days in the army of the British Raj. The soldier had lost his ability to speak, and most of the doctors thought he'd had a stroke. "But my father did some detective work and found that several weeks earlier the soldier had received a letter from his home village informing him that his mother had died." The soldier had gone to his sergeant and said, "I want the day off because my mother—" But the sergeant denied his request without letting him finish the sentence. The soldier then went to his major, his colonel, and all the way up, but no one let him finish the sentence with "my mother has died."

"Finally," Deepak said, "the man lost his speech because his subconscious mind said, *It's no use. Nobody is listening.* So my father went to the patient and said, 'I heard you lost your mother. What happened?'

And the patient started to cry. His speech came back. The story was being acted out by his body."

There was a time when I would have assumed the man in Deepak's story was faking it. Everything I've learned recently about telling to win, however, has convinced me that mind-body circuitry is real and that, whether we realize it or not, stories tap directly into those circuits. Our backstories and those of our listeners are always lurking under the surface, poised to spring into action. As I discovered the hard way in Thailand, we ignore them at our peril. In fact, the more we deny or try to run away from them, the more we are at their mercy. But Deepak was saying that if we actively *confront* them, then we can convert even the most dangerous time bombs into valuable treasure.

RULE THE STORY THAT'S RUNNING YOU

Deepak's remarks brought to mind the many powerful entrepreneurs and leaders I know who have personal backstories that might qualify as sinkholes. My run-ins with school bullies can't hold a candle to the childhood poverty, broken homes, exile, and loss that are common elements of these remarkable life stories. Yet somehow these individuals managed to break the patterns of their negative past and script a positive future. Many of these leaders drew on tales of their own early frustrations, as the designer Norma Kamali drew on her childhood desire to feel good about herself, to inspire and tell and retell a new story of purpose that became their personal brand. Others refer to the oral stories that shaped their youth as cautionary tales of how *not* to conduct themselves. Some of the most powerful leaders and entrepreneurs I've known, however, converted their seminal backstories into the organizational know-how and drive that enabled them to build empires.

Serial entrepreneur John Paul Dejoria is one such phenomenon.

Today his primary company, John Paul Mitchell Systems, produces more than ninety products sold through 90,000 hair salons worldwide, with annual retail sales topping $600 million. But some sixty years ago little John Paul was living with his brother and single Greek immigrant mother in Echo Park, near downtown Los Angeles. John Paul's mother didn't have enough money to buy Christmas presents, but John Paul and his brother loved to look at the mechanical puppets in the Christmas window displays, so they took the trolley car to Bullock's department store. The year John Paul was five his mother pointed out a woman in a navy suit who stood in front of the store ringing a silver bell.

"Boys," she said to John Paul and his seven-year-old brother, "I'm giving you a dime. See that lady ringing the bell? Go over there and put it in her bucket."

John Paul didn't understand. In 1950, a dime was a lot of money to a kid who didn't have much. Why did he have to give it away?

"That's the Salvation Army," his mother told him. "They need it more than we do. In life, you'll always run across people who need it more than you do. Always try and share. I know it's a lot for us, but it means even more for them."

John Paul thought about what his mother had said, and as he and his brother put that dime in the bucket he felt a thrill he'd never forget. His youth from then on was anything but easy. While still in grade school he got up at three in the morning to fold and deliver newspapers. At nine years old he sold Christmas cards door to door. Later he sold Collier's encyclopedias. He joined the U.S. Naval Reserve, then did everything from pumping gas to repairing bicycles in an often unsuccessful attempt to avoid homelessness. But through all his struggles, the story his mother had told him—which he heard to mean that success unshared is failure—remained with him. And while visiting my house in Hawaii some thirty years later, John Paul told me how that backstory ultimately guided him from poverty to fortune.

Dejoria was in his early thirties when he teamed up with hairstylist Paul Mitchell to develop a new line of hair care products, which they launched on a loan of just $700. "I slept in my car for the first two weeks and we started with one product line and a story that captured the stylists' interest." Drawing from their own experience working in salons, they keyed their tale to an audience of stylists who worked hard, often owned their own salons, and were strapped for money and pressed for time. "At the back basin," Dejoria told them, "you condition hair, you put it on someone's head, you wait ten minutes, rinse it off. Ten minutes of your time, more water, it all goes down the drain." Then, having proven his empathy for them, John Paul told how they could reduce these problems dramatically. "Ours is a leave-in conditioner that the beauty industry has needed for years. When you cut the hair, your scissors slide through it easier. You get a cleaner cut. When you blow dry the hair, it's already been conditioned." The story was about fulfilling need. "Their need, not mine." To cap it off, John Paul guaranteed his sales to salon owners; if they didn't sell their inventory, they could return it for a full refund, so they'd never lose money on his product. That story, of course, was a direct descendant of the seminal story of John Paul's mother and the gift of the dime. The ideal that underlies both stories is commitment to the greater good.

Dejoria has told variations of his childhood epiphany story with every product he makes, including Patrón tequila (packaged in recycled materials and providing work to artisan craftsmen in Mexico) and John Paul Pet products (tested *by* and *for* animals rather than *on* them). And financially, just how well has this story delivered for Dejoria? According to Forbes, he has a net worth of more than $4 billion. Not bad for a guy who used to live in his car!

ROCK LEGEND GENE SIMMONS, otherwise known as "The Demon" of KISS, is another backstory survivor. Recently Gene e-mailed me a photo from his BlackBerry as he stood onstage in front of sixty thousand screaming fans in Chile. This man was pushing sixty in a business notorious for short-lived careers, and he'd been an international icon for more than half his life! He also had appeared in dozens of films and television shows, created cartoons, and starred in his own reality series. Yet this titan of entrepreneurism had also had plenty of flops, some of which I unfortunately participated in. Back in the 1970s my partner at Casablanca Record and Filmworks, Neil Bogart, had the inspired idea that we should release solo albums by each of the four KISS band members simultaneously. I loved the concept, even though I knew it was a naked ploy to make four times as much money as our typical single KISS album release. Gene was suspicious of the plan, since not all the band members possessed solo potential. But avarice was invented in Hollywood. Nothing could stop us. We shipped gold. The public returned platinum. Fortunately, Gene took the losses in stride. "I'm a child of risk," he said when I asked if he regretted our gamble. He'd begun life as the immigrant son of a single mother, and he never forgot it.

Whatever KISS's ups and downs, Gene's own brand remains a juggernaut of merchandising and licensing. His enormous home office is a living museum of KISS-related products and services, from comics to toys to lifestyle gifts, books, trophies, and memorabilia of all descriptions. Literally overwhelming the senses, they fill every nook and cranny of a space the size of a warehouse. And it was here that we met to discuss Gene's secret to success.

Gene didn't mince words. "My mother's story, which she lived and told, is my connection and filter to almost anything I do," he said. "My mother was born in Hungary, and at fourteen years of age, she was in the concentration camps of Nazi Germany. She told me how she watched her entire family be wiped out, how at age fourteen she was doing the hair of the commandant's wife to survive."

Backstories don't get much more negative than that. But instead of letting it bury him, Gene translated his story into a vow of determination. His personal mantra became: *I, too, will survive, whatever it takes—even if I have to be a chameleon.* "My life has been a zigzag of back and forth," he said, "so I had to be flexible. But who I am is not the outside; who I am is the inside. I know where I'm going, and I'm convinced in what I'm going to say."

Survival became a whole lot more interesting to Gene after he moved from Israel, where he was born, to America. "Television and movies were such a culture shock. In America, you could fly through the air; you could wear masks. There were comic books and horror movies. Everything here was larger than life." To succeed, Gene figured, he, too, needed to become larger than life. And his desire to survive was now matched by his desire to succeed. "I'll be damned if anybody is going to stop me, and I'll be double damned before I stop myself from succeeding."

To this day, Gene's mother's Holocaust story drives him, but long ago he turned this tale of adversity to his advantage. Although he knowingly lets it run him, he never lets it run him down. He often shares this story when he starts a new enterprise, and credits it further for his refusal ever to put all his business eggs in one basket. He unabashedly tells his partners, "It's you and me, buddy. We laugh and cry together." Yet for all that togetherness, he keeps each of his business interests separate. No way will Gene Simmons ever cross-collateralize his efforts or bet the whole farm. This policy doesn't preclude failure, but it contains losses while recognizing the necessity of risk that is embodied in his mother's story. This backstory gives Gene the grit to rebound from failure instead of crumbling under it. And that resiliency has provided the springboard for his brand and career. Whatever may go wrong, Simmons will survive.

IF THE LION DOESN'T TELL HIS STORY, THE HUNTER WILL

Unfortunately, some of the backstories that threaten to sabotage us are told by others. It may seem as if these tales—or frequently *tall* tales—are out of our control. But these stories, too, we ignore at our peril.

If the lion does not tell his story, the hunter will is an African saying that I wish I'd learned back when I worked for Sony. The hunters we had to contend with in the early 1990s were the American media, and they were sharpening their story-telling spears before I even got in the door.

Remember, there were no blogs in those days, no company websites or YouTube. As the only gatekeepers between corporate America and the public, the mainstream media controlled both the flow and the content of every story. And because Sony, the Japanese electronics giant, had bought the iconic American company Columbia Pictures Entertainment and named me CEO, I was depicted as the poster boy for the sellout of America. My Japanese owners dismissed the premise that this was a significant financial story, so I followed their lead and let the herd decide what was heard. I realized, you can't fight folks who buy ink by the barrel. That was my first mistake.

In 1995, after leaving the company, I partnered with Sony to form Mandalay—a multimedia company that I'm still helming fifteen years later. At the same time, I assumed I was bowing out of the media's ongoing story of Sony's entertainment investment. Even as I made this exit, however, Sony Corp. President Ohga was tidying up the corporate books in preparation for his move up to the chairmanship of Sony's global empire. He claimed he "wanted to make some healthy room for the man who followed him." So, at the end of his tenure as president, he approved a $2.7 billion write-down, which was announced just two weeks after I left Sony.

Much of this sum reflected the excess Sony had paid six years earlier for Columbia. Now, I was fully prepared to take responsibility for decisions I'd made as CEO, and there's no doubt we'd suffered some significant financial losses at the end of my tenure. But much of the write-down consisted of acquisition costs that had been incurred before Sony purchased our public company and named me CEO of the new venture.

Nevertheless, the coincidence of my departure from Sony, my own participation, and the timing of the write-down fueled the imagination of two writers who decided to exploit the media's now familiar story by bundling it into a book. Not wanting to dignify or validate it, I refused to cooperate. Strike two.

My reticence allowed the authors to tell my part of the story their way—which I would experience later to my detriment. The book was dominated by the antics of my former business partner Jon Peters, even though he'd left shortly after arriving at Sony, and my tenure as CEO continued for four more years. The book also ignored the company's many successes during this period. In 1992, for example, Sony Pictures was highly profitable, with sales of $2.4 billion, a 33 percent increase from 1989, the year Sony purchased Columbia. To be sure, in my last year we also had losses, but the authors failed to mention contributing factors such as the appreciation of the yen against the dollar. In 1993 alone currency fluctuations caused Sony's net income to drop by 70 percent. You'd have to be superhuman to make enough box office hits to offset a financial blindside like that—even if you weren't up against more than $300 million owed in annual interest payments on inherited debt, plus $100 million in annual "goodwill charges" taken over forty years against Sony's purchase.

And yet I still did not directly refute the story these authors peddled or, more important, tell my own. Instead, furious and angry, I blamed them, the media, their publisher, even the readers that believed them or paid that story forward. I let the backstory they told run me. Strike three.

Finally it dawned on me that I'd struck myself out of the game. Even if I couldn't prevent these writers from telling or selling their story, I should have swung at it with my own!

That epiphany changed everything. Instead of ducking, I began to confront the inquiries and direct the conversation about my future business activities. The more clearly and calmly I corrected misinformation, while admitting mea culpa for mistakes I'd actually made, the less power the media had over my emotions.

Like so many of my other detours on the road to success, this episode proved a useful, if painful, lesson: If your audience has a negative story about you or your product or business, you'd better confront it. As famed author Salman Rushdie once said, "Those who do not have power over the story that dominates their lives, the power to retell it, rethink it, deconstruct it, joke about it, and change it as times change, truly are powerless, because they cannot think new thoughts." Once you lose control of your own story, you'll need double the muscle to get that power back.

This lesson is all the more critical in today's age of digital media. When negative stories start to circulate online, changing the narrative—and quickly—becomes especially imperative. So, late in 2009, when bloggers began to tell a potentially damaging story casting Rich Rosenblatt's new enterprise Demand Media as the villain of digital content creation, he immediately went into action, rallying his team to correct the story with maximum force by recasting his company in the hero's role.

The controversy erupted around Demand's ability to produce some four thousand pieces of original content each day by employing more than ten thousand freelance contributors. The crux of the hostile narrative was that Demand Media was a "content mill." An article in *Wired* magazine actually triggered the drama by comparing Demand Media's system to Henry Ford's production line for cars in the early twentieth century. This story was repeated at cocktail and dinner parties and percolated throughout the company. Unlike me, Rosenblatt wisely seized the energy of his attackers and flipped it in his favor.

"Henry Ford kept the inner workings of his production line a secret," Rosenblatt told me at the time. "I'm going to challenge the critics by telling them all what makes us tick. Our platform powers over three billion conversations every month. On the other side of the Demand chain are thousands of content creators who will tell you Demand Media is a hero to them, their families, and their careers. I'm going to confront the criticism with a manifesto that reflects the story they tell."

This document was challenging to craft, Rosenblatt told me, because it had to serve as a guideline for the official story his team would tell, yet not restrict their ability to tell it forward and discuss it individually in their own ways. While the first priority was to rebut "the content mill–Henry Ford story and the nastiness that's been dumped on us recently," the manifesto also had to reflect the full breadth and depth of Demand Media's business.

The ultimate goal was not necessarily to change the minds of the critics but to put new words in the mouths of Demand's most valuable audience—its content creators and consumers. "We will refer back to it and it will be the foundation of much more to come," Rosenblatt said. "It will spiral, but it will spiral on our terms, not theirs."

RIDING THE STORY THAT RUNS YOUR AUDIENCE

It's September 2008. Strains of "Here Comes the Bride" float through the garden of the Bel-Air Hotel. But the bride is a guy, and so is the groom, and the minister . . . is Alice Walker! In the audience with me are Quincy Jones, Oprah Winfrey, and many of the other luminaries who made the 1985 film version of Alice's Pulitzer Prize–winning opus *The Color Purple.* Now we've all come to celebrate the marriage of producer Scott Sanders, who, with Quincy and Oprah, coproduced the Tony-winning *Color Purple* on Broadway. As I watch Scott and his partner, Brad Lamm, exchange vows, I recall how much difficulty Scott had convincing Alice to agree to his plan to put her novel on the stage. The obstacle, if only Scott had realized it, was Alice's backstory.

In 1997, when Scott first approached me to help him secure the live stage rights for *Color Purple,* he'd just left Mandalay, where he was president of our TV operation, to launch his own television and theatrical production company with the financial backing of multibillionaire Phil Anschutz and Carnival Cruise Lines owner Micky Arison. Warner Bros. controlled the rights Scott sought, and I was happy to approach Terry Semel, then still chairman of WB, to vouch for Sanders's professional credentials and passion for the project. Semel agreed to license the rights, but only if Scott first secured Alice Walker's blessing. Although she no longer held the legal rights, it was understood that *The Color Purple* was still Alice's baby.

I knew Scott to be a superb salesperson, but I warned him that Alice was not an easy sell. I told him about my first pilgrimage to her home in Northern California, back when I still wore a ponytail and backpack, to ask her to entrust the film version of her story to a white man from Boston whose affinity for her struggling Southern black heroines was dubious at best. I told Scott the story I'd shared with Alice about my grandmother, with whom I was extremely close, who used to read out loud private letters from people in our family and in her past. Those letters introduced me to my heritage and taught me to honor the truth of these people's lives. Since Alice's novel was told through letters based on her own heritage, my backstory echoed the heartbeat of her material and demonstrated that I understood the power of personal narrative. I'd said to Alice, "What if I could bring the people you most admire to execute your story in a film that preserves your voice and the characters you created, and resonates with that same authenticity?" When she asked who I had in mind, I named Quincy Jones, an old friend with whom I'd done movies in the 1960s and '70s and a giant talent within the African-American community. Little did I know that just prior to my visit Alice had fallen in love with a short piece of Quincy's music. So when his name came up, she later told me, it seemed like a stroke of magic—and in the backstory of Alice's life, magic plays a large and respected role. The movie we made together went on to win eleven Oscar nominations!

The moral of my tale to Scott was that he needed to pay attention to Alice's backstory as well as his own. I called Alice and asked her to take the meeting. And with that, he made his way up to her house and told her how moved he was by her story of a woman who, against all social odds, found the person she loved. He said he passionately believed there were emotionally resonant stories in the book that never made it to the screen, and he wanted not only to showcase those narratives, but to enrich them in the stage medium through the music that he felt the story had in its soul. Scott promised Alice that if he couldn't do a stage version at least as well as the movie, he wouldn't even try.

Unfortunately, Scott put his accent on a seriously wrong syl-*la*-ble. What he didn't fully realize was that the backstory running Alice at this time, and which she continuously told herself, centered on the *negative* fallout from the film version. She told me later that she'd taken an immediate liking to Scott. "I think he was coming from just that place of enthusiasm." But there was a big but. He didn't seem to be aware that the black community's reaction to the film had taken a major emotional toll on Alice. Black critics accused her of colluding with "White Hollywood" to demonize black men. They called her a sellout and mounted campaigns attacking the film, even comparing it to the notoriously racist silent movie *Birth of a Nation*. "They were still going strong five and six and seven years later, writing about it and vilifying me. . . . That's the part that Scott didn't know."

Had Scott known, he might have told a story that addressed those sensitive concerns and set Alice's mind at ease on their first meeting. Instead, she told him no.

Fortunately, Scott was truly dyslexic in thinking that "no" meant "on." He enlisted Quincy Jones and Diana Ross to vouch for him. He flew Alice to New York to introduce her to the leading lights of Broadway. He won her over through sheer conviction, goodwill, and persistence. And when Oprah signed on as a third producer, Scott wisely enlisted her to help him bring the African-American audience into the theater to see and support Alice's story. The show went on to be nominated for eleven Tony Awards, including best musical, and grossed more than $100 million. But this all took eight long years. Even recently, Alice confided to me, "I wished many times that he had understood. . . ."

KNOWING ALICE'S TRUE BACKSTORY might have helped Scott craft a shortcut to victory. But how? As I cast my mind back over similar negotiations in my own life, I recalled a competition that I, like Scott, had lost because I didn't know my listener's backstory—but that also taught me how a true master of telling to win can turn psychological narrative into professional leverage.

It was the late 1980s. My business partner, Scott Sternberg, and I had gotten word privately through Larry King's agent, Bob Wolfe, that Larry was interested in pursuing new opportunities beyond CNN's *Larry King Live.* So Scott and I created a global talk show called *Wired* with Larry in mind and prepared to give him an ownership stake in it. We knew he didn't own his CNN show, and he wasn't earning a lot of money working for Ted Turner. But this was a big deal that required big bait. Roone Arledge at ABC also was vying for Larry, and Ted Turner did not want Larry to leave the Turner network.

Over several meetings with Larry, Scott and I laid out our concept for a show that was more robust and multifaceted than the straight-talk format of the *Larry King Live* show, and we made sure he understood that our offer was twice the size of his CNN deal and would give him ownership. I was so confident that we'd capture his attention and interest, I never even thought to tell Larry a story. When he passed, electing to stay on CNN, I was baffled. How had Turner persuaded him?

Later, over coffee at his Beverly Hills home, Larry told me what happened. I learned that Turner hadn't told a story either. But he knew his audience well enough to seize the reins of the backstory that ran Larry and turn it in Ted's desired direction. He did this by making one simple demand.

Turner said, "Just tell me, 'Good-bye.'"

Those two words unleashed a cascade of memories and emotions bottled up in Larry's backstory. Larry could not speak them. Instead he told his agent, "I'm staying."

Turner had known that the story running Larry was dominated by the untimely death of his father. Deep down, Larry always felt his father was disloyal for leaving him when he was young. Turner knew Larry had issues with disloyalty. By pushing the emotional button nested in that backstory, Ted ruled the day.

PRESSING YOUR ADVANTAGE DOESN'T have to be quite that adversarial, though. Sometimes knowing your audience's backstory can help you frame your front story to win them over in a positive way. The first time I can recall doing this was back in the 1970s when I sold David Begelman on *Midnight Express.*

David was chairman of Columbia Pictures when I left my job there as studio head to form my own production company. Always supportive of me, David agreed to distribute my first film, *The Deep.* After its great success, he was willing to finance a riskier project based on the true story of a young Long Island boy caught smuggling drugs out of Turkey and sentenced to life in prison. However, David agreed to sign on only if I was cross-collateralized, that is, if I applied my profits from *The Deep* to any potential losses on *Midnight Express.* No filmmaker wants to risk the biscuit this way, but I so much wanted to make this next picture that I agreed.

Near the end of the development phase of the project, I began to get wind of a very bad personal story that was overtaking David. Early in 1977 the actor Cliff Robertson revealed that David had forged an endorsement on a $10,000 studio check that should have been paid to Robertson. The IRS launched an investigation and found that Begelman had forged several checks, totaling $40,000, to cover his gambling debts. This was a relatively insignificant amount by Hollywood standards, and because Columbia had prospered during his tenure, he remained head of the studio. Nevertheless, the government investigation now had a red-hot light trained on David's every move.

Early in 1978, David secured an early cut of *Midnight Express* for a screening with Norman Levy, Columbia's head of domestic sales. Clearly uncomfortable, David sat in front of me and twitched through every frame. When the film ended, Norman gave me a nod of approval. David, however, said, "This is a brutal picture. I don't think it's releasable. What will the Drug Enforcement Agency say? I'm just not comfortable that this is the kind of film Columbia Pictures should do." And then, smelling my panic, David cleverly offered to release me from cross-collateralization if I'd release Columbia from the distribution deal.

This offer seemed unnaturally generous. If I didn't accept, I risked going down with the film. But on the way upstairs I thought, *I just can't do it.* When we reached his office, I said, "David, this is not a story about criminality. It's a story about the pain of injustice. This kid may have been guilty, but the punishment so far exceeded the nature of the crime. They wanted to take his entire life away. Can you imagine the sympathy the audience will feel for him?"

Without realizing it, I was aiming straight for David's backstory. Because he was deeply worried that his whole life was going to be taken away for kiting three checks, he couldn't help seeing the film as a reflection of his own story. By reframing the criminal in *Midnight Express* as a victim of injustice who heroically perseveres, I gave Begelman both a glimmer of hope for his own situation and an incentive to support the film. Instinctively, I'd used telling to win as the secret sauce.

Fortunately, Norman then chimed in, saying he thought Columbia could make money on the film. David glared at Norman, and in that glare he hatched a plan. He'd make a bet with me. We wouldn't do any U.S. test screenings. Instead, the film would do or die at the Cannes Film Festival. If the reception in Cannes was underwhelming, I'd fall on my sword.

I swallowed hard and agreed to David's gamble. At Cannes the audience sat in dead silence all the way through the end credits. Then the lights came on and two thousand people stood up and cheered.

Sadly, life did not follow my artful framing. David struggled with depression for years afterward and ultimately committed suicide. I couldn't change the ending for him, but *Midnight Express* went on to win two Oscars, including Best Screenplay and Score, and six Golden Globes, including Best Picture. It was a huge commercial success, ultimately on David Begelman's watch. And the DEA wound up supporting the film.

But as with so many of the stories I told in the early phases of my career, my telling to Begelman was instinctive rather than calculated. I found the right words through serendipity rather than design. I aimed the story toward my target automatically, rather than intentionally. And I relied on my audience to listen, instead of using telling to win to *guaran-*

tee me his attention. In short, I didn't understand that to turn purposeful stories into a game-changing success tool, you have to know how to get ready . . . get set . . . and tell!

aHHa!

- Own your backstory so it doesn't sabotage you when you tell your *front* story.
- Be active in your own rescue; confront the stories that others are telling about you.
- Leverage the backstory that rules your listener; it can be a powerful ally.

PART TWO

THE ART OF THE TELL

PUTTING YOUR STORY TO WORK

CHAPTER FIVE

Ready . . .

*T*he Olympics are coming! The Olympics are coming!.
Though the 1984 Summer Games were still two years away,
Los Angeles was in a lather of anticipation. Every businessperson in town wanted a role in this enterprise, and I was no exception. At the time, my company was producing movies, television, and
music. I loved sports and sensed that this historic athletic event right in
our own backyard could be the opportunity of a lifetime. But how? What
exactly was my goal? What did I want to accomplish at, for, and with the
Olympics? Who was the audience I needed to persuade? And how best
could I appeal to their interests and win them over?

No one would let me in the door just because I wanted to be part of
the action. And the big-ticket roles were already taken. ABC had locked
up production of U.S. television coverage of the games. And the LA
Olympic Organizing Committee, headed by Peter Ueberroth and Harry
Usher, was in charge of the opening and closing ceremonies, physical
venues, and athletic events. So I had no shot at producing the physical or
broadcast action . . . but what about the music? At my previous companies, Casablanca and Polygram, we'd created the soundtrack albums for

Flashdance, which sold platinum, and *Midnight Express,* whose score won the Oscar. A role related to music would be congruent with my experience and interests.

Suddenly I had my goal—or so I thought. My company would produce the music for the Twenty-third Olympiad. Not only would this make us participants in this historic celebration, but also it would create a world-class credit for my company.

With great expectations, I set up a meeting with Harry Usher, general manager and gatekeeper to the Games' ultimate power broker, LAOOC president Peter Ueberroth. Harry seemed a promising audience because he knew me and knew I had experience and credibility in the music arena. Still, I prepared in advance to make sure I aimed for his top interests. My research revealed that the LAOOC's goal was to make this the most successful and profitable Games ever, thus demonstrating that the Olympics could be a powerful economic engine. To appeal to Usher's interests and prove that my proposition possessed both authenticity and congruence, we'd need to offer use of the music to the LAOOC for free. Our economic benefit would come from sales of the album.

Confident that I had the right audience and the right proposition, I went to meet with Usher on his turf at LAOOC headquarters. Unfortunately, at that point in my career I still thought that the right data and strategy constituted the keys to the kingdom. Usher had just a few minutes for me, and I spent them laying out our credentials and tallying up the revenue streams that new music could add to the Games.

Usher listened dutifully, then said, "I'm not sure. Go see Ric Birch at David Wolper's office. They're producing the opening and closing ceremonies, and maybe they can use some music. Maybe they'll get it." Translation: Usher *didn't* get "it."

I retreated, bruised but not yet beaten. The problem seemed to be "it." Usher couldn't feel my proposition's emotional resonance. I'd targeted a goal that had no heart. No wonder I'd failed to move him. But where was the heart of my offering? I could feel it, but I didn't know how to tell it.

A month later I was sitting in a lodge in Africa doing preproduction research for a documentary about lowland and mountain gorillas. Suddenly a cacophony erupted in our audio engineer's room next door. I heard trumpets! Drums! Immediately I recognized Charles Fox's iconic theme that was the signature for *ABC Wide World of Sports.*

In my mind I saw the familiar images of athletes performing, with the concluding shots of the guy careening off the ski jump and crashing into the snow as the show's host, Jim McKay, narrated, "The thrill of victory and the agony of defeat. . . . *The human drama of athletic competition.*" Filled with excitement and anticipation, I followed this clarion call to the engineer's portable television and was instantly transported to an athletic drama on the other side of the world.

This was my "it"! By telling the story of how I'd been emotionally transported by a piece of music all the way from Africa to a specific event on the other side of the world, I could illustrate the call to action that our Olympic music segments would deliver to audiences worldwide. I well knew from my work in the movies how the right score could combine with visual images to rivet people's attention. Great music can encode the whole story of a film and give it emotional unity. And, if the impact of Bill Conti's tune "Gonna Fly Now" for *Rocky* was any indication, the relationship between music and visuals only intensifies when the story revolves around sports. The music we produced would encode and unify the emotional drama of the 1984 Olympics in a series of signature themes! *That* was the heart of my goal—my "it" factor.

Back in Los Angeles I did some research and discovered that, although music had played a limited role in the Olympics since the 1930s, no one had ever created a whole suite of world-class themes specifically for one Olympiad. We weren't just talking elevator music or background noise. We'd employ the greatest composers in the world to create a unique musical signature for each athletic event so that listeners would instantly recognize what sport they would expect to see. Each piece would serve as a call for audiences to participate both physically and emotionally in the human drama of that event. The musical seduction would begin weeks in advance in promos, and continue during coverage of the actual Games. The music would call to audiences in the venues at the physical Games. And it would prompt audiences to remember these Olympics for years afterward through our soundtrack album of all the themes.

Now that I owned the heart of my goal, the ideas flowed as I prepared anew to tell my story. But which audience should I tell first? It would take a flock of geese to deliver this golden egg, and each represented a different set of interests.

I decided the LAOOC's official endorsement, signified by the graphic stamp of those Olympic rings, would be key to telling and selling my proposition to anyone else. And since Ric Birch was my only way back to Usher, Birch had to be my next audience.

I arranged to meet Birch at LAOOC headquarters—the venue where he was most likely to view me as an Olympic contender—and told him that my idea for the Olympiad was nested in an experience I'd had in Africa. Then I told him that story, concluding with my call to action, "Through the rainbow of talent we'll bring to the composition and performance of this music, we'll honor the spirit of the Olympics and dramatically enhance all audiences' experience of the Games."

Ric smiled. "I get it," he said.

And so it began. With Ric's backing, we told Harry Usher the Africa story. Now he got it. ABC Sports producer Roger Goodman heard my story, and he got it. With ABC's network buy-in I moved on to CBS Records CEO Walter Yetnikoff. We had an existing business relationship, and we'd share the profits of this album, so it was an easier tell. But Yetnikoff was interested in music that would sell far into the future, so I emphasized the collectible value our recording would have, especially if we attracted the highest possible caliber of composers.

With Yetnikoff's backing, I told my story to Grammy- and Oscar-winners John Williams, Quincy Jones, and Bill Conti. To appeal to their interests, I emphasized that the Olympic audience was estimated at 2 billion people—all of whom would hear their music. But I also had to defuse the prejudices that some of these artists had against the "Holly-wood machine." If it looked like I was trying to cash in on the Olympics at their expense, they'd turn me down. So, turning standard practice on its head, we promised that they'd retain all publishing rights to their com-positions. Suddenly everyone got it and wanted in. We filled out our ros-ter of talent with Giorgio Moroder, Bob James, Burt Bacharach, Carole Bayer Sager, Christopher Cross, Toto, Foreigner, Herbie Hancock, and Philip Glass. Now we just had to deliver the goods.

With ten months to get all these diverse artists to write, perform, and record their compositions, I'd wake up every night in a cold sweat, pic-turing a packed LA Coliseum, a conductor raising his baton, and . . . no music. But finally came the day when composer John Williams and David Wolper, who was in charge of the opening and closing ceremonies, called us down to the scoring stage at MGM to listen to a rehearsal of William's Fanfare. As the first ten notes poured forth from that 101-piece orchestra, my eyes filled with tears. I felt the whole experience we'd been through finally coming to fruition. The music proved every bit as moving and powerful as my story had promised.

We did more than reach our global audience. We moved them. John Williams's Olympic theme won a Grammy. The final album cover was imprinted with the Olympic rings and bore a gold seal that read, "The Official Music of the XXIIIrd Olympiad Los Angeles 1984." And every Olympiad since has had a soundtrack of its own.

PREPARATION IS THE MASTER OF SUCCESS

Today I see clearly why my initial pitch to Harry Usher failed and my later story succeeded. Before even attempting to tell my story, I should have much more sharply defined my targets, from the heart of my goal to the what's-in-it-for-them. To move my target audiences to action, I'd needed to ignite their passion, and to do that I had to put them inside the *experience* I was offering, not just the business plan. The keys to the king-dom weren't and never could be purely informational.

In retrospect, this episode shows just how much preparation matters in mastering the art of the tell. Back in 1983 I may not have fully under-stood that a story was what I needed to tell, but I did realize that there's a reason marksmen don't shout *"Fire! Aim! Ready!"* While no one can guarantee that you'll hit your targets, if you don't bring them into focus, you're almost certain to miss.

That may sound obvious, and yet executive search guru Bill Simon told me recently that lack of preparation is the number one reason why executive candidates fail to win over prospective employers in job in-terviews. Simon is a senior client partner and managing director of the media, entertainment, and convergence sector at Korn/Ferry Interna-tional, the behemoth search firm that specializes in high-level global re-cruitment and talent management. I'd engaged him on several occasions to headhunt top leadership candidates for my companies, so I knew he *only* represented individuals who were supremely qualified and experi-enced. That made his remark all the more alarming. If these folks didn't prepare to get themselves hired, how would they prepare to lead organi-zations, persuade customers, manage employees, and sell products?

Simon explained that arrogance and self-righteousness can mis-lead potential executive hirees into thinking they don't need to prepare. Instead of doing the advance work required to shine a light on their at-titude and aptitude, some fall back on their résumés. This usually is a fatal mistake, he said, because the essence of what audiences remember is wrapped not in the tellers' résumés but in the way they tell their stories.

When I asked how he advises his clients to prepare, Simon said he tells them first to set their goals and make them clear. "Transparency is a trite word these days. Everybody uses it about the workplace and busi-ness, but it's actually very important. The story has to have a purpose, it has to be relevant, and it has to have a conclusion." He paused and repeated for emphasis, "Even in a business situation, there has to be a reason for telling the story."

To illustrate what he meant by "purpose," Simon mentioned the candidate who'd wowed the UCLA search committee in 2009 when we were working together on hiring a new dean.

WHAT'S THE HEART OF YOUR GOAL?

Our committee was seeking a leader for one of the country's premier schools of film, theater, and digital media, with alumni giants such as *The Godfather* director Francis Ford Coppola. For months we'd been hunting for three top candidates to advance to the chancellor for his final decision. Then Bill Simon lured Teri Schwartz to meet with us.

Teri was the founding dean of the School of Film and Television at Loyola Marymount University, but it wasn't her credentials that impressed us. What immediately captured our attention was the way she began her two-hour interview with a story that told us she'd done her homework on *us*.

"The problem UCLA faces is obvious," she began. "It's hemorrhaging funding and resources. But, more important, your school has lost its vibrancy. A new dean must change the culture and create a new story for the school. Economic well-being will follow collective response but never precede it."

She told us this was a once-in-a-lifetime opportunity to help the school reimagine itself for the twenty-first century. But change wouldn't come without a certain amount of internal struggle, since UCLA was a mature institution. The hero of our story—our future dean—would have to be someone who could galvanize everyone from students to administrators to go down a very new and special road.

"It's not about me," she said. "It's about a vision for a great school whose graduates will become industry leaders and inspire change for a better world." That vision was the heart of Teri Schwartz's goal for her story.

But it was the way she narrated this goal that captivated and stayed with me. Teri concluded her story with the magical analogy of our school as a reflecting pool into which every person associated with the school would drop a new quality of diversity, innovation, and technology. All these drops would ripple outward into the world and into the future, and each ripple would reflect our individual and collective vision and participation.

Teri's story paved the way for an engaging and energetic interview, after which she met with us as a group and individually several more times before we made our final decision. Through all these meetings, her opening story and, in particular, her metaphor of that reflecting pool continued to resonate. By articulating the heart of her goal so clearly in the context of our problem, Dean Schwartz established an emotional connection that served her well. We advanced her to the chancellor as one of the finalists, and just a few weeks later she was hired.

BUT DO THE SAME rules of preparation that govern the art of telling to get hired also apply to the art of telling to sell a commercial product? To find out, I turned to brand powerhouse Lynda Resnick. With her husband, Stewart Resnick, Lynda owns and runs Roll International, a $2 billion corporation with more than four thousand employees and product lines as diverse as Teleflora, FIJI Water, and POM Wonderful. As the overseer of all their marketing and branding, Lynda always has the ultimate goal of turning her companies into robust businesses that benefit the purchaser and deliver an economic windfall. And she unapologetically credits the art of the tell for her success in this enterprise.

"I don't do companies that don't have a story," she told me, "because if they don't have a story, they don't have a business."

Resnick's father is Hollywood veteran Jack Harris, who produced such cult classics as *The Blob* and *The Eyes of Laura Mars*. So she grew up not only listening to stories but watching her dad develop them. That legacy taught her that the first rule of the tell is to give the audience an emotional experience. So the heart of the goal for each story she tells is the feeling she wants her audience to have. But this call to emotion has to serve her larger purpose, which is what she wants the audience to do. In other words, the call to emotion has to *move* the audience to heed the call to action. Whether Lynda wants her audience to finance, make, sell, or buy products, she knows she first has to find a way to connect them emotionally to that product.

Lynda told me that she never just makes up the emotion she wants her audience to feel. Instead, she finds the heart within each product. "Think inside the box," she said. "The answer to the problem lies within the problem itself." If you can succeed in telling a story that makes your audience feel as if this heart is beating for them, she told me, they will buy your product in order to own the story. Case in point: Jackie Kennedy's fake pearls.

In 1996 Lynda noticed that Sotheby's was auctioning a string of imitation pearls from the estate of Jacqueline Kennedy Onassis. She wanted to buy them to replicate as collectibles through the Franklin Mint, which the Resnicks then owned, but first she had to tell their story in a way that would gain her husband Stewart's support. He assumed the necklace would sell for the listed value of $300 to $700, but Lynda warned him the pearls were more likely to sell for at least $25,000. Then, before he could object, she showed him the heart of her goal through photos of Jackie wearing the necklace while in the White House. One showed little John John on her lap pulling at the pearls. "She wore them in nearly every picture ever taken of her," Lynda told her husband. "They're an icon of an icon." Immediately, he got it: Any woman who wore an exact replica of these pearls would feel as if she were channeling the queen of America's Camelot. So what Lynda was really buying was the story of Jackie. She would then package this story through the replica pearls and tell it to her employees, media, and customers, giving each and every one the experience of Camelot's queen. They'd then tell the story forward to inspire others to buy the same necklace.

The Resnicks ended up paying $211,000 for the necklace, making these the most expensive fake pearls in the world. But owning them gave Lynda the right and the ability to analyze and copy them, right down to "the sterling silver clasp and the three little cubic zirconiums and the silk cord and the seventeen coats of lacquer." More than 130,000 of these exact replicas sold at $200 apiece, for a net profit of millions—all of it told and sold through story.

Lynda impressed me with her absolute dedication to authenticity. The reason it was so important to her to own the originals was that they gave her both the standing and the ability to produce the truest possible replicas and to own and sell the story the pearls told. Even though these pearls were copies, they were copies with credibility. "It has to be real," she said emphatically. "The promise of the story has got to deliver. If it doesn't deliver, who would care?"

IF ANYBODY KNOWS HOW to create stories that deliver on their promise, it's Pat Riley, the legendary basketball coach who took the Los Angeles Lakers to four championship titles in the 1980s before moving to the Miami Heat. Riley's probably had more champagne poured over his head than he's actually consumed. I've known him for years and seen him use the art of the tell in a thousand different ways to motivate and guide his players. But it was the story he told to win the 2006 NBA Championship that made the most lasting impression on me.

The Heat weren't even supposed to get into the play-offs that year. But with rookie Dwyane Wade and former Lakers superstar Shaquille O'Neal on fire, they moved steadily up until they were ahead three to two in the finals against the Mavericks, with the last two games of the series scheduled in Dallas, the Mavericks' home court. Hoping for a historic match, I decided to go down to Dallas with life strategist Tony Robbins, who was also a friend of Riley's. We called Pat and asked him to help us get tickets for the seventh game. He insisted we come for the sixth. I said,

"But I want to be there for the last game." He said, "I'm only going to give you tickets for the sixth."

We couldn't figure it out. Why wouldn't he let us see the seventh game? A bit annoyed, we flew down for the sixth, and lo and behold, the Heat won the championship that very night! *There was never going to be a seventh game.*

But how could Pat have known that in advance? Later, when he was a guest at one of my UCLA graduate courses, I asked him the question. He said, "I told my team a story."

Riley had felt certain his team could beat the Mavericks as long as they were *convinced* they could. But he realized well in advance that the Mavericks would have a huge advantage in Dallas. Statistically, the team with home-court advantage wins more than three out of every four series in the play-offs. And the Heat's handicap would be most intense in the seventh game. "Obviously," Riley said, "we didn't want to go down there and have to play that seventh game." So his goal was to stoke his players' desire to win in the sixth.

But how? Instinctively, Riley knew he needed to put his players inside the positive experience of a win in game six that was hard, fast, and definitive. And he needed to make that goal *feel* real and achievable, to synchronize their mind-set with his purpose.

What did he do? He took a gamble and told his team the whole story of their victory in a single line. "I told everybody to pack for just one day—not two days, three days, or four days—just one day of dress and change." That elegant short story telegraphed Riley's intention that there be no seventh game. The Heat wouldn't need a second change of clothes, his implicit tale told them, because they were coming home the night of the sixth game as NBA world champions. He told it. They felt it. And they did it.

Looking back, I realize that Pat Riley had told me and Tony a variation on that same story when he refused to give us tickets to the seventh game. Why didn't we get it? Because we weren't its intended targets! The heart, body, and soul of Riley's core audience had to be transported until they owned his goal. We were merely spectators.

BUT WHAT ABOUT COACHING a business team? Surely the heart of the goal in a purposeful management story takes on different dimensions. Rob Pardo, executive vice president of game design at Blizzard Entertainment, a division of market leader Activision, told me about one such story—a tale he told his designers when developing World of Warcraft.

In his hit-dominated business, Pardo said, the possibility of a billion-dollar upside is very seductive, but failure also comes with the territory. Game development is tremendously complicated and unpredictable. "Making a game is like making a movie while inventing the camera at the same time. We're building brand-new technology to support a game while the game itself is being designed." As lead designer for World of Warcraft, Pardo's ulterior goal was to inspire his design and execution team to take the risks necessary for true innovation. The problem was that the stakes were so high. "Games are very expensive to design, build, and execute into the marketplace," he said. "And how do you tell your team *not* to play it safe? Once they put in months and years of time and energy, they naturally want to see their product on the shelves."

It seemed counterintuitive, but as he prepared to tell his team to become more innovative, he realized that the heart of his story's goal was a dramatic change in their feelings around failure. "I had to prove to them that their work wouldn't be wasted, that we always learn from their efforts and what we pay forward is their knowledge and experience. Failure is part and parcel of how you succeed as a great game designer."

But he couldn't just exhort them to fail. He needed to gain their trust and move them to feel what he was talking about. Suddenly Pardo had the perfect story—a tale of public, painful, multimillion-dollar failure that he himself had survived.

He told his designers, "A few years back we acquired this company up in Silicon Valley that did the first Diablo games. The original Diablo in 1996 was an action role-playing game that debuted at number one across the country, but after the success of Diablo II, no further versions worked well enough to release. I was trying to work with the company to get a good game-design vision, but their leadership changed. They lost designers and were never able to get it going." Eventually, Blizzard decided to close down the company. "I interviewed all their designers to decide who we were going to bring down to Southern California, to Blizzard South. And it was a very human experience because it's not just canceling a game. They'd worked on these new games for multiple years, and they'd failed! They weren't going to have anything to show for all that effort. I looked into everyone's eyes knowing the human cost."

But, Pardo told his new team, what he'd been looking *for* in those faces was energy, curiosity, and pride. He wanted to find the designers who recognized that all their "failed" effort had actually yielded valuable assets. He knew that some Diablo employees had taken from their failures ideas and insights that they were eager to apply to new games. These were the people Pardo kept on to help him chart Blizzard's future.

"Our hit rate probably isn't that much higher than anybody else in the industry," he said to conclude his story. "The difference is that when failure is inevitable we embrace it, canceling multimillion-dollar games with years of investment before they ever go public. Failure can be the fulcrum to do it right and better next time."

Pardo's story delivered the message: "If World of Warcraft is destined to be one of those casualties, then so be it—as long as you designers hold back nothing in your efforts to innovate." "By being willing to risk failure in the pursuit of success, we lose some financial capital," he said, "but we pay the intellectual capital forward. Our goal is not to fail intentionally, or to pretend we enjoy failure, but it is to be *willing* to fail in the pursuit of greatness."

The team got it. By 2009 11.5 million subscribers were playing World of Warcraft worldwide, and 8.6 million units of the game had sold in the United States alone, making it one of the fastest-selling PC games of all time. More important, Blizzard's more than twelve hundred employees rave about working for the company. The *Orange County Register* cited Blizzard as one of the top places to work in Orange County, and a current employee said one reason why was that he was "empowered to make decisions and learn from them."

ARE YOUR MOTIVES AUTHENTIC AND CONGRUENT WITH YOUR GOAL?

Whether you're a CEO, salesperson, volunteer organizer, or small business owner, your listeners will never fully connect to you, buy into your proposition, or join your parade unless they can trust you. And only if they respect your motives and empathize with you as a fellow human being will they feel that trust. To tell a compelling story, then, you need to be authentic in your passion for your goal, and that passion needs to be congruent with your experience and commitment. If you don't believe me, just ask Wally Amos.

Most people know Wally as the founder of Famous Amos Cookies, but I first met him back in the 1970s when he was a talent agent with the William Morris Agency. Here was a guy who'd dropped out of high school, gotten a job in the agency mail room, and within one year risen to be William Morris's first African-American agent *and* the first to book The Supremes, Simon & Garfunkel, Marvin Gaye, and many other legendary performers of that era. As he told me some three decades later, "My dream back then was to be a big-time show business manager. If the clients were important, then I was important, because to get them, you had to go through me. That's the whole show business mentality."

But there was a problem. "I never felt a part of show business. I was in it, but I never felt that I actually belonged." Much as he wanted to be a celebrity among celebrities, Wally didn't feel authentic in Hollywood. So what did he do? He followed the recipe of the aunt who raised him— literally. By baking cookies according to her recipe, he felt real again. "It was a way for me to release the tension, the anxiety. It was just me and the cookies."

Then he started bringing those cookies into the office. "I'd see a casting director, a producer, a director, or studio exec like I did with you, Peter, and before we'd talk about the clients I was selling, I'd open the Ziploc bag and start passing out cookies."

How well I remembered. "Those cookies were fantastic."

He nodded. "For five years, people would always say, 'You ought to sell them.'" Finally, fed up with show business, he did just that, with financial backing from his client Marvin Gaye, singer Helen Reddy and her husband Jeff Wald, and United Artists Records president Artie Mogull.

"I swear," Wally told me, "I made a commitment to chocolate chip cookies not to be famous, not to have a chain of stores, but just to have fun and be more in control of my life. The very next morning, I was a new person. I had a new purpose."

What changed was that Wally's purpose suddenly lined up with who he really was. He felt authentic because his recipe came from the aunt who took him in and turned him around when he was in trouble as a kid. She'd given him love and goodness, and he was now putting that same heart into his baking. He felt congruent now also because he was staking his livelihood on an enterprise that he believed in body and soul. "The cookie is a representation of how I feel about life, you know?" he told me. "That cookie is me."

Just as he'd used the cookies as his calling card in the talent business, now, as he passed the cookies out to the media, customers, and investors, Wally would tell the story of how his aunt's love and care had translated into the love and care that went into making his cookies. In no time he became the hero of a story called Famous Amos, baked into a cookie that melted your heart. However touchy-feely that may sound, it worked to build a national brand so irresistible that it was ultimately bought by the Kellogg Company and is still going strong thirty years after Wally sold it. Even though the cookies are no longer made with Wally's expensive premium ingredients, they are still popular nationwide because of the emotional attachment to his founding story. Wherever Wally goes, fans still call out to him, "Famous Amos!"

BACK IN 1993 I was privileged to spend a couple of days in the company of one of the most authentic leaders on the planet. Nelson Mandela, the leader of South Africa's anti-apartheid movement, had called me to ask if I, as CEO of Sony Entertainment, would host a 75th birthday party for him in Los Angeles. This was only thirty-six months after Mandela had been released from nearly three decades of imprisonment for opposing his country's white-minority rule. Later in 1993 he'd be awarded the Nobel Peace Prize, and the following year he'd become president of South Africa's first truly democratic government. But when I received this phone call, the political fate of South Africa was still uncertain. Mandela was playing a pivotal role in the plans for a Government of National Unity, a highly unusual and daring proposition that was to include both South Africa's old regime and new leaders from multiple racial groups and political parties. Few in the West could imagine such a government succeeding after the bloodshed and hatred that forty-five years of apartheid had fomented. But the new government would need diplomatic, cultural, and (most important) economic support from the West. So Mandela was coming to America to change the prevailing view of his country and raise support for his peaceful vision of a new South Africa. Of course, I agreed to offer my full support.

He asked if, in addition to hosting the party, I could arrange for him to meet privately with certain business leaders. So I was able to spend several days watching and listening to Mandela. There was one story he told that in particular made irresistible his call to action to participate in South Africa's future.

"In my twenty-seventh year in jail," he began, "a guard I had come to know well whispered to me that I was soon to be released." Mandela said he could see that the jailer was excited for him. The man considered this a moment for jubilation, but Mandela himself had a different reaction. "I was sad for this man with whom I had so frequently talked. He didn't understand that my spirit and beliefs had never been locked in his prison. My body could be contained but the story of my dreams could not. He didn't understand that the only prison that takes away a man's freedom is one that does not allow that man to dream."

Then Mandela transferred his story to a broader stage and began to talk about his country. The heart of his goal was for his people to feel the same freedom he felt, to believe they could realize their dreams. Otherwise, futility and despair would imprison the soul of his nation and the country would be lost.

Then he delivered his call to action. "I've come to America," Mandela said, "to invite you to invest not only financially, but also through your reputation and belief, in my country. I invite you to tell our story to your friends and acquaintances, to spread the word of the future that is possible in my country. I invite you to help keep alive the potential for our young people's dreams to be realized."

Mandela's authenticity was so clear and gave his story such resonance that his telling reached straight to and through the heart of every person in his audience. Inspired and motivated, his listeners wrote checks and volunteered their intellectual and reputational capital to help him realize his goals. Later they'd tell their own story, as I've done many times, of listening to Nelson Mandela and feeling the sincerity of his conviction that South Africa could transition to democracy without revenge killings or political chaos. And thanks largely to the beacon of Nelson Mandela's leadership, his vision of that peaceful transition came true.

IRONICALLY, THE BETTER SOMEONE knows you, the harder you may have to prepare to prove your authenticity. I was the audience for this lesson a few years back when my daughter Jodi appealed to me to invest in her new clothing company. Already in her thirties, she had her master's degree and had been planning to become a teacher. Suddenly she did an about-face and announced she wanted to manufacture designer lifestyle clothes around yoga. She needed hundreds of thousands of dollars to start up, and all I could think was *Why me?* Followed in quick succession by *Why this?* and *Why now?* She had no business, retail, wholesale, or design background. As her father, I knew this better than any other investor she could have approached. In fact, I knew it too well. I was her toughest customer, and to me at the outset, everything looked wrong with this picture.

But authenticity is a powerful persuader. Whatever story you tell, if you are perceived to be authentic, your audience will hear you empathetically and be more likely to embrace your passion. When someone shows a genuine drive to overcome all obstacles, that's compelling, because to succeed you have to have true conviction. Jodi proved her passion to me with a story that I knew to be true but had never before considered as a catalyst for my daughter's career or my investment. After all, it was one thing to be her fan, quite another to be her business financier.

She told me how, as a young girl growing up in Los Angeles, she longed to be part of the glamour she saw all around her. But she always felt as if she were on the outside looking into a world where everyone else looked and felt better than she did. The problem was that her body did not conform to the thin, lithe bodies celebrated in the magazines that she constantly perused. Jodi struggled with her weight. She didn't have a model-perfect figure, and she knew most other people didn't either. She loved fashion but wondered why so few great-looking clothes looked good on women who were shorter than five-ten or bigger than a size 4. She felt that fashions should be designed inclusively, so that no one, regardless of size, shape, or social status, felt excluded. Lifestyle active wear, in particular, should make everybody look good and feel both fashionable and comfortable. Unfortunately, such a thought never seemed to occur to most designers of these fashions. Finally, Jodi decided that, since no one else was making those clothes this way, she would do it herself. The vehicle was her yoga practice. She would make clothes that every woman could wear to feel comfortable enough for yoga *and* fashionable enough for the magazines.

Listening to my daughter tell me her story with a sense of purpose I'd never heard before, I knew this was a mission from the inside out, not outside in. It rang true in a way that her ambition to become a teacher never had. And this story would ring true to her customers, too, because it proved she understood and shared their experience and was designing a product that was emotionally satisfying as well as practical. Her narrative told me to override my concerns about her lack of technical expertise, especially when she showed me that she'd done her business homework as well and was truly ready to roll with a line of active wear she was calling Beyond Yoga.

Once she was up and running, Jodi continued to sell her product by telling her own authentic story. She told versions of it to her vendors, customers, and the media. It resonated with everyone who heard it, but made a particular impact on those who shared Jodi's experience. Oprah Winfrey, for example, has been challenged by her weight her whole life. Oprah embraced Jodi's ethos and wore her clothes on the cover of *O* magazine. In a short period of time Beyond Yoga's sales grew from $80,000 to $5 million, and today the line itself has grown beyond yoga into lifestyle apparel and is known as "i am BEYOND." I may have been my daughter's toughest audience at the start, but her story made me both her proudest and most satisfied investor.

WHO'S YOUR AUDIENCE?

The most successful story tellers are also attentive story listeners. They understand that it's more important to be interest*ed* in their audience than to appear interest*ing*. Why? Because what they learn about their audience will determine how they tell their story. They might tell the same story to two thousand customers at a convention, then to fifty employees at a marketing meeting, and then to one competing CEO over drinks at a resort, but each telling has to be different. Otherwise it will become boring—a fate equal to death in the art of the tell. As organizational leadership expert Warren Bennis told me, "Boredom occurs when you fail to make the other person interesting."

What interests your audience will always shape the way they hear your story, so it's incumbent on you to harness that interest to your advantage. The word "audience" is deliberate here. If you think of your listeners as an audience, you'll remember that what matters most is the emotional experience you're rendering and that, to tap that emotion, you've got to figure out a way to hook their attention. Business story tellers don't have the benefit of a darkened movie theater or soundtrack to interrupt the pattern of the audience's thoughts. So how do you break through the mental cacophony inside your listeners' heads to capture their interest? Knowing who they are is essential.

What's their age, gender, education, personality? Where do they live, and where do they come from? Most important of all, what do they want and need? Armed with this insight, you can employ *their* interests to tailor a story that will achieve *your* goals.

WHAT INTERESTS THEM?

Nobody understands the art of wooing a business audience better than my astrophysicist friend Gentry Lee. As chief engineer for the Solar System Exploration Directorate at the Jet Propulsion Laboratory, Gentry is on a perpetual mission of human persuasion as he calls for funding from Congress and corporations for JPL's interplanetary robotic missions; coordinates numerous JPL programs requiring collaboration by multiple teams of engineers; educates the media; recruits scientists to his team; and inspires schoolkids to become the next generation of astrophysicists. Whatever his audience, Gentry's sales tool of choice is always telling to win. And the key to telling a story that resonates with listeners, Gentry told me recently, is to understand that audience's value structure. "In business of any kind," he said, "if you're going to tell a story to get the other person to see or do something, you have to know what the audience is going to respond to. What are the resonant chords in your audience? Frame your story to hit those emotional chords."

Sometimes, Gentry said, the most resonant chord is fear. "People are afraid of the future, so if I can show that what we learn through inter-planetary exploration will reduce their uncertainty about the future, then they'll get why they should support our mission."

How would fear help Gentry persuade a congressman who has his eye on the federal deficit to support the Mission to Mars? "Once upon a time," Gentry would tell him, "Mars was a lush planet with a climate a lot like ours. It had air and water and possibly life. But now it's barren. Why? What happened?" And then to strike the chord of fear, he would ask, "Could the same fate be in our future on Earth?"

Then, Gentry said, he'd go on to describe some of the clues that the Mission to Mars would be looking for, what they expected to find, and what implications those findings could have for scientists' understanding of our future on Earth. "Could our findings on Mars help us redirect our manifest destiny and save our planet? Let's go there together and find out."

If the resolution of your story can somehow allay the fear you've raised, Gentry explained, then telling that story will sell your proposi-tion. With an audience of students or young scientists, however, Gentry might tell the same story, but with an emphasis that aroused curiosity and a sense of adventure rather than fear. "I believe that we are going to find an Earth-like planet close enough that a multigenerational space-craft could get there," he'd tell them. "It will have water and oceans and an atmosphere like ours. Picture us like the early American pioneers in wagon trains. I can see streaming groups of human beings going off on this multigenerational trip to a true new world. Wouldn't you want to be part of that story?"

Gentry's overriding message was that to make your audience care, you need to know what they care most about. Family? Status? Home? Adventure? Security? The most powerful stories begin by placing a core concern at the center of a threat, promise, or possibility that the audience has never before imagined and now cannot ignore. "That value proposition," Gentry said, "has to be right at the forefront of the story."

GENTRY'S WORDS CAME BACK to me when I discussed the art of the tell with Dr. Robert Maloney, director of the Maloney Vision Institute and clinical professor of ophthalmology at UCLA. Maloney was the first surgeon in western North America to perform LASIK surgery as part of the original FDA clinical trials. What I wanted to know was how he figured out what story to tell his patients to help them overcome their fear of the knife. After all, this procedure involves a laser cutting a flap in the cornea—the surface of the eyeball. It's not for the faint of heart.

Coming up with the right approach was tricky, he replied, because he had to give full disclosure, and the negative possibilities could easily take over the story, discouraging people from getting procedures they needed. Initially he'd struggled with this conundrum and tried to soft-pedal the warnings, but many still had unwarranted doubts. Finally, by listening more closely to his patients, he discovered that the value proposition they actually cared about most was trust. They needed not guarantees, but reassurance.

So, without altering the facts that enabled them to make an informed medical decision, Maloney began telling his patients, "No matter what happens, I'm going to be here to take care of you." Then he'd tell them the story of what he expected to happen with their surgery. As before, he'd cover the negative information about problems they might have to struggle with. But then he would conclude the story with a resolution that satisfied their *emotional* interests. "I am never giving up on you," he'd promise. "Even if there's a problem, we're in this together walking side by side." And with this subtle shift of emphasis he changed his story into one of relationship and friendship. His call to action was for his patients to trust him enough to make the leap into uncertainty, and they have by the thousands. In fact, Robert Maloney has personally performed more than fifty thousand vision-correction surgeries.

IN 2009, GAREB SHAMUS, founder of Wizard Entertainment, came with his partner Peter Levin to talk me into investing in their online venture Geek Chic Daily, a daily online newsletter for pop culture fans that highlighted the latest in cool yet geeky comics, toys, games, movies, technology, and gear. Little did I know that I would be on the receiving end of a story tailored with masterful care to appeal to my personal interests.

Shamus's publications include *Wizard* magazine, considered the most influential in the comic book, toy, and character-based genre, as well as *ToyFare* and *FunFare* magazines. He also owns and operates the Big Apple, Chicago, Philadelphia, Toronto, and Anaheim Comic-Con festivals, which are like Woodstocks for comic fans. Gareb, in other words, is a guru of geeks.

Since Peter Levin had first introduced me to him a few months earlier, Gareb had observed that I, too, was making products that were very youth-centric. He'd also noticed that I was a few decades past my twenties and had no direct voice in the conversation of my youthful audience. Sensing that these vulnerabilities concerned me, Gareb used them with great precision to interest me in his digital newsletter and website for popular culture enthusiasts.

At the outset of our meeting he literally laid my concerns on the table by presenting physical evidence that I was out of touch with a vast new realm of business opportunity. He showed me some of the comics and graphic novels that he published through his Black Bull publishing imprint. He gave me a copy of *Wizard,* which he had started fresh out of college and which spawned a magazine and entertainment empire that has since branched out into toys, role-playing games, and Internet media.

He presented me with a program from his most recent Comic-Con, describing it as "the largest comic book and popular arts convention in the world!" As Gareb had predicted, I did not recognize a single one of the items he showed me. And this served as proof positive that I was not capitalizing on this valuable and intriguing market. Why did I need to tap this market? Because this same audience would buy many of my entertainment products. The more Gareb showed me, the more I wanted in.

Once he'd hooked my interest and shown me what was potentially in this deal for me, Gareb proved his authenticity by telling me his own backstory. He'd traded sports cards as a kid in the 1980s, then gotten into comics when his parents started selling them at their card store. But he always wanted more information. "I didn't know what artists and writers were working on what books," he told me. "There was really nothing that told me what was coming out, what was new, and what was exciting. I felt like I was totally out of the loop. That's when I came up with the idea for *Wizard* magazine."

Savvy guy. Even as he was talking, I could tell he knew how totally out of the loop I was feeling at that very moment. But what he did next was story telling genius and sealed the deal.

"Remember the movie *Big*?" he asked. Of course I did. The 1988 Penny Marshall film featured Tom Hanks playing a little boy trapped in a grown man's body. "Well," Gareb said, "when I was a young boy, I saw that movie and recognized that all older people had kids inside them." Then he reminded me of the scene in which Hanks and his much older boss—the owner of a toy company—play a "Chopsticks" duet on a walking piano. This experience put the older man back in touch with his youth and with the audience he was trying to reach. It also created an emotional bond between him and Hanks, as the spirit of youth. Gareb understood that I was like that older guy who needed this relationship to tap into his young audience, and Gareb was Hanks's counterpart. Geek Chic Daily, his story implied, was the piano that we could both play to bring our worlds together. If I became his partner, I would gain the currency I badly needed to tap into the demographic that was Gareb's tribe.

Once I had that currency I could sell my products as a tribal insider, regardless of my age.

Because he'd done his homework on me before he walked in the door, Gareb told his story in a way that resonated with my head, heart, and wallet. In other words, he appealed to what interested me, what I wanted, and what I needed. I joined Gareb and Peter as a third partner, and Geek Chic Daily launched in October of 2009.

I WISH GAREB HAD BEEN around to instruct me back in 2003 when Bruce Stein and I hatched what we thought was a grand slam business proposition guaranteed to light up the Starbucks empire. Bruce possessed just the right credentials for the challenge. He'd served in senior management at Mattel, Inc., Sony Interactive Entertainment, Inc., and Kenner Products, Inc., and we'd known each other since 1989, when he acquired key merchandising rights to our first *Batman* movie. I'd seen that he had a sixth sense for the interests and needs of retailers. However, as we'd learn, some retailers are not like the others.

We were high on confidence as we flew up to Seattle to sell our proposition to Starbucks chairman and CEO Howard Schultz. We didn't know Schultz, but we had an introduction from Indigo and Chapters CEO Heather Reisman, who'd partnered with him to put Starbucks into her bookstores, and so he received us as colleagues. This was no small compliment, considering the relative scale of his empire. Starbucks was expanding by thirteen hundred new stores that year, and their grand plan was to have forty thousand locations worldwide.

Respecting his valuable time, we immediately began telling him our business proposition. Our idea was to install, at no cost to Starbucks, one large plasma screen per store, in the open space above customer reach, thereby using real estate that was currently going unused. Content would be programmed from a central source but be specifically targeted for the location and time of day at each shop, so the nature of programs would be different in the morning and evening, and on the East Coast and West Coast, and in urban and rural locations. Schultz wouldn't have to pay for content, and there'd be no interference with the baristas or other employees, since everything would be controlled from a central site. The HD video screen would play with closed captioning, but customers could pick up sound via Ethernet or phone connection. And after hours, regional store managers could use the screens for training purposes, with content that Starbucks generated and controlled.

Furthermore, we told him, there'd only be a total of ten minutes of advertising in each hour, and all ads would be subject to Schultz's approval, with revenues to be shared. He'd also be able to advertise his own products throughout the programming. Then we showed him scientific data proving that people consume more food when watching television, at our ballparks, and at location-based entertainment events. The bottom line was that these screens would increase his profits in multiple ways.

But wait! There'd be an additional jackpot down the road, when the programming became so well established that Schultz could turn the whole process on its head to launch a "Starbucks Live" network for cable broadcast.

It sure sounded good to *us*. Howard, not so much. He listened appreciatively and a few days later said, "No, thanks. I'm in the business of selling coffee."

What did he mean? How had we missed our target? For months afterward we tried to figure out what had gone wrong. Finally, I did what I should have done long before we flew to Seattle: I put myself in Howard's shoes to see what interested *him*.

Belatedly, I realized that Schultz's own bedrock story casts Starbucks as his customers' "third place"—a home away from home and office where they can relax and feel like it's *their* place. In this story, the customer is the hero, who decides not only what beverage to drink, but also how to spend time in the store—reading, or working on a laptop, or chatting with friends, or listening to music. Starbucks provides choices, but the customer owns his or her experience, and that's the story Schultz wants them to tell forward.

If I'd paid attention, I'd have known Schultz would never go for a proposition that treated his guests as a passive audience. He was interested in their *active* engagement in the Starbucks story. No wonder we'd failed! We'd aimed squarely at a goal Schultz had no interest in. If only we'd prepared properly and been interested instead of trying to be interesting, and honored his story with a proposition that aligned with it, we might have had a different outcome.

WHAT ARE THEIR PREJUDICES?

The flip side of interests are prejudices. One attracts, the other repels. The teller who ignores audience prejudices is asking for disaster. And be warned, prejudicial symbols lurk everywhere, even in seemingly innocuous details.

Over the course of my career I've seen prejudice undermine the art of the tell on numerous occasions. The most memorable of these, strangely enough, revolve around a demonic teller who actually employed prejudice to his advantage. Because his call to action was to hate, Adolf Hitler could whip millions of his countrymen into frenzy by telling them stories that fed their prejudices against the Allies, the Jews, the Gypsies, the handicapped, and anyone else that didn't fit his Aryan profile. Yet Hitler's own crimes against humanity were so heinous that most people today react with equal and opposite prejudice against anything associated with him or his Third Reich.

This prejudice rose up to take a nasty bite out of our company's 1997 release of *Seven Years in Tibet,* the film version of the true story of Heinrich Harrer, an Austrian mountaineer who, during World War II, became the tutor and close friend of Tibet's future spiritual leader, the young Dalai Lama. Harrer's story of spiritual transformation is a powerful testament to peace, understanding, and humanity. In the entire movie there is a single shot of the star Brad Pitt wearing a Nazi swastika, to indicate Harrer's reluctant submission to the Third Reich early in his life. Nevertheless, before the film's release some journalists saw this single image of the dreaded symbol and, without watching any actual footage, categorized *Seven Years* as a Nazi movie. Jewish media called for a boycott, and no matter how many times we or the artists told the real story, we couldn't overcome the power of that visual artifice. The symbol of the swastika on Brad Pitt aroused such powerful prejudices that it hijacked our whole story.

At my home in Hawaii a decade later, I told that story of *Seven Years in Tibet* to my guest Mark Shapiro, who, together with Washington Redskins owner Dan Snyder, was financing Tom Cruise's upcoming World War II film, *Valkyrie*. I warned Mark that prerelease publicity pictures of Tom Cruise, his film's star, brandishing a Nazi insignia would probably arouse some of the same prejudice that had sideswiped our story. Unfortunately, some photos of Cruise in a Nazi uniform, wearing an eye patch no less, did make their way into the media early on and created a misperception of the film as a pro-Nazi movie. Audience prejudice once again took its toll, negatively impacting box office earnings.

I've also been on the receiving end of a tell that activated my own prejudices. In 1992, when I was CEO of Sony Pictures, I made a trip to Berlin with Sony Corporation's leadership Norio Ohga and Mickey Schulhof to visit the planned site of Sony's new European headquarters. We had just finished building a huge multiplex theater in Manhattan, complete with the latest Sony technology, and Ohga was in love with the idea of developing more state-of-the-art real estate. In Berlin he wanted to create Sony's corporate headquarters with executive offices adjacent to an entertainment mega-center housing a multiplex, an IMAX theater, restaurants, and a food court. Since I'd played a key role in planning Sony's New York 67th Street multiplex, he wanted me to champion this new development as well. So far so good. Berlin sounded like a dream canvas on which to paint a portrait of Sony's future.

Schulhof, a licensed jet pilot, flew us over on the corporate jet. We landed in a small mid-city airport and taxied under a massive overhang that seemed out of all proportion to the short runway. I wondered aloud what the story was behind this architecture, and Ohga said enthusiastically, "This is a great airport—Tempelhof. Hitler built this airport in the thirties! It is famous."

"Great," I said. "Hitler." I didn't think I needed to point out that he wasn't exactly my hero.

Apparently I was mistaken. Ohga completely missed my sarcasm. He was too busy charging ahead with his vision story of Sony Center as a gleaming citadel of technology that would rise from the ashes of Berlin's wartime past.

A few minutes later we were standing in a wide open field directly across from the Mercedes-Benz world headquarters. Ohga seemed to have a little extra steel in his strut as he told me Sony had already completed the purchase of this property—an enormous parcel of land smack in the middle of the rapidly expanding city. This was bigger and better than New York for what we wanted to accomplish. It almost seemed too good to be true.

"How come all this prime real estate was available?" I asked. "Was it a park?"

"No, no park." Ohga gestured at the bare ground and began to tell his story. "Back in 1945, this was a famous place. Down underneath here was Hitler's bunker—"

"Hitler's bunker!" I let out a yelp, the whole toxic story flooding my brain. "You're building Sony headquarters on Hitler's bunker? You can't be serious!"

Ohga said matter-of-factly, "Peter, you work for Japanese. We were allies with Germany in the war." In other words, Ohga felt no prejudice against Hitler, so what was *my* problem?

I thought but didn't add, *could you possibly have chosen a worse place to tell the story of your grand new corporate vision?*

I couldn't stop thinking that this was the place where this mass-murdering monster had hunkered down. The story of Hitler and his victims instantly overwhelmed whatever Ohga said next. I had to get away from there, and I had little intention of participating in a project that I now saw as venerating the Holocaust.

It took all the political finesse I could muster, but I succeeded in absenting myself from Ohga's new pet project, and I never returned to that grassy plot, before or after it was transformed into the 2.1-million-square-foot Sony Center that opened in 2000. But now I wonder, was there any way Ohga could have told his story to win my support? I can only think of one, and it would not have been easy. He'd have had to acknowledge and then somehow defuse my prejudice against Hitler. But apparently that never occurred to him. Instead, by simply ignoring my prejudices, he sabotaged any chance of my active participation before he even began to tell his story.

WHAT'S THEIR OPTIMAL CONTEXT?

Getting to know your audience also means figuring out the place where they will be most receptive to your tell. On the golf course? Over lunch at a quiet restaurant? At home or in the office? To identify the place where listeners will give you their full attention, you need to look, listen, and locate their comfort zones. This sounds simple but can pose some challenges, as I discovered with director Tim Burton when we were wooing Jack Nicholson for the pivotal role of the Joker in the first *Batman* movie.

Batman was a long haul for our production company. Although it would turn out to be the grandfather of all comic-book movie franchises, the eight years we spent in development were fraught with uncertainty. The key to that movie was attitude. Its $40-million-plus price tag at the time seemed stratospheric, so we couldn't afford for the picture to appeal only to kids. That's why, as its producers, we brought on director Tim Burton, who'd given *Beetle Juice* its memorable edge. Tim persuaded

Beetle Juice himself—Michael Keaton—to play Batman, and by 1988 everything was coming together. All we needed was a world-class villain.

Nicholson was the man. He'd made *The Last Detail, Five Easy Pieces,* and *Tommy* for Columbia Pictures during my tenure there, and we all knew he'd make a formidable Joker. But the clock was ticking, and although he claimed to be interested, he was slow to make up his mind. Finally he said, "OK, I want to meet Tim Burton." He told me to bring Tim up to Aspen, where Jack had a home.

It made sense that Nicholson would want to meet the filmmaker, especially on a project like this, where direction was going to be crucial. So we took the Warner jet to Aspen. Tim, a notoriously quirky character with a penchant for the macabre, was immediately out of his own comfort zone. Not only was he unaccustomed to the country, but all the pressure was on him to come up with a story to win Jack now, or the movie might never get made. That story would tell how Burton, with Nicholson's help, intended to revolutionize cinema with a new kind of supervillain, a more complex character—an antihero of sorts, with a look that had never before been seen on the screen. It wasn't the size of the role, but the impact of the role that would resonate. This was a villain the audience could root for and would pay forward.

Then Jack upped the ante. He called soon after we landed and said, "Let's go horseback riding."

As I hung up the phone, Tim said, "I don't ride horses."

I answered, "You do now. Get ready."

Whether Jack had done research on Tim and was testing him, whether he thought he might be too quirky to work with, I had no way of knowing. But I knew we didn't want to launch the relationship with a no. You have to make your audience feel that you're comfortable and willing to go the distance with them. If Jack lived in Aspen and wanted to go for a ride, then we had to ride on his terms, not ours. Tim didn't get to choose the context in which he'd tell his story.

The next morning, as Tim stood looking up at his horse, I could almost hear him thinking, *Oh my God. This is harder than making the movie.* But he did it. I suspect that was the last horse Tim ever went near, but out there on the trail, as we rode across the meadows of Jack's comfort zone, Tim passionately told his story of how he and Jack together would change movie history. That context put Jack in exactly the right mind frame to hear Tim's story. By ride's end, he was in.

FINDING THE RIGHT CONTEXT in which to tell his story was also crucial for Michael Milken in one of the biggest endeavors of his career—a voluntary commitment that began in the 1970s and is still on-going today. When Milken invited me to his house recently to introduce me to his story, I wasn't sure what to expect. He'd been a major influence on medical research, as well as one of the most powerful and successful men on Wall Street, and he began our discussion by asking about my minor-league baseball business. But the connection between his interests and mine became quite clear as he told me his story.

"In 1993 I was a forty-six-year-old dad," he recalled. "I went to the doctor and told him I wanted a complete physical, including a PSA test for prostate cancer. I knew a fair amount about cancer because I'd been involved in supporting research for twenty years. But I really knew nothing about prostate cancer except that my good friend Steve Ross, who was CEO of Time Warner, had just died of prostate cancer at age sixty-five. The doctor said I was too young for a PSA test, but I eventually convinced him.

"Well, not only did I have prostate cancer, but I had lymph nodes one hundred times normal size and my life expectancy was twelve to eighteen months. I had kids and a great family, and I didn't want prostate cancer to take me out of my game."

Milken fought back with an aggressive regimen of hormone therapy and radiation. He changed his diet and embraced some alternative therapies in addition to conventional treatment. Within months, his PSA dropped to zero. His prostate cancer was in remission. But his remission set him on a mission—to change the trajectory of this disease and to expand on his longtime goal of accelerating medical progress.

Milken realized that, while public awareness of breast cancer was soaring, prostate cancer had no public face or story. He decided he'd change that by telling his own story in his own voice, in that way spurring middle-aged and older men to get tested and pass the message through their own stories. But what was the optimal context for telling his story?

Wanting to reach the largest possible multigenerational audience of men, he chose as his ideal context the game of baseball. Baseball is all about stories. The park and the game create a stage, and there's space between innings to tell and listen to stories, to absorb a call to action. And not only are the fans largely male, but so is virtually everyone on the field and in the clubhouse. That expanded Milken's cast of tellers. "If I communicate the message, fine," he said, "but Ken Griffey, Jr., and other major players telling their dads to go get checked, that would have a much different effect. And statistically many managers are going to be diagnosed with prostate cancer themselves, because they're older. So the strategy was to make every manager a sponsor of the effort for their team. Then let's get a player rep, like Terry Steinbach, whose father had prostate cancer, to reach out to other players and pull it out of the dark. And most important, let's get someone who's in the clubhouse talking to the guys when they're all interacting. Let's get the team equipment manager and strength coach involved. The only way to get them involved is to make it their story. It's their ballpark; they own it."

Soon Milken was headlining his story: KEEP DAD IN THE GAME. After all, he was a dad, and baseball was the perfect context for an intergenerational story to be told to and about dads. "Our idea was to culminate the event on Father's Day. Starting on June 1, through Father's Day, I'd travel around the country with former Hall of Famers visiting major-league ballparks every day. The first year, 1994, we went to about ten cities. Since then Tommy Lasorda has traveled with me every year."

For fifteen years—and counting—Milken has been generously telling his story forward, and the impact on the fight against prostate cancer is staggering. The month that the most number of men get checked for their PSA is the month of June—the month of Father's Day. Since Milken started telling his story to "Keep Dad in the game," the number of men dying from prostate cancer has dropped to half of what had been projected. And still he keeps expanding his story's baseball stage, which is why he was talking to me about telling it next in minor-league arenas.

Meanwhile, Milken has expanded his own life's work by telling his story. There may have been a time when the name Michael Milken was associated mostly with finance, but in 2004 that changed forever. *Fortune* magazine ran a cover story of a very different nature about Mike Milken. Headlined THE MAN WHO CHANGED MEDICINE, it was all about how his story was keeping Dad in the game.

INEVITABLY, THE CONTEXT IN which you tell a story colors the story you tell. The trick is to use that color to your advantage. Jason Binn, CEO and founder of Niche Media, has mastered this trick so completely that he's actually turned story telling context into a multimillion-dollar enterprise. While the rest of the magazine industry is plummeting, Binn presides over a veritable empire of upscale luxury magazines in highly targeted communities, such as the Hamptons, Aspen, Los Angeles, Manhattan, Miami, Boston, Philadelphia, Washington DC, and Las Vegas. His business strategy first came to my attention when we became acquainted at a symposium in Fiji in the late 1990s.

"There are ten markets in the United States," he told me then, "that really move the needle for any lifestyle or luxury brand of product or service, and in each of those markets there are four hundred people that inspire and motivate others through the way they dress, the way they act." His grand plan was to key into those "market makers" in the top ten markets through his local magazines, then have them tell their own stories and attract national advertisers. "Insiders to insiders" is how he put it.

He could do that because he literally went to the homes of these people and discovered what interested them where they live. "Before I launch a magazine," he told me, "I live there. Whether it's six months straight or every other week, I make sure that I'm ingrained in that community." But he doesn't just live the context, he leverages it into his magazine's content. For example, he recalled visiting an art collector at her home in Venice, California, to persuade her to write for *Los Angeles Confidential*. He walked into her house and saw a huge print by local artist Ed Ruscha. Jason told her, "I can see with my own eyes that you're someone who lives the LA life, and we want to help you celebrate the life you live and share that with your community." Then, after she'd agreed to write for him, Jason would tell the story of their meeting and her painting and her participation to both local and national advertisers so they'd all benefit as part of the same insiders' club.

The story of context as content has been so successful for Jason that he now has advertisers coming to him and demanding, "Why aren't you in this market? We'd be behind you if you were in that market." It seems only natural to assume that a good thing would work everywhere, but Jason is emphatic. "No, it's never going to be everywhere. That's not my intention. I would only want to tell my story where this particular audience is."

What's the take-away that Jason Binn delivers to everyone on his food chain? That the best stage on which to tell your story is your audience's stage, and the best way to locate that stage is to get to know your audience.

BUT ALL OF THIS scoping out of goals and audience interests still leaves wide open the process of selecting and shaping the specific story you're going to tell. After the marksman shouts, *"Ready!"* he doesn't go straight to *"Fire!"* There's a middle step. The same is true in the art of the tell. Ready as you may be, you've still got to find the raw material for your story. How do you shape this material into a three-part challenge, struggle, and resolution? How do you insure that it works as emotional transportation? You can't move your audience until you've *Set!* your story.

aHHa!

- To tell a great story, make preparation your partner.
- Demonstrate authenticity and congruence; they're the rails on which your story rides.
- Show you've got skin in the game.
- Aim for the *heart* of your goal—emotionalize your offering.
- Be interested in what interests your listeners, and they'll find your story interesting and your goal compelling.
- Remember, the context in which you tell your story colors the story you tell.
- Be dialed in; your listener's prejudices can hijack even your best story.

CHAPTER SIX

Set . . .

Former president Bill Clinton once said that politics is "about giving people better stories." Well, no one told a story to better political purpose than Clinton himself. His mastery of the art of the tell, in fact, played a key role in persuading my wife and me to offer our active support when he first declared his run for the presidency. We'd known him since his days as the "Education Governor" of Arkansas, when we invited him to speak at a luncheon at the Beverly Hills Hotel benefiting Education First, an organization that promoted quality public education nationwide. Knowing that celebrity was a political currency that he'd want to tap, I gathered six hundred members of the Los Angeles entertainment community to hear him, and Clinton dazzled us by telling one compelling story after another that highlighted the country's need and opportunity for improving public schools. His telling sparkled with intellect, passion, and heart, and we were convinced that Bill Clinton was bound to be President.

Then, early in the 1992 primaries, he was pummeled by allegations of Vietnam draft dodging and sexual infidelity. He lost New Hampshire, which as a liberal Democrat he should have owned. Not since 1952 had a candidate won the presidency without first winning New Hampshire, and since the Golden Rule of politics is "Money flows where the vote goes," this loss put Clinton's organization in fiscal crisis. One of the chiefs on his staff called me the morning after the primary to say that for Clinton to move on to the next key primary state, they'd need to raise $90,000 by the end of that day. And since I was then CEO of Sony, he hoped I would reach out to the Hollywood community on the governor's behalf.

The sum they requested told me just how bad things were. This guy was running for President of the United States. An ask for $500,000 would have made sense, to push to the finish line. But an eleventh hour $90,000 to move the campaign just one stop signaled that the campaign was teetering on the brink.

"Do you really think you can win?" I asked, signaling my own doubt.

"Of course," he said, "or we wouldn't be asking." But campaign finance rules strictly limited to $1,000 the amount of money any individual could donate, so if I was to reach Clinton's total I'd have to put my credibility on the line with a whole lot of people. I needed the candidate himself to persuade me that he really had a chance.

Clinton came on the line. "Hello, Peter, this is Bill."

Then there was a long pause. Looking back I can imagine mental calisthenics being performed at the other end of the phone as Clinton searched for just the right story content that would move this particular audience—me—to his particular goal.

Finally he said, "Have you ever seen the picture *High Noon*?"

He knew I had. How could I be a movie executive and not? *High Noon* is the classic 1952 Fred Zinneman western starring Gary Cooper as the heroic sheriff Will Kane, who spends most of the movie preparing to face off against a notorious gang that's due to arrive on the noon train. Kane expects the community to back him up in this fight, but only one young boy has the nerve to stand by him as he waits for his moment of truth.

Clinton didn't recite the story of Kane's urgent, lonely contest. He didn't need to. He just said, "Peter, this is *High Noon*."

Ahha! Those words transported me emotionally, and I immediately got it. When the noon whistle blew in the movie, the hero faced his demons, inside and out, and braved his way to victory. And that's just what *our* hero, Bill Clinton, would do if I played the role of that lone supporter and backed him despite the odds.

I don't know if Clinton is actually a movie buff, but he sure knew where to look for story material that would resonate with the entertainment community. After we hung up, I made a beeline for Sid Ganis, head of all marketing for Sony, who'd later become president of the Academy of Motion Picture Arts and Sciences. Over a quick cup of coffee I told him my story and asked for his how-to advice. Sid said, "Simple. Call everybody we know who depends on us and tell them that same story."

We both started dialing our Hollywood A-list. "You know *High Noon,* the movie?" we asked each person. Of course they did! "Well, this is *High Noon* for Bill Clinton. We need you and your wife each to give a thousand dollars, and we need it now, before the noon whistle blows. In our case, high noon is four p.m."

Almost everyone was emotionally transported through the familiar yet unexpected content of this movie story. We collected the checks that afternoon. At four o'clock I called Clinton's chief of staff. "It's *High Noon,*" I said, "and you've got your money. Now take on the bad guys and win."

Clinton's winning streak began then and did not let up. When he got off the plane in May to campaign before the California primary, I was waiting at the airport with a thousand people. He saw me from the top of the steps and put up his thumb. The story was far behind us now. Clinton's team was headed for the White House, and Ganis and I would be sharing the joy as his guests at the inauguration.

THAT EPISODE WITH CLINTON left no doubt in my mind that, in the art of the tell, story content is the Holy Grail. But stories are lurking everywhere. We all experience living stories every day, and we carry story treasure troves in our heads from books we've read and movies and television shows we've seen. With all that potential content and more to choose from, how do we set up the right story to tell for a given purpose? How, for example, did Bill Clinton set up *High Noon,* out of all the stories he could have told to persuade me?

Sure, it made sense for him to tell a movie story to appeal to a movie guy. But there are thousands of movies he could have selected, including comedies, tragedies, and action adventures. What made *High Noon* perfect was the way it mirrored Clinton's intention to overcome the odds against him. He didn't have to spell it out; I got the association automatically. Our hero, like Kane, would stand up when everybody else sat down. Clinton believed in his own ability to take on the bad guys and would keep on fighting until he'd won. Conveniently, through the stalwart young kid who helped to make victory possible, the movie's story also painted a role for me. And because I had personally experienced the emotional drama, urgency, and ultimate exhilaration of Kane's struggle through the movie, this familiar story immediately triggered my empathy for Clinton's experience in his campaign. I was moved emotionally to support the man we'd all come to call the Comeback Kid.

WHO'S YOUR HERO?

Communications consultant Bob Dickman, who coauthored *The Elements of Persuasion,* made a comment at one of our story conclaves that reminded me why heroes play such a critical role in purposeful stories. "All the passion in the world won't do any good," Bob told us, "unless you have some place to put it. That's where the hero comes in. By hero, I don't necessarily mean Superman or a grandmother who rushes into a burning building to save a baby, but the character in the story who gives the audience a point of view. The hero's both our surrogate and our guide."

In other words, the hero is the character that your listener will identify with. Why is this identification important in the art of the tell? Because, if your audience experiences the story through your hero, and the story leads your hero to embrace your call to action, then your audience automatically will hear your call too!

Simply stated, your hero is the person, place, product, or brand that enables your audience to feel the change your story promises. Remember, business stories, just like novels and movies, consist of three parts: the challenge, the struggle, and the resolution. And the hero's the character who faces the challenge and fights through to the resolution. That may sound obvious, but as I discovered during the making of *Rain Man,* the hero is sometimes surprisingly hard to pinpoint, and until you do, you have no story.

The story of *Rain Man,* which my company produced in 1988, focuses on an autistic savant, played by Dustin Hoffman, and his much younger, manipulative brother, played by Tom Cruise. From the beginning of the movie's development, I'd thought the point of the story was to shine the light on the extraordinary life of an autistic savant. But we went through three directors, none of whom could find a way to tell that story, before Barry Levinson signed on. Barry understood that our story needed to achieve a purpose beyond entertainment. His goal was to move audiences to change the way they respond to and care for people with severe disabilities. In the story Barry told, the younger brother, Charlie, tried to take advantage of his brother Raymond, but ultimately came to appreciate him. That sounded fine to me, but I still thought Raymond, with his almost supernatural skills, was the hero of the story.

After Barry screened his director's cut for us, I had only one suggestion. "It's terrific," I said, "but couldn't Dustin at the end just turn and give a little wink or something to Tom? Like saying to the audience, 'I get it. My life's going to be OK, I've seen the light.'"

Barry gave me a long-suffering look and said, "You don't get it. Dustin's not the hero."

He wasn't? But Dustin Hoffman was our star (and, as it turned out, headed for an Academy Award for this role). Tom Cruise was only in his mid-twenties at the time, and I'd perceived his as a supporting role. Nevertheless, Barry patiently explained, regardless of star power, the hero of a story is the character who makes the hard decisions and actually *feels* meaningful change happen within himself. Dustin's autistic character was passive—he was incapable of changing his own life, much less experiencing emotional transformation. It was Tom Cruise's character, Charlie, who made all the key decisions and ultimately changed his own life and point of view. It was by changing himself that he changed life for his brother, so *he* was the hero of this story.

The lesson of *Rain Man* was brought home to me years later when I interviewed Tom Cruise on my AMC television program *Storymakers*. Tom recalled Barry Levinson telling him, "Look, this picture rides on you being able to make this transition credible, because everybody's going to step into your shoes. Everybody's going to say, *What if my wife had an accident and was brain damaged? What if I had a son or a daughter who had this? What if my father had Alzheimer's disease? How would I have to change to manage that problem?*" The hero had to be someone who could embody the purposeful goals of the story that Barry was telling.

Barry's purpose went beyond just selling movie tickets and entertaining people. He intended to move audiences to change the way they related to the physically and mentally challenged. And he succeeded. While *Rain Man* won four major Academy Awards, including Best Picture, the audience heard a call to action that echoed far beyond Hollywood. In letters that poured into our offices, moviegoers told us that the film had inspired them to be more compassionate, supportive, and proactive in dealing with the people in their own lives who had autism, Alzheimer's disease, and other disabling injuries or illnesses. The lesson they took from the story wasn't how to count cards like Raymond, but how to transform their own attitudes and aptitudes. We didn't get a single letter from an autistic person or a savant. We got them from people who followed the lead of our true hero.

TELLER AS HERO

"In every story there's one person who can make the difference," Pat Riley recently told my UCLA graduate students. "That's your hero." As a legendary pro basketball coach, of course, Riley is used to telling stories that cast his players as heroes. But sometimes when you tell a story, you need to paint yourself as the hero. How do you do that without seeming pompous or self-centered? Riley offered a perfect example from the very first season Magic Johnson played with the Lakers, when Riley was the Lakers' assistant coach, back in 1979.

"That season," Pat recalled, "we ended up in the NBA finals, against the Philadelphia 76ers. Then, at the fifth game in Los Angeles, Kareem Abdul-Jabbar sprained his ankle and went down in the second half. The greatest NBA scorer in history, and we lost him for games six and seven. So even though we're ahead three to two, players are coming to me saying, 'We're going to get beat.' Well, Magic Johnson heard this, and he went berserk. Nineteen years old, trying to get his guys back into the fray, he said, 'I know what the problem is. All of you guys are afraid because Kareem isn't here. Well, I'll be Kareem.'"

So the story that Magic told, breathed, acted, and played for the next two games was that he was the team's hero, aka Kareem. "We get on the plane for Philadelphia," Riley recalled, "and 1A is Kareem's seat. Even when he was sick, nobody ever sat in 1A. He'd put a sign there: DON'T SIT IN MY SEAT. I'M KAREEM. But Magic sat in his seat and said, 'Hey, I'm Kareem. I'm here.'"

In Philadelphia, Magic, who was point guard, played Kareem's position at center the whole practice. "In game six," Riley said, "the greatest game ever played by a rookie in the NBA was played by Earvin Magic Johnson. He had 42 points, 15 rebounds, 13 assists, 7 steals. We won 123 to 107. And he was Kareem." The next day, the *Los Angeles Times* headlined the real hero of this story: IT'S MAGIC. That year the Lakers won the NBA championship and Magic won the NBA finals Most Valuable Player Award.

The irony is, Earvin Johnson's greatest act of magic was the story he told to move his team into believing he was *their* hero. It was a pretty gutsy story for a rookie, but he pulled it off because he knew he was up to the role and because his ultimate goal was to benefit them all. And therein lies the moral of the story for other purposeful tellers who dare to cast themselves as heroes. True teller-heroes are generous as well as powerful. They never lose sight of what's in their story for their audience. And they only cast themselves as heroes if they know they can deliver.

LISTENER AS HERO

"I am not your hero." This was news to me. I was talking to the Dalai Lama, the highest and most holy of all Tibetan Buddhist leaders and the greatest of all political heroes to hundreds of thousands of Tibetans, both inside Tibet and in exile. But what the Dalai Lama meant was that he was not the hero of the particular story I needed to tell.

The problem we faced back in 1996 was the Chinese government's condemnation of our film-in-development *Seven Years in Tibet*. One of the first co-ventures between my company Mandalay and Sony, this film paid tribute to the courage and humanity of the Tibetan people through the true story of Heinrich Harrer, who met His Holiness as a young boy during World War II and served as his teacher up through the Chinese invasion of Tibet in 1950. Even before we started principal photography, Chinese officialdom had gotten wind of our plan to show the brutality of China's invasion while paying homage to their enemy, His Holiness, and they were hopping mad.

The Chinese government had no direct leverage over us. Our director, Jean-Jacques Annaud, who previously had made *Quest for Fire* and *The Name of the Rose,* had already made a stealth mission into Tibet to capture the documentary footage he needed. We were planning to shoot the rest of the film in India, where the Dalai Lama lived and headed his government in exile and where we had access to plenty of Tibetan actors and extras. We had already spent millions of dollars on our sets there and had Brad Pitt committed to star as Harrer. The Chinese waited till the last minute before we started photography to pressure the Indian government to shut us down, thinking that would prevent the picture from ever getting made.

Despite our best lobbying efforts, the Indian government buckled, first refusing to license the film for production, then insisting we leave the country. To make matters worse, Martin Scorsese was hard on our heels with his film *Kundun,* a biopic about His Holiness. In fifty years there had never been a film about the Dalai Lama, and suddenly there were two. Knowing that Scorsese would be safe shooting his picture in Morocco, we decided to find a similar location—well away from China's sphere of influence. We doubled down our bet and moved our production of the film to Argentina.

But although we were still several months ahead of Scorsese, we couldn't seem to shake the Chinese. Buoyed by their ability to pummel India into submission, they now took aim at Sony Entertainment's parent company, the electronics giant Sony Corporation. China threatened that, regardless of where we made the film, they would pull the plug on Sony's electronics business in China if Sony distributed *Seven Years in Tibet.* This was when I asked the Dalai Lama to be our hero.

I'd had the good fortune to be with His Holiness on a number of occasions, and I thought that if he raised his voice on our behalf, the media might tell a story that could force the Chinese to back down. The Dalai Lama knew better. "You must make Sony your hero," he said.

So I turned to John Calley, then head of the motion picture studio at Sony, and told him our problem, calling on him, the listener, to step into the hero's role. Then I narrated the story of this hero's journey.

He and Sony faced an urgent dilemma, I told him, with two choices, both of them risky. Sony's electronic empire was a source of national pride that far outreached its entertainment divisions. How could Sony risk as important a trading partner as China for the sake of a movie? On the other hand, I suggested, if he did not persuade Sony to stand up for this film, the company's reputation for artistic integrity would suffer. As studio head, Calley knew that the right thing to do was to protect the artistic flame and not allow it to be extinguished by the Chinese or any other political pressure.

Then I told him the story that Jean-Jacques Annaud had told me of his film *Quest for Fire,* about a prehistoric tribe that hasn't yet learned how to make fire. When alien tribesmen steal their last blazing log, three warriors must travel in search of a flame to replace the fire their tribe has lost. They encounter saber-toothed tigers, mammoths, and other dangers, but the fate of their people rests on their finding and keeping the flame. In just this way, I said, Sony Pictures' Japanese parent company was charged with keeping the artistic flame alive. Despite the current threats by China, Sony could show itself to be a staunch defender of creative rights and thus become a hero to all current and future producers of music, television, and film products. I told Calley that this crisis was actually giving Sony the opportunity to turn adversity to advantage.

John heard the call to action in the story, and it motivated him to advocate on our behalf to Sony's corporate leadership. At his urging, Sony didn't back down. Our movie was released in 1997, three months ahead of Scorsese's. And although Sony's business relationships with China, especially in their electronics divisions, took some hits, the corporate leadership persevered and Sony's international reputation for creative integrity soared. My listener had indeed become the hero and carried the day to solve our problem.

CAN TELLING PEOPLE STORIES of their own heroism actually change the world? Bill Haber thought so, and he was willing to leave the company he'd cofounded twenty years earlier to prove it. That company, Creative Artists Agency, is one of the premier talent agencies in the entertainment business. I was among Bill's early clients. But when he left in 1995, this Hollywood agent was determined to become an agent for global change. He wanted to put his talents to work helping the most vulnerable of the world's populations—children—and so he became a leader of the nonprofit organization Save the Children.

The problem he faced right off was the scale of the organization and the scope of need that it served. "Save the Children has forty-one different branches internationally," he told me. "Except for UNICEF, it's the largest nongovernmental, nonsectarian organization for children in the world. We service thirty-five million desperate children. But how do you raise potential donors' interest in thirty-five million children? Telling people you need to pay for four thousand employees, five million meals, and six thousand pencils doesn't move them. Human beings instinctively turn off when numbers get that large and impersonal. We're wired to respond emotionally one to one. So our story had to turn the listener into the hero for that one child. Our story had to be that every single child has a story, and if you save one child's life or make one single child's life whole because of what you do, then you've made a difference that matters. Through that one life, you can change the world."

This approach to the art of the tell applied, Bill told me, to the stories he told to donors, government sponsors, and Save the Children's own staff and volunteers. Whether his purpose was to raise money, recruit staff, affect policy, or ignite political support, his best story was always you can save one child. You can be the hero.

"It's not about thirty-five million children," Bill said. "It's about being the hero in the story I told about one nine-year-old girl I met in Tripoli, Lebanon, who couldn't go into the school because her family didn't have five dollars to buy a uniform. Or the story I told of the kid in Croatia who had to wear a hat because he'd pulled out all his hair after seeing his sister decapitated in their living room by a piece of shrapnel. When I talked to people at Save the Children, I'd tell them, 'You can make more money other places and you can have easier lives and you don't have to be shot at or bombed, as we were when we went into Sarajevo. You could go take other jobs and have a regular life, but you choose to do this to save that one child's life.' "

But not any child's sad story will do, Haber said. When the overall purpose is as serious as Save the Children's, you can walk a very fine line between moving people and shocking people. "When I came here, their most successful advertising was that Pulitzer Prize–winning picture of a little kid dying with the vulture over it. I told them, 'I cannot be here and have that picture. You've gone too far.' That's not the way to tell the story. You can't win people's hearts by horrifying them. Very quickly, they'll turn away to protect themselves."

To open the way for the audience to play a heroic role, the story has to hold out hope, Bill said. The solution that Save the Children has adopted is to tell the story through the mechanism of sponsorship. "Sponsorship is where you spend twenty-four dollars, which goes to one child. Then the child writes you. You get a picture of the child, which puts a face on the major character of a story in which you personally participate. This story proves you are the hero changing the world. That's really what moves you, and then comes the key to the whole thing: You tell this story to your family and friends, and the story you tell of 'your' child, the call to action that you answered, and how that action made you feel—that story persuades them to become sponsors. And so it goes."

This approach both attracts and retains donors from year to year, because heroes naturally feel invested in the children they help to save. In 2008 Save the Children received more than $33 million in child sponsorships. The recruitment of donor heroes also has been hugely effective in securing corporate donors. In 2006 Save the Children's sponsors included more than a third of the top global brands ranked by *BusinessWeek*. "Just tell people that they can make a difference in one child's life," Bill said. "That's how you change the world."

Putting your listener in the shoes of the hero clearly makes sense if your call to action involves risk or sacrifice—or if you know your audience will have to overcome some resistance to fulfill your purpose. By moving the listener to feel like the hero at the end of the story, your telling can supply the needed motivation to push past the listener's own reluctance. But what if your goal is simply to inspire people to buy your product?

CUSTOMER AS HERO

In 1996, as a walk-on fullback at the University of Maryland, Kevin Plank came up with the bright idea of selling T-shirts made out of women's lingerie fabric. Plank had noticed that his cotton workout clothing soaked up buckets of sweat that weighed on him and slowed him down on the field, so he dreamed up an undershirt made from Capilene, a lightweight fabric that keeps its shape and color and wicks sweat away from the skin to keep the body cooler in summer and warmer in winter. At twenty-three, he put all his money into developing a prototype with superior moisture wicking technology, which bore the label Under Armour. To show proof of process he gave the product for free to his friend and colleague athletes. His rationale was that these 250-pound linebackers defined toughness, so if *they* embraced the product, they'd change the whole perception of its fabric. Lo and behold, the apparel caught on. In fact, Jeff George was featured on the front page of *USA Today* in his Raiders uniform with an Under Armour turtleneck—and Jeff wasn't even one of the players who'd received the product for free. The phone rang off the hook with calls from athletes. But how could Plank now transition the story of this product to the general population?

When Kevin came to my office in 2009 to leverage some of my sports entertainment relationships, he shared with me the story he'd told to broaden Under Armour's appeal. "I now had to make the customer my hero," he told me. "Like telling the Superman story in reverse, I had to make them believe that it wasn't the obvious Superman costume but Clark Kent's T-shirt that would give them the liftoff they really needed." That was a tall order, but his team knew how the product could perform and all its operational characteristics. Kevin told them to tell an aspirational story, and the aspiration was whatever goal their customers came in with. "We didn't just say, 'How may I help you?'" he explained. "We asked, 'What do you want to be? Do you want to play varsity? Be the best? Lose twenty pounds? Whatever it is, you'll get there with Under Armour.'"

The theme of Plank's story was that every Under Armour product helped the customer perform like a pro. Under Armour would provide the physical assist and the emotional propulsion, but it was the customer who would break higher and higher personal records. And telling his story with the customer as hero proved to be the game-changer for Plank's company.

Today Under Armour is worth nearly $1 billion, and Plank makes sure that every one of his 2,400 employees tells a version of the customer-as-hero story every day to consumers, retailers, media, and athletes. Because customers' goals are constantly changing, so is the story Under Armour must tell to keep them in the hero's role. That's fine with Kevin. "My job as chief story teller is not to push, print, bind, and you're done," he said. "Our story's a living, breathing, changing thing. We're a different company every six months." And that story continues to move hundreds of thousands of customers to buy and extol his products.

PRODUCT AS HERO

Sometimes there's no way around it; the product *is* the hero. At least that's how Lynda Resnick tells the story of POM Wonderful. In addition to marketing brands such as Teleflora and FIJI Water, Lynda and her husband Stewart's company, Roll International, is the biggest producer of almonds, pistachios, clementines, and pomegranates in the world. And the story Lynda told me about POM left no doubt that her product was its hero.

In 1986, Lynda and her husband bought 120 acres in California's San Joaquin Valley. On those acres they found trees that they thought were pistachios. Turned out they were something called pomegranates. At the time, Lynda told me, few Americans had any idea what pomegranates were, much less what they were good for. So the Resnicks did some research and uncovered the story of the pomegranate's history, its versatility, and its suspected health benefits. Could this history mean they were sitting on an antioxidant superhero?

Tracing the journey of the pomegranate's cultivation around the globe and back four thousand years, they discovered that this round red hero was such a symbol of strength in Persian culture that the army of Xerxes carried spears with pomegranates instead of spikes on the tip when they invaded Greece in 480 B.C. In ancient Egypt, pomegranate juice was used to treat maladies from dysentery to stomachaches, as well as intestinal worms. In India the pomegranate became a symbol of prosperity and fertility; in China, of fertility. In Israel it was said to help prevent heart disease. And after the heroic fruit had displayed its cancer-fighting prowess in Europe, its picture was added to the British Medical Association's heraldic crest in tribute.

The historical anecdotes spurred the Resnicks to increase their acreage of pomegranate trees to eighteen thousand and fund scientific research to investigate the benefits extolled in these stories. By 2009 they had spent $32 million on medical studies and found that the storied benefits were true. Pomegranate juice had a particularly beneficial effect on prostate cancer and type 2 diabetes, as well as cardiovascular disease. Now they could take the history of the pomegranate and power it with proven scientific truth to tell their customers, retailers, and the media a story that made their product the hero.

Lynda put together the best sales team in the world to make personal calls on the top management of every retail supermarket chain. She took a page out of her successful Jackie O Franklin Mint strategy and instructed each sales rep to tell store managers face-to-face the true stories of this heroic fruit that could save lives. "Then we let them taste this delicious juice," Lynda said. " 'You should be drinking it,' we told them and we're going to put you on the list, so you get it every month. And they all tried it and bought it and moved it by telling and retelling its remarkable story."

As Lynda said, sometimes you have to "think inside the box" to find not only your story but also your hero. But what if your "box" is not a manufactured or packaged product, but a location?

LOCATION AS HERO

Frank Lowy is now chairman of the massive Westfield Group, the largest publically traded real estate company in the world. Westfield globally operates 119 high-quality regional shopping centers, valued at more than $62 billion. But back in the 1980s, along with his numerous multinational enterprises, Frank was chairman of our public company Barris-GPEC Entertainment before we sold the company to Sony. Frank was always a shrewd and decent man who thought relationships had to be earned one customer at a time, and he's passed that ethos on to his son Peter, Westfield Group's managing director. I met with Peter Lowy at their San Fernando Valley offices recently to propose a co-venture to build a professional minor-league baseball stadium in the Valley, which despite being America's twelfth largest market has no professional sports team. I told Lowy how Mandalay's minor-league parks and professional baseball teams weren't just about winning and losing. More important, these locations provided a valuable opportunity for fans to gather socially, relax, and enjoy themselves in a comfortable family-friendly atmosphere. Peter Lowy replied that Westfield has built its monumental success on the back of a similar strategy, which showcased every Westfield location as the customer's hero. While our sports co-venture would be thwarted by the major-league baseball franchises that controlled the Valley's territorial rights, the insights that Lowy gave me that day shed a whole new light on the art of the tell.

He pointed out that at Century City, near my home, Westfield tells a story of the location as hero springing into action the moment customers enter the shopping center's parking lot. "We installed red and green bulbs over every parking stall so people can instantly see where a space is available. That cut down their time in the garage by eighty percent. That means customers are more relaxed, and they have that much more time to shop." And I knew as a customer myself that anyone who'd ever had the pleasure of parking in that garage would pay forward the location as hero by telling friends their story of this experience.

Being a hero, Lowy said, means not just giving the audience an experience that makes a positive difference to their lives, but also exceeding their expectations. Then they will tell that experience forward as a story. "Like a restaurant, we can't afford to cultivate a new customer every day. We have to keep them returning and win them as advocates through the story of their experience with us. Beyond that, there's nothing unique about having the Gap or Bloomingdale's or other stores. It's the way we make our location a hero in their story that differentiates us."

For example, Westfield's research showed that their customers are predominately women and nearly half bring children. So Westfield created parents' rooms. "If you've got little children and you need to breast-feed or change them," Lowy said, "we have the perfect environment. Or if you just want a break because your kids are little, there's a television there, soft toys, mats on the floor. You have baby-changing stations, diapers, wipes, even a microwave. It's unbelievably clean. And we wouldn't charge for it in a million years." In short, every Westfield location gives people—for free—an experience that they just can't get in any other shopping center.

Lowy tells his "Westfield-as-hero" story to train everyone from architects, retailers, and engineers, to the customer service employees in each mall. Why? Because when the hero delivers, the customer will go forth and tell this story, sending others to Westfield locations. And for the hero to deliver, all the people who represent or work at the location have to tell and uphold the same story. "The first contact the customer has is usually with the least paid, lowest person on the rung who works at that location. It could be the security person. So the security person better be well trained. You've got to tell them, 'Customers will tell you what they think and you've got to listen to them. You've got to be empathetic and then you've got to be sympathetic. You do those three things and you'll find out what they want. Only when you know what they want can you exceed their expectations.' In other words, you can't be your audience's hero unless you're interested in your audience."

But even Westfield isn't master of the universe. Sometimes bad things happen at good locations. That, Peter said, presents Westfield malls with an opportunity for even more heroic action. "A customer loses her purse, and Westfield will send her home with cab fare. So, do you think she comes back? You bet! More important, do you think she tells others? All the time! Here is the story about our location I love telling my guys. I got a letter from a woman complaining our mall in Northridge was dirty. So I wrote her back, 'Thank you for your complaint. I must tell you, we don't own that mall in Northridge, but I would much rather you shop at our mall in Topanga. Here's a $250 credit, please come to our mall instead of that mall.' She has since come back, thanking me, sharing how often she's retold this story to others."

If you don't work in a location-based business, the idea of location as the hero of a story may sound like a stretch. But Peter Lowy knew the power of oral narrative. He viewed his customers as an audience. His retailers were secondary characters like players on a stage. And his brick-and-mortar location was the proscenium. His goal was to render an experience for his audience that was resonant and memorable and would engender their trust. By telling a story in which Westfield's location would always come to the customers' rescue, he's succeeded in motivating ever more customers to come back to Westfield's locations.

TRIBE AS HERO

During my expedition to New Guinea in the early 2000s, the owner of one jungle lodge where we stayed told me a highly purposeful—if amusing—story in which the whole tribe was the hero. Because this small encampment above the Sepik River was the only commercial establishment for miles, it was vital to the local economy. And foreigners were particularly valued, as they made up most of the clientele and brought hard currency into the area. So when the story of 9/11 first filtered to the staff, they were very worried that their guests' tribe was under attack. Few, if any, of the employees had any schooling, so the manager, sensing their anxiety, showed them America on the globe and told them, "Here's where the attack happened over here in New York and here's where we are way over here." He thought that would make them feel more secure. He misread them.

The staff's goal was to protect Americans from the terrorists whose attacks were threatening their livelihood. They wanted to be active in our rescue. But they couldn't understand that these attacks had taken place ten thousand miles away. All they knew of geography was the globe the manager had shown them.

They must have gone back to their village and told and retold the 9/11 story until it delivered a call to action that they could comprehend, because the next morning the whole tribe showed up at the lodge with spears and bows and arrows at the ready and took up positions around the camp grounds. The terrorists, they'd concluded, would run away from New York and around the back of the globe the manager had shown them, then sneak up on the lodge from the other side. "We will defend you," they told the American guests. "Our tribe stands with those who stand with us." In other words, they would be our heroes.

COLLECTIVE HEROISM CAN MAKE for a powerful, purposeful story, especially when the call to action benefits the whole tribe. Back in 2000 I was invited by former secretary of defense William Cohen to participate in an eye-opening program called the Joint Civilian Orientation Conference, which enabled members of the U.S. military to tell their collective story of heroism in order to raise support for their tribe.

The JCOC brought together opinion leaders who could influence the media, public, and government and sought to persuade them that the most valuable asset in the military was not its weapons technology but its human technology. To accomplish this, the Department of Defense sent a group of about twenty-four of us into the heart of America's military to hear, unedited, individual stories of this tribe's commitment and heroism. For one week we traveled from military base to submarine, from aircraft carrier to air force base. At the outset I'd thought of the nation's defense primarily in terms of tanks, guns, bullets, planes. But that perception radically changed as I got to know the people who actually man the guns, steer the ships, fly the planes, interrogate the prisoners, cook the food, drive the trucks, and administer the vehicles and personnel. These people told me story after story, each one echoing the core message of the others in its own unique way. That message was conveyed in one particularly poignant story told to me on the USS *Enterprise* at sea in the Atlantic.

In the captain's mess, the tall, handsome Hispanic pilot who'd flown me in was sitting next to me. Twenty-nine years old, he said he'd joined the Navy right out of college and had been flying for four years. His pride in his work and his accomplishments shone more than his medals. There was a sad edge to his voice when he said, "My service commitment is up next year and I'm probably going to return to civilian life."

With a little encouragement, he told me he had a wife and daughter, and another child on the way. They lived in base housing in Norfolk. He'd married young, and his wife dropped out of college when he was transferred. She worked part-time for minimum wage at a Wendy's but would have to quit when the baby came. "Look." He put down his fork. "I love being a pilot. I love my plane and my squadron. I love being part of the military. I'm proud as hell of the job I've done here. I consider it my duty. But I also love my family, and I have a responsibility to my wife and kids, too. The way it is now, I can't fulfill both these duties. I have to choose one or the other. Sir, I can't go on having my family on food stamps."

"Food stamps?" I could not believe I'd heard him correctly.

"You do what you have to, sir, to make ends meet."

All week other servicemen and -women had thanked us for coming and told us they wished more citizens could see what they really do. They said they often didn't feel appreciated or respected. This pilot's story brought their dilemma into cutting focus because it reflected the reality for so many members of the U.S. military. The stakes were not bullets and steel, but flesh and blood.

This tribe's heroic story called for action. We heard them and knew we had to support these brave and dedicated men and women, for their sakes and for our own. And that's precisely why the JCOC had encouraged us to get into the trenches. If we heard directly from the heroes themselves, we'd feel compelled to go out and retell their stories, adding our own sense of urgency with each retelling, in talks and conversations, phone calls, movies, articles, and the then-emerging Internet. I heard that call loud and clear and began to answer it as soon as I returned home. I phoned my senators and my congressman and told them the stories I'd heard and experienced. At events and in the boardroom I told influential colleagues. "What matters most in the military are the people," I always concluded. "They're taking care of us, and we have to take better care of them."

WHETHER THE RIGHT HERO for your story is your tribe, product, location, customer, audience—or you the teller—will depend primarily on your goal. If you need your audience to trust in your personal leadership, you may need to assume the hero's mantle yourself. If you want them to step up and take what they will perceive as a risk, you may need to cloak them in the hero's role. If you want them to choose your brand over someone else's, it makes sense to shine the light on the heroic virtues of your product or location. And if you want them to support, promote, or select the activities of your group, be it the U.S. military or your organizational team, then it may be best to fire up a story about the heroic virtues of the tribe. But even after you've determined who you need in your hero's role, the story still must be shaped and textured. And for that, you will need raw material.

FINDING YOUR RAW MATERIAL

In my courses at UCLA over the years, my graduate students often ask where they can find source material for purposeful stories, given that they've barely begun their careers. Based on my experience, I tell them that narrative is always lurking, ready to give emotion to information, shape to experience, and propulsion to purpose. But as organizational story guru Steve Denning said at one of our narrative conclaves, the key is not to expect to find a story fully born, perfectly framed and ready for use, but to constantly stockpile fragments that have the potential to become stories. "Once you have enough material to tell a story, then you have to perfect it."

Thinking back over the stories I've told in my own career, I've found that the most effective story material usually comes from firsthand experience. When you narrate an event that has actually happened to you, it's natural to infuse your telling with the emotional highs, lows, and inflections you felt at the time, whether you were the hero or a secondary participant in that drama. Your personal feeling will ignite your listeners' empathy and carry them along on your emotional journey. Plus, personal experiences are easy to remember and tell with authenticity because you lived them.

FIRSTHAND EXPERIENCE

Frank Sinatra was not called the Chairman of the Board by accident. Right up until his death in 1998, he was a force of nature. Singer, dancer, actor—he was the leader of the Hollywood "rat pack," with Dean Martin and Sammy Davis, Jr., in the 1960s and won more than eleven Grammy awards and thirty nominations, plus an Academy Award for his performance in *From Here to Eternity* in 1953. But as I knew from firsthand experience, he was also a complicated human being.

In 2006 one of my sons told me of his embarrassment at a school event, when he was admonished by a teacher I knew to be a decent and honorable fellow. I tried to explain that people are sometimes confusing creatures, and no one experience completely defines them. The words were barely out of my mouth when I realized I was talking about Frank Sinatra, with whom I'd had an encounter something like my son's with his teacher. After sharing that story with my son, I got to thinking that Sinatra's human story would make a terrific theatrical film. I did some research and found that no theatrical movie had ever been made that did justice to Sinatra's unique persona. So I decided that Mandalay should undertake this goal.

Gary Lemel, who had run the Warner Bros. film music operation for decades, had known Frank, and he helped me set up a meeting with Tina Sinatra, who was in charge of building her father's legacy. But Tina was no easy mark. As the keeper of the Sinatra brand, she oversaw a veritable empire of music and merchandising rights, and she was ferocious in making sure that any license she granted honored her father's name and reputation. Lemel and I knew we'd have to tell her a powerful story if we were to get the rights to portray Frank Sinatra's life and music, without which we'd have no film. Fortunately my firsthand experience with Frank gave me the material I needed to set my story.

I told Tina that in the 1970s, when I was a very young man running the West Coast studio at Columbia Pictures, Columbia chairman Leo Jaffe called to say that Dean Martin was woefully behind schedule on a special project he was doing for the Matt Helm film series, and I had to go down to the stage and "get Dean cracking." Of course, Dean was a huge star then, so I asked John Veitch, our head of physical production and a veteran of such confrontations, what my best approach was. Veitch suggested my only approach was to go face-to-face and personally get Dean out of the trailer where he was holed up.

Then I told Tina how I'd made my way to the back lot, prepared to ask Dean one polite but clear question: "What can I do to help you get this project finished?" I passed through a gaggle of crew and cast who were impatiently waiting, but I didn't realize they were waiting for the drama to unfold as one of the suits—me—came down to cajole Martin into action.

I knocked on the door once, then a second time. Suddenly it shot open and there was Frank, as in Sinatra, demanding, "Who the hell are you?"

"Dean saw me," I told Tina, "and said, 'He's a good kid, Frank, the head of the studio.' I edged in and Frank squared off. 'What do you want?' he demanded. I started to say we wanted Dean to finish up, but before I could complete the sentence, Frank threw open the door and bodily pushed me out into our chortling onlookers. Then he began to berate me, saying I had no experience, no business being there, and nobody gave a damn what I had to say. As for Dean, he'd come out when he was good and ready! I retreated, humiliated, furious, and thoroughly discouraged as the whole crew watched my debacle.

"For the next months," I told Tina, "every time I heard Frank's name or music it would trigger a complete replay of the whole story, and the same hateful emotions would sweep through me."

Tina looked at me warily, unsure where I was going with this unflattering story about her father. But then I moved her forward to a big Hollywood award event about a year later, when I was sitting with our key execs and several top actors at the table next to Sinatra's. "He glanced at me several times, and the whole embarrassing experience came ripping back. I thought, *Oh my god, not again.* But as I was leaving, I could not avoid passing his table. Suddenly, his arm shot out to corral me. I thought, *Here goes.* But then Frank pointed at me and said loudly to everyone in earshot, 'This fella's head of Columbia and he is one smart cookie. You watch, he's going to make a mark on this business. Columbia's lucky to have him.' He patted my hand and looked in my eyes and smiled that melting smile of his. In a single line he propelled me from the depth of fear to the height of pride."

As I told Tina this story, I kept my eye on my goal: to persuade her to sell me the rights to make a movie about her father. My story proved that

I had what it took to honor the whole human truth of Sinatra. It showed that I understood the complexity of his character, warts and all, and that I appreciated both his dark and his light sides in work and play.

Because Tina had experienced her father's complexity so many times in similar scenes, she immediately got that I understood it. In fact, she said, based on her own firsthand experience, her father never would visit Dean Martin when Dean was working at a studio unless Dean had put out a 911 SOS call to his best pal. "Maybe he was going to cry, maybe he was about to tell him the bottom line to something that was life-and-death, and you walked in. And Dad chewed you out to save him. If he thought you were a schlub, I don't think he would have done it. If he thought you were a suit, he might have done it just to be pissy, but I think he was pissy in defense of a moment that was a very serious moment for Dean, because Dad was very mannered, and politeness was not out of his realm."

She went on: "Look, when someone sits down with me to talk to me about doing something with the estate, I'm a businessperson, but first I am a daughter. I have a responsibility to other heirs, people we're already contracting with, and the legacy. I come from an instinctual place. I learned from Dad to see and smell out a bullshitter at five hundred yards. That's why he put the legacy in my hands twenty-five years before he died. So the first thing I do is assess the character and authenticity of anybody trying to tell me or sell me anything. I hear with my heart and ears. I can't help it. They're not separated. What he did and did not do in his lifetime is what we perpetuate today. I'm an extension of his story. I think you get it. Let's go!" And with Tina's blessing, we brought Universal Studios into the mix to finance the acquisition of the rights and the development of the project.

Everybody faces challenges and struggles to resolve them. In other words, we all live stories every single day. If you pay attention to these experiences and are good at remembering not only what happened but also what it meant to you, then you're constantly stockpiling prime story content. But firsthand experience is not your only source. Purposeful stories also can be distilled from people you've observed or events that you've witnessed, even if you didn't directly play a role in them.

WITNESSED EXPERIENCE

Early in George Lopez's career as a comedian, he got a rude awakening. After a show where he'd performed a stand-up routine that borrowed in attitude from popular comedians like Richard Pryor and George Carlin, a critic said to him, "You're trying to stir the pot, but it's not your pot. Nothing that you're saying is yours; it's mundane." Lopez had to look up "mundane" in the dictionary, and when he did, the definition hit him like a kick in the head: "to say something that means nothing."

That kick struck a spark that turned into a bonfire for Lopez. "Most people from my neighborhood would have said, 'Fuck that guy.' But I listened to him; I learned to listen." And listening, as he told me recently, became the basis for the stories he told to climb to the top ranks of comedians in America, and to establish his philanthropic endeavors.

My kids attend the same school as George's, so when I began my exploration of the art of the tell, I naturally sought him out. In 2005, *Time* magazine had named George Lopez one of the twenty-five most influential Hispanics in America. He not only did stand-up before sellout crowds, but he'd starred in his own network sitcom, hosted his own TV talk show, and was a major figure in philanthropic circles. I wanted to know how he found his raw material and why he thought it resonated with audiences.

Lopez told me that after he'd absorbed that criticism all those years ago, he realized that if he really wanted to stir the pot of audience reaction, then it had to be a pot he'd witnessed from the inside—his own Mexican-American community. And whether his call to action was for audiences to laugh, fight, hire him, buy his products, or give to his causes, he was now determined that his stories had to tell the whole truth of this world as he saw it.

"I struggled in the beginning to find an identity," Lopez told me, "because when I was a kid I didn't have one." What he meant was that he was always trying to escape who he was and where he lived. He never knew his father, his mother left him when he was young, he never even had enough money for a coat, and he always wanted to avoid witnessing what he saw every day. "So when I started to tell stories, they didn't have a bottom. I was making it all up."

But as that critic's spark caught fire, he realized he needed to find his center. "And my center was my grandmother who raised me. My grandmother never left me even when times were hard. She left husbands, left kids, never left me." He also knew, though, that his grandmother was no angel. "When the San Fernando earthquake happened near us in 1971, we had very little damage to our house, and yet my grandmother was at the church every day getting free food. I came from a family that was always about taking and never about giving. It just didn't seem right to me."

Worse yet, when George questioned his grandmother about taking the food that other people needed more, she rebuked him: "What's it matter? Nobody's watching."

Even at the time, George thought, "I'm watching. Aren't I somebody?" But he never acted on this thought until he started thinking about what it really meant to have a center. Suddenly he realized that having a center meant having enough gravity to tell the truth about what he witnessed and also having enough self-regard to try to do the right thing. His reputation might be built on what others witnessed of him, but his character was built on his actions when he had no witness other than himself. This realization made him vow to engage in at least one "random act of kindness" every day, whether or not anyone else was there to see it. This became the center point of his philanthropy and his determination to work to change the very conditions his comedy would illuminate.

Recognizing that humor feeds on the paradoxes of life, Lopez decided to tell the story about his grandmother, first in his stand-up, later on his television shows, and eventually through his charities. He also told other stories he'd witnessed in his community growing up. "We hit our women and we buy them sunglasses," he'd say. "We drink and then order the kids around and can't remember the next day how we treated the kids at night." Nothing was fabricated. He took the raw material for his stories from his community and told those good, bad, and ugly stories in order to change the community. It was like holding a narrative mirror up to his culture.

Then he discovered that the stories he told struck a chord with people far outside his community. It turned out they'd witnessed the same contradictory behavior in their own cultures. "It's an economic thing and it's a world thing," George told me. "People in India do the same thing as people in Germany and people in Poland and people in Russia." So he was stirring their pot by stirring his own. "When I sold out the Radio City Music Hall for the first time, I had the most diverse audience, and they all got it."

You don't have to be an actor or a comedian to mine witnessed experience for purposeful stories. Arne Glimcher has built one of the most prominent art galleries in the world, the Pace Gallery, on the back of stories he tells about the artists he represents. These include giants of the art world such as Chuck Close, John Chamberlain, Jim Dine, Elizabeth Murray, Kiki Smith, Lucas Samaras, Joel Shapiro, and Robert Rauschenberg, as well as the estates of Alexander Calder, Agnes Martin, Louise Nevelson, Pablo Picasso, Ad Reinhardt, and Mark Rothko. Glimcher not only knows these artists personally, but he makes it his business to watch them as they work, because that's how he collects the stories that he tells customers. He's used these stories to persuade me to buy art from him on numerous occasions.

"I'm not a picture seller," Arne told me on one of my recent visits to his New York gallery. "I'm a narrator." That's important, he explained, because collectors consume stories about artists in a way they can't consume the physical art. They can look at art and be stewards of it, but no matter how much money is exchanged, the soul of the art always belongs more to the artist who created it than it does to the collector. Stories can bridge the gap. "Being in the studio and seeing the artist develop the work, you're the only person in the world who'll ever see that. People will look back at these as finished works. You're the only one who was there to witness the artist's unfolding narrative." So when Glimcher tells collectors the story of what he sees during the creative process, that makes them feel privileged and motivated to buy the work.

Arne understands narrative as well as he understands art. He's produced more than seven motion pictures, including our 1988 film *Gorillas in the Mist*. Back then I thought it curious that the owner of an art gallery would have such a feel for the kind of story telling we do in Hollywood, but the more I got to know Arne the more I understood that the art of the tell is fundamental to all aspects of his career. And the most valuable raw material for his stories comes from his close and fascinated observation of the world around him.

He pointed out that there's more to witnessing story material than just seeing and remembering. To tell a story about something you've seen, you have to observe closely and thoughtfully. When Glimcher is in an artist's studio, he's not just watching, he's asking questions and looking for insights. "It helps me to understand the work in another way. What are the systems that are creating these works? What's the motivation of the artist? If I can absorb that, I can impart that to customers. I don't just sell art. I sell the story behind the art and the artist." Collectors consume that story with their purchase of the work, and when they share the art with their friends, they pay the story forward.

Then he told me a story about a Chinese performance artist, Zhang Huan. "He collected ash from incense used in offerings at temples around Shanghai. He cast a nineteen-foot Buddha in aluminum, and the mold was then turned upside-down and packed with tons of incense ash, and at a certain moment, six guys removed the mold, leaving one mold on the face with a pole propping it up. The Buddha stayed perfect for about three seconds and then started to crumble. They took the face mask off and the head stayed for about three seconds. Then the face melted, the ash fell, the head fell off, and in ten minutes, the whole sculpture turned into a mound of ash. Now it was about resurrection, Buddhism, the idea that the end is the beginning of something else—magic." And this magic endures through the story of that performance, which Glimcher tells and retells to collectors in words and through the artist's video documentation of the event, which is for sale.

When I'd arrived at the gallery that day I'd never head of Zhang Huan. But Arne made the passion and power of this artist's creativity irresistibly compelling. Driven by Arne's story, I became interested in purchasing Zhang's work and in 2010 made the trek to his gallery outside of Beijing to see how he put together his magic.

METAPHOR/ANALOGY

One of the most memorable and instructive stories I've ever been told was actually wrapped in a metaphor. It was the early 1970s, when the whole movie industry was going through a serious financial crisis, and I was a very young studio head at Columbia Pictures. We had a deal with Jack Warner, the legendary founder and recently retired chairman of Warner Bros., to make his first movie with us, a film version of the stage play *1776,* and late one day we were having a meeting at Warner's home to discuss his plans to bring on Peter Hunt to direct the picture.

During a lull in the conversation Warner asked me casually, "How are things going for you at the studio?"

Ordinarily I was so intimidated by Hollywood giants like Warner that I was practically tongue-tied, but his question caught me off guard. He knew that I was just a few years out of graduate school and that many of Columbia's senior executives were based on the East Coast. He seemed genuinely interested, and I answered honestly, "By the end of each day I'm overwhelmed." Then I found myself venting: "It's like a tidal wave. People just keep coming into my office with one problem after the other. It never ends."

Warner said, "Let me tell you a story. Don't be confused. You're only renting that office. You don't own it. It's a zoo. You're the zookeeper, and every single person that comes in the office comes with a monkey.

That monkey is their problem. They're trying to leave it with you. Your job is to discover where the monkey is. They'll hide it, or dress it up, but remember you're the zookeeper. You've got to keep the place clean. So make sure when you walk them to the door, they've got their monkey by the hand. Don't let them leave without it. Don't let them come back until it's trained and they have solutions to their problem. Otherwise at the end of the day, you'll have an office full of screaming, jumping animals and monkey shit all over the floor."

Then he said, "Think of that visually. Make them all take their monkey problems away and come back with a solution."

After that, I noticed that visitors to my office invariably would wait until the last possible second to reveal the monkey in their briefcase, their pocket, or the person they were with. But if I just watched and waited, the real problem would come popping out. Then I could hand it right back to the person who was trying to foist it off on me. Warner's metaphor became a valuable managerial tool, and I told it forward often in my career.

Many years later, when Ron Meyer became the chairman of Universal Pictures, he asked me over lunch one day what the best lesson was I had to pass on to him. I told him, "Stay out of the monkey business. Here's how." Meyer laughed at the time. Later on, he thanked me. I told him to thank the late great Jack Warner. I was just passing the story along.

THE BEAUTY OF METAPHORS and analogies when used as story material is their economy. When they work, all the emotion and meaning you need can be delivered in a single image, sometimes a single word. I don't think game designers have a corner on the telling of stories through metaphors, but it just so happens that two game designers with whom I had recent meetings told precisely this type of story.

The first was Dan Rosensweig, former CEO and president of Guitar Hero, the $2 billion franchise of Activision Blizzard. Rosensweig was a highly sought after executive who'd been COO of Yahoo! and a major player in private equity. I was curious what story Activision Blizzard CEO Bobby Kotick had told to lure Rosensweig into his world of gaming. It turned out Kotick's story was actually a single metaphor—that of a canoe shooting through rapids.

Why had that metaphor been such a perfect device? Because Kotick, who'd served on Yahoo!'s board when Rosensweig was COO, knew his old friend's penchant for exciting new ventures. Rosensweig always wanted to be an active participant in his ventures, never just a passenger.

"If you're going to be in a canoe," Kotick told him, "it's better for the canoe to go with the rapids instead of against them. In rapids, you're going to hit walls; you might flip over or somebody might fall out of the boat, but if you're in with the right people and the current is moving in the right direction, then you're likely to succeed. And I'm the right people."

How did that story resonate with Rosensweig? He told Kotick that throughout his career he'd sought opportunities to leverage technology for the future, which meant joining companies that moved with the currents of technology instead of against them. "The two things that young people are using today are the Internet and gaming. For the first time, the Internet and gaming are coming together. And if this is the river of change, then you're right, I have to decide who to be in the canoe with."

Rosensweig heard the metaphor's message, he told me, and he saw the rapids not as the problem but the opportunity. "Traditional companies usually get beaten by the challenger, but I saw Bobby reposition Activision to be the leader. He saw and told me how gaming was going to get bigger, that connectivity to the Internet was going to change the business model around games. Bobby didn't want to be dependent on hit-driven games based on movies, because he thought—incorrectly, as it turned out—that the movie market was going to decline. So the metaphor of the canoe moving with the rapids made me realize how we'd leverage Internet and gaming together."

At the time the two men spoke about working together, Kotick's Guitar Hero was the sixth best-selling franchise in the history of gaming, selling 40 million units around the world within five years. Before buying Guitar Hero and merging with Blizzard, Activision was less than half the size of its direct competitor, and within four years, Bobby had grown the company to be two and a half times bigger. In one year the number of people who played Guitar Hero online doubled. Kotick could simply have pitched those numbers to Rosensweig, but a numbers pitch would have lacked the sense of adventure, exhilaration, and camaraderie that he wanted to arouse in his listener. So he told his story through the metaphor of a canoe racing faster and faster through the technological rapids but with just the right people to make sure they had the ride of their lives and emerged as leaders.

Rosensweig got it. He jumped into the canoe in March of 2008, and by 2009, some 2 million gamers per week were playing Guitar Hero through the Internet.

A FEW WEEKS LATER, I was meeting with Will Wright, who designed The Sims, the best-selling PC game in history, and cofounded the game development company Maxis, now part of Electronic Arts. He also produced the game Spore, based loosely on the science of evolution, which sold 406,000 copies within three weeks of its 2008 release. At the time we met, though, Will was in the middle of a transition from EA to run an entertainment think tank called Stupid Fun Club. This new group would develop new intellectual properties to be deployed across multiple fronts, including video games, movies, television, the Internet, and toys. He said it was an exciting proposition but sometimes challenging to explain to the talent he needed, so he'd resorted to telling the story through a metaphor—in this case, the metaphor was *Switzerland*.

Wright explained his problem by describing what he'd gone through to persuade one very talented programmer to join him. "He'd worked with us for many years on Sims, but he was seriously considering leaving programming and games because he had a lot of interest in independent filmmaking, toys, and Web technologies." Having worked in large companies, this programmer thought of creativity as an either/or proposition, as in "I can't be a programmer if I'm going to be in toys or in film or games."

"He was right," Will said. "These large companies are designed as single-purpose intellectual property–generators, and then perhaps if an innovation occurs, it will migrate to other disciplines without their further participation. This makes most creative people feel like they have to fill one of these pigeonholes and there is no position where they can be involved in all of them."

Wright's challenge was to reverse that thinking and prove that he was creating a land where boundaries between fields like television, film, games, and toys didn't exist—a neutral land where imagination could run free. "I realized I had to initiate the intellectual capital and the product in the white space between these fields, in a zone where we'd be free to work with all these guys in the most productive fashion."

So he told the programmer that what he really wanted to do was create intellectual property in neutral Switzerland. "Then we'd take that thing out of Switzerland to all the different areas so no one medium would fall subservient to another."

The metaphor of Switzerland told the story of a small, landlocked country surrounded by mega powers, recognized and able to do business with all yet beholden to none. Immediately the programmer got it and was happy to come on board. "He knows he's going to be involved in a lot of linear story telling experiences, reading scripts, but also programming. So for him, it feels like it's maximizing his skill set, instead of being forced to abandon one skill set to acquire another."

Switzerland, Will added, was a perfect metaphor because it carried no ego burden and needed no operation manual or translation.

INFORMATION SCENARIOS

Most of us will naturally find story content where we work, in the stuff that fascinates us. Sometimes that stuff is people and relationships that lend themselves to obvious human stories, but sometimes the stuff is information—not statistics and data, but information about the world that lives, breathes, struggles, and strives around us.

I recently had the pleasure of meeting Dr. Shirley Pomponi, executive director of Florida Atlantic University's Harbor Branch Oceanographic Institute, who told me that for decades scientists like herself have been exploring and testing marine organisms to find out what treasures they might offer for human use. These organisms, primarily animals that live on the bottom of the ocean, have evolved an arsenal of chemical weapons to defend themselves against predators, against things that want to grow on top of them, kill them, eat them. Some of these marine-derived chemicals have shown promise in preliminary clinical trials against severe terminal diseases. With that proof of process, Pomponi is going to pharmaceutical and biotech companies to persuade them to invest in further exploration. But to do this she has to break through their traditional thinking that cures are found in the lab—and not on the ocean floor. How does she achieve this breakthrough? By converting research into stories—or information scenarios.

Pomponi explained that potential investors often can't understand how anything profitable could come out of Harbor Branch's marine research. "Why, for example, would a sponge produce a chemical that is useful against cancer when sponges don't get cancer?" She said that was exactly the obstacle when she tried to raise funds to study one particular deepwater sponge. "They didn't get it."

To help them get it, she told the story of another deep sea creature that has proven the process. "It's a snail found deep in the Pacific called a cone snail and it can be very dangerous because it has a little harpoon that's connected to kind of a string that leads to its venom duct. When it strikes its prey that harpoon injects this venom into a fish. That fish can be much bigger than the snail, but when the snail injects its toxin, it paralyzes the fish. One component of the venom causes the fish to convulse. Another component anesthetizes the fish; another component starts sending other chemicals into the fish that cause the fish to start to disintegrate so that eventually the snail can completely engulf that fish and eat it."

By the time she reached this point in the story, I was practically cheering for this snail, which she described as a little aquatic David triumphing over the Goliath fish. Even though the snail maybe had something a little sinister in that venom and harpoon, I was dazzled by its inventiveness. There was no doubt in my mind that this snail was my hero.

"So here was a simple animal whose ultimate objective was to kill the fish so he could eat it," Shirley continued, "but to do that he produced this whole suite of chemicals that each did different things. Scientists took the snail and removed the toxin from its venom gland. They started isolating the different chemical components and testing them. One chemical caused spasms; another caused lethargy; but one chemical acted as a painkiller! So the researchers convinced a pharmaceutical company to start testing it on other animals and eventually developed it into a drug for humans."

Every beat of Pomponi's story is information that marine biologists have discovered scientifically, but she transports her listeners emotionally by shaping that information into a scenario about one memorably feisty little snail. Pomponi told the story to every potential partner in her sponge research, from pharmaceutical companies to federal funding agencies. Why? Because the message hidden within it was that the ocean is brimming with cures and treatments that can benefit humans and pay off handsomely for investors. "So rather than just saying, 'Let's look for things that will kill cancer cells,' I'm telling them, 'Let's look at these marine animals' stories and figure out how can we apply their benefits to human health care.'"

Has it paid off? "We collected a sponge in the Bahamas that we'd never seen before, and were able to identify a molecule that had anticancer activities. We sold that idea, licensed that discovery, to a pharmaceutical company that then put it in clinical trials, and we actually cured one woman who had pancreatic cancer. We don't know the results of the other clinical trials yet, but we are very optimistic." And now she can tell the story of the heroic sponge to sell her next deep sea adventure.

BOOKS AND MOVIES

As Bill Clinton demonstrated when he prompted me to recall the plot of *High Noon,* movies and television shows provide excellent purposeful story content. So do stories originally written as novels or short fiction.

Best-selling phenomenon Nora Roberts certainly knows how to turn fiction into entertainment gold. Over the last twenty-seven years, an average of twenty-one Nora Roberts books have been sold every minute. She's had the number one ranked title on the *New York Times* best seller list more than 155 times, and there are more than 300 million copies of her books in print. Several years ago I convinced Nora to sell me the rights to a number of her best-selling novels, including *Angels Fall, Carolina Moon, Montana Sky,* and *Blue Smoke,* and we turned them into movies for Lifetime. But writing an entertaining story is one thing, and telling it orally to build a business is quite another, so when I heard that Nora had opened an inn near her home in Boonsboro, Maryland, I wanted to hear and see this businessperson in action.

When I got to Nora's quaint little town, her hotel, Inn BoonsBoro, was right there on the corner of the main street in a beautiful old heritage building, originally built in the 1700s. But as Nora gave me a tour of her new venture, I quickly realized that the architecture and history of the building were only part of the experience she was selling. Her most important lures were the stories she told to every guest or member of the media who visited the inn. Why? It wasn't just because each room was designed to echo one of those stories. It wasn't because these fictional stories held the key to the eventual story guests would tell and retell about their experience after they left. It was no accident that all the stories had happy endings.

The specially selected stories nested within the Inn BoonsBoro come from books about romantic couples written by some of the greatest novelists in history and are narrated by members of the staff to every guest. There's a suite for Marguerite and Percy from *The Scarlet Pimpernel;* Nick and Nora from Dashiell Hammett's *The Thin Man;* Titania and Oberon from *A Midsummer Night's Dream;* and Westley and Buttercup from William Goldman's *The Princess Bride.* There's also an Eve and Roarke suite after the *In Death* novels that Nora writes under the pseudonym J. D. Robb. All of the stories have ups and downs but end happily ever after, and each of the rooms is detailed like a stage set to replicate the atmosphere of the literary romance it's meant to evoke. Guests experience the stories through period furnishings and decor, even through soaps and scents. In my room, the Elizabeth and Darcy suite, the aroma of English lavender transported me to the era of Jane Austen's *Pride and Prejudice.*

Nora has a clear purpose in selecting the stories told at and through her inn. Not only do the tales give the enterprise a distinctive brand that is congruent with Nora's brand as a romantic novelist, but these specific stories also are meant to inspire each couple who stays at the inn. Her mission is not just to run a hotel, but to give her guests the feeling that they, too, can live happily ever after—especially while staying under her roof.

A BOOK OF A VERY different kind, the Bible, provided the raw material for the story that ultimately persuaded me to invest in Bethany Hamilton. I'd first heard of Hamilton on Halloween day back in 2003 when I was at my home in Kauai and she was out surfing and a shark bit off her arm. Just thirteen at the time, she not only survived but was back in the water a few months later. Just a short time after that, she placed fifth in the National Surfing Championships and made the U.S. National Surfing

Team! When I read the news, I thought she must have a lot of grit, but I didn't think much more about it until 2009, when producer David Tice came knocking on my door to sell me on a small independent film to be based on Bethany's autobiography, *Soul Surfer.*

But instead of transporting me to the *heart* of his goal for this movie, Tice kept pitching numbers and budgets. I knew nobody says, "Hey, let's go down to the AMC theater, I hear there's a film there that came in on budget." So I passed on his project.

Then some time later, in one last attempt to get our involvement, Tice prompted Bethany to visit me when I was in Kauai. She wore a sleeve-less top and no prosthetic arm and seemed completely at ease. I was impressed and asked where her self-confidence came from. She credited her deep-seated faith. Her belief in Jesus Christ, she said, had guided her and her family through the aftermath of her attack.

"And now I see the bigger purpose for my life," she told me.

"You mean as a surfing champion," I said, thinking that was the center of her story.

"No, purpose from God," she explained. "To help others know His love." Then she quoted a passage from the Bible, about the child prophet Jeremiah. " 'For I know the plans I have for you,' says the Lord, 'plans to prosper you and not to harm you, plans to give you a future and a hope.' "

Reading up on Jeremiah later, I learned that he came from a long line of prophets but was only a little boy when God told him he was to be a special prophet. Jeremiah balked because he was so young, but God told him not to be scared and promised to protect him. It wasn't easy. This child was sent to preach to the king and tell people things they didn't want to hear, but Jeremiah powered through because he believed God was behind him.

Bethany told me that afternoon in Kauai that the verse in Jeremiah gave her hope—that even in times of crisis, faith makes it possible to turn suffering into a blessing. (She's living proof!) "I want to inspire other people to never give up, no matter what happens," she said. "That's why I hope this movie gets made."

Bethany told her story through one simple Biblical passage, but I heard it loud and clear. Not only was the Jeremiah story more compelling than the producer's budget figures, but it also told me why our film would appeal to a wide audience. Bethany's story, I realized, would draw teens, surfers, and *Jaws* fans—*and* it would speak to a huge group of Christian moviegoers.

"I'm in," I told her. And when I told Sony Pictures president Peter Schlessel her tale, he said, "We're in too."

In the spring of 2010, I was back in Hawaii to watch the start of filming on *Soul Surfer* with Dennis Quaid, Helen Hunt, and Carrie Underwood—and the young star AnnaSophia Robb playing Bethany. While there, I asked Dennis if I could interview him for my national television show *In the House.* When he agreed, I asked what made him take on this small independent picture. His answer was simple. It was the story Bethany told about her and her family's faith during their ordeal. "God's the only way you're going to make it," he said. "He's the glue that holds everything together. That certainly has been a comfort in my life."

Bethany's telling tapped into a crisis Dennis experienced in 2007, when his newborn twins nearly died after mistakenly being given a drug overdose in the hospital. His story of faith, like Bethany's, had seen him through. How could he not star in her story?

HISTORY

Finally, one of the richest sources of story material is history, with its vast wealth of legends, myths, and true adventures. Unbeknownst to me, this was the arsenal that mega-magnate Kirk Kerkorian tapped when he turned his artful telling on me back in 1988.

Kerkorian had made his fortune developing some of the largest resort properties on the Las Vegas Strip, but he got into the movie business with the purchase in 1969 of MGM and, later, of United Artists. I first met Kerkorian when my company was developing *Rain Man,* which UA would distribute, and based on that association, Kerkorian decided we were candidates for a different kind of business venture.

In 1988, he was looking to sell a portion of his interest in MGM to someone who would manage the business while he offered the balance of his interest to the public. When Kerkorian asked to meet so he could tell me what he had in mind, I was beyond flattered and very nervous. Kirk, after all, was a Billionaire when "B" really meant something. He'd been running a huge chunk of the entertainment industry for nearly two decades and was known as the kingpin of dealmakers. Oddly enough, though, he didn't want to meet in his office but in the coffee shop of the Hilton Hotel, and not the fancy coffee shop, either, but the coffee shop with Formica tables and no tablecloths.

As soon as we sat down, he pulled out a small buckslip with the famous MGM lion logo stamped at the top. "Are you familiar with this lion's roar?" he asked.

"Of course," I said. "That lion must have roared at the start of a thousand of the greatest movies of all time." And instantly scenes from all those historic MGM movies—*The Wizard of Oz, Ben-Hur, Gone with the Wind, An American in Paris, The Thin Man,* and *Singin' in the Rain*—began to play in my head.

Then Kirk began casually to narrate MGM's history. He reminded me that two of the greatest producers in Hollywood, Louis B. Mayer and Irving Thalberg, had begun the story of MGM. He told anecdote after anecdote to illustrate the legacy of glamour and majesty that was bound up in this storied company . . . which my partners and I now had the opportunity to run.

"It would be a fantastic move for your career," Kirk said. "We're all excited about *Rain Man,* but you could take the history of MGM and grow it into something even bigger than anything you've ever done."

Then, as he continued to hold me spellbound with scenes of MGM's glorious past, Kirk began scribbling the terms of the deal on the pad, below the lion. I hardly looked at the numbers. The emotional pull of this iconic company's logo and history virtually blinded me. I remember asking once, "Well, we'll have to see the current properties and the assets," but really I could hardly wait to run straight into the jaws of the historic story, embedded in that famous logo, that Kirk was telling to snare me.

I walked away from the Hilton in a state of euphoria. Back at our film company offices I told my partners the stories Kirk had just told me that we were about to own. Fortunately, I didn't tell the stories quite as well as Kirk had. Our chairman listened carefully and then said, "I think we'd better examine the latest chapter of this history."

We proceeded to go through two extreme days of meetings with all the current MGM executives to see what Kerkorian really had to sell us. We quickly discovered that recent history had not been kind to the grand old legend. The company's glory days clearly had been left in the dust, and its future looked anything but glamorous. Unfortunately, by this point the deal had mysteriously been leaked to the *New York Times* and *Variety*—as if to cement us into MGM's narrative.

It was mortifying to have to pull out after the public announcement, but the experience taught me an invaluable lesson: never underestimate the pull of history when it's artfully told.

WHERE'S THE EMOTIONAL TRANSPORTATION?

What's in your story that will move your audience emotionally to your call to action? This is a crucial question when setting your story content. If you want listeners to help you achieve your purpose, they need to be able to feel your call actually resonating inside them. In fact, when I visited veteran television news journalist Anderson Cooper to explore his style of telling stories, he remarked that even if your only goal is for them to hear you, you still need to move their emotions.

This lesson came home to Cooper in the strongest possible way when he was in New Orleans covering Hurricane Katrina for CNN. His experience of the disaster was so overwhelming that he couldn't play the straight-faced objective reporter. He had no choice but to reveal his own personal anguish and frustration through the stories he selected and the emotionally vulnerable way he told them. Cooper's stories resonated powerfully with millions of viewers, and all across the country people told and retold the stories of Katrina not as Cooper had seen them but as he had *felt* them and in turn made the viewers feel them. His coverage of Katrina rocketed him to superstardom as a CNN ratings magnet and ushered in a new style of broadcast journalism, dubbed "emo-journalism," which since has spread across the network landscape and even into print and radio news.

But it seemed to me that stories about women and children clinging to rooftops would be difficult *not* to emotionalize. I assumed the opposite to be true for stories about inanimate objects, such as automobiles. However, my old friend Al Giddings proved to me that, when it comes to cars, emotion is all in the telling.

I first met Giddings when he was the best underwater cinematographer in the business. We did *The Deep* together and later a documentary about discovering the real *Titanic,* which inspired James Cameron to tap Al to help him make his *Titanic*. Together they put the emotion into a rusted piece of metal twelve thousand feet under the ocean and told it as a story that moved audiences to the tune of more than $2 billion. But a few years ago, Al suffered ear damage that ended his diving career, and he shifted his technical passion to vintage cars.

Specifically, he was seduced by the classic roadsters and touring cars manufactured by the Willys-Overland Motor Company between 1914 and 1933. "The combination of their art form and the physical function is very appealing to me," Al told me. "And these particular cars have had no exposure. I tripped over this, saw something that I thought was very provocative, and pursued it maniacally, excited about the history, art, and engineering." These cars were so rare that, in some cases, only one car of a given model still existed. One by one, Al began to track down 1930 Willys Knight 66B Plaidsides. He bought them, even if they were only shells of their former selves, and then spent up to six thousand hours on each one to restore them to mint condition.

Eventually Al began to show the cars at local auto shows. But he noticed that the judges gave all their feedback in terms of technical specifications. They didn't seem to get what moved Al as he researched each automobile's design and history. To Al, these weren't hunks of metal and leather but works of artistry.

Giddings saw that to separate his entries from the competition he'd have to emotionalize these driving machines for the judges the way Jim Cameron had emotionalized the sunken Titanic by venerating the people who took its maiden voyage. What Al needed was a story of challenge, struggle, and resolution that would put a human face on these machines. Since everyone who restored vintage cars shared a similar passion, his own story gave him little advantage, but the history of the men who *originally* designed and built his cars offered a distinctive tale that could give him an edge over competing exhibitors. Those who'd shed blood, sweat, and tears had the real power to move judges to Al's favor.

So Giddings started telling the judges the story of these two men—Amos Northup and John Willys—as part of the presentation of his cars at every show. "Having produced his two millionth car in the 1920s, John Willys was second behind Henry Ford. Willys was a brilliant strategist and firebrand, originally a sporting goods dealer in New York. He'd seen an Overland 1909 go by his shop, and ran down the street after it to write down the name of the car. He quit the sporting goods trade, sent a check for $5,000 to the factory, bought six Overlands, sold them immediately. The following year, he sent the little Overland company a ton of money. They were supposed to build about fifty or sixty for him, but the company failed. He went charging up there on a train, hired all the people back, had money transferred from New York, put the company back on its feet."

Then Al cut forward fifteen years, to 1929. "Willys had sixty-six thousand employees. But there was so much competition then. So he went to Amos Northup, who was a very famous but very quiet, reserved guy, the finest designer in the world. Northup suffered from depression and

SET . . .

was high-strung, but also brilliant. John Willys went to Northup knowing he was a perceptive designer of sweeping lines and was moving away from that square look of the 1920s into the 1930s. He told Northup, 'I want to blow everybody away with something that's absolutely stunning, and I want you to design the 66B Willys Knights for 1930.' Northup proceeded to design the most beautiful of the 66B cars—the Roadsters and the Phaetons, four-door convertibles. But then the stock market crashed. Only three left-hand-drive Phaetons were built in 1930 for the New York, Chicago, and LA shows, because of the financial catastrophe in America."

And here, before the judges, Al waved a hand, because these three Phaetons—the only ones left in the entire world—were the cars that he'd lovingly restored for these competitions. "During the Great Depression," Al said, closing his story, "Willys Overland declared bankruptcy."

The judges' attention and wonder were captured by the way Giddings breathed emotion into metal and leather as he told his story. He'd moved them with awe, admiration, anxiety, sadness, and surprise. Then they awarded him prizes. In 2009 Giddings won the Antique Automobile Club of America's highest national award. These accolades have brought prospective buyers running with offers of millions of dollars for Giddings's beloved cars. Although, for the moment, he's not selling, there's no doubt that he's leveraged his "car stories" into real economic value. From mettle to metal to millions, this is emotional transportation at work.

BUT HOW CAN YOU make sure *your* story has the power to move people in the direction you actually want them to go? This was the question that confronted Mark Shapiro in 2006, when he became CEO of Six Flags, one of the world's largest chains of amusement and theme parks. At the time the company was staggering under $2 billion in debt and its reputation was tanking as a result of poor maintenance, aging rides, and an increasingly scruffy and even dangerous customer base of teenagers who used the parks as hangouts. Coming in the door, Mark knew his only way out of this monumental problem was through it. Although bankruptcy promised to be a necessary phase of the reorganization process, he couldn't let the company's problems doom its prospects. He had to focus on the opportunity to build the business, debt or no debt. And in Shapiro's mind that opportunity hinged on his ability to train every member of the Six Flags team to tell stories—in, around, and through the experience of park attractions—that would resonate emotionally in a positive way not just with teens, but also with parents, grandparents, tweens, kids, the media, boards of directors, and shareholders.

Shapiro had learned the business value of telling stories when he was head of programming at ESPN. That's when we first met, as I was constantly pitching programming ideas to him that related to Mandalay Sports Entertainment's hockey and baseball teams. He invited me to speak to ESPN employees at a convention in Orlando, where I talked about the art of the tell as emotional transportation. Mark already understood that narrative is the essential component of sports entertainment—stories lurk in every game and captivate fans—so he and I connected over our appreciation of the art of the tell and became fast friends.

Mark's vision story for Six Flags came from his own experience. "When I was a kid, I saw Six Flags as a Disneyland in my backyard. It was a place where you could get caught up in the theater and the majesty and the imagination of Bugs Bunny and that whole world, and yet have all the drama and tension of thrill rides. Back then, rich story telling was woven through the rides and the attractions. Good theme parks take you back to a time and place in your life when you had the ability to wonder."

The problem that Mark saw at Six Flags in 2006 was that customers walked from ride to ride with nothing in between. "There was no story telling. There was no innovation and wonder. That was all gone. You can't get caught up in a fairy tale or any kind of good story when the look is so decrepit." But he also saw the opportunity to resurrect the story he remembered from his boyhood, of a theme park as a stage of dreams—and make it even richer.

Mark's goal was to turn his employees and customers alike into active participants in Six Flags' rebirth. To achieve this goal, all staff members of every park would have to contribute to the creation of a state of wonder so strong and consistent that visitors would remain enthralled the whole time they were on Six Flags premises. "Even though you're waiting three hours, you're getting into the unfolding drama surrounding these rides." You can't just stick up a ride, Mark explained, and call it Batman. You have to tell people the story. Who is Batman? What could he do? Who did Batman battle? Who was Batman out to save? Mark knew he had to constantly remind customers of what was familiar about the story, yet also give them something unexpected. "If you can envelop them in a story around the ride, they'll be that much more immersed in the experience."

Shapiro's first and most difficult audience had to be the thirty thousand employees in the massive Six Flags organization who hadn't a clue what he was talking about when he said, "We're in the emotional transportation business." "These employees were essentially carnies," Mark explained. "All they ever knew for years was how to run a carnival. The concept of telling a story was foreign to them. It's not even like they didn't believe. They had no idea what story telling was. They just thought Six Flags was about 'Build a huge ride, market it, and they will come.' They had to understand it was our job to evoke a certain visceral emotional response in every single guest." Why? Because only that response would move people to repeatedly spend the kind of money and time at Six Flags that the company needed to thrive. And only this response would prompt them to pay the story forward through word of mouth.

Mark knew he couldn't just tell his employees *about* this visceral response; he needed them to *feel* it directly in the most powerful way possible—as an emotional catharsis. So he'd tell his own seminal story of going to Six Flags as a kid and feeling the wondrous sensation that he'd entered Disneyland in his backyard.

How did Mark make that story come to life? "Through the look, feel, senses, and sensibilities that all play roles in feeling," he told me. "So if there's entertainment in the midways, if you're caught up in the story as you stand in line, the ride will be that much better because you're caught up in the tale before you ever get on the ride. I tell my advertisers, research shows that when the senses are turned on through the telling of stories, the consumer will embrace and recall a message that much deeper."

To help his employees actually feel the power of emotional transportation full throttle, Mark showed them a reel of clips from some of the most moving films of all time. He included heart-stopping scenes from classic dramas like *Sophie's Choice* and *Streetcar Named Desire*, from tearjerkers such as *Shane* and *Old Yeller*, from comedies—*Tootsie, Some Like It Hot*, and *The 40-year-old Virgin*—and from macho pleasers like *The Godfather, Crimson Tide*, and *Rocky*. As short as they were, each of these scenes evoked a visceral human reaction—tears, gasps, laughter, chills. By the time the reel ended, every member of the audience understood that they'd all been on an emotional roller coaster of fear and desire— and that same emotional ride was what Shapiro wanted every guest at a Six Flags theme park to experience. Every attraction should deliver not just a physical thrill but also an emotional one.

Not only did Mark and his employees wrap a moving story around and through every ride, but they also began selecting vendors who'd add new forms of emotional transportation within the parks. "When it came time to serve ice cream," Mark said, "Cold Stone Creamery was the one. Why? Because Cold Stone Creamery is experiential. From the minute you walk in, they're singing songs, enveloping you in this story of fun. You pick different candies, make a concoction like you're Willy Wonka, and that story fits and serves our larger story. Johnny Rockets, same thing. I go into Johnny Rockets, they sing to you, and suddenly you're in a diner in the fifties and sixties. So even the food is experiential and fun at Six Flags."

The bottom line is that people will pay extra, stay longer, and spend more on food and merchandise when they're moved emotionally by the story they're experiencing. And they will tell the story of their experience forward, thus selling the brand to others. Two and a half seasons after Shapiro took over Six Flags, his story of emotional transportation was paying off handsomely. Park customers were staying an average of forty-five minutes longer and spending 21 percent more per visit than they had before. In 2008, Six Flags enjoyed its most successful summer season ever, narrowing corporate losses and increasing both sales and attendance. Unfortunately, external conditions beyond anyone's control, from the economic downturn, to rising gas prices, to the swine flu outbreak, took a toll on the theme park business worldwide in 2009. These conditions forced Shapiro and the board of directors to now seek that repackaged bankruptcy to relieve the burden of debt he'd inherited. Even as he announced this decision, however, Six Flags chairman Daniel Snyder praised his current management team for "exceeding every operational goal we set out three years ago." A short time later, with the company's financial restructuring complete, Shapiro decided to move on. All indications are that his mastery of emotional transportation will keep Six Flags on the right track.

Telling oral stories may not be quite as complicated as telling stories through a theme park, but listening to Mark Shapiro, I was reminded that setting your story still only gets you another step closer to your goal. Once you've identified your hero, shaped your raw material, and made sure it's emotionally moving, you've still got to perform and deliver that story so it reaches its target. If Ready and Set are phases 1 and 2 of the art of the tell, then what is involved in phase 3?

aHHa!

- Heroes come in all shapes and sizes—teller, listener, customer, product, location, and tribe; choose the hero that fits your goal.
- Your firsthand or witnessed experience is the best raw material for your story.
- Use metaphors and analogies to fire up imagination and illumination.
- Engage the powerful narratives in books, movies, and history to emotionalize your call to action.

CHAPTER SEVEN

Tell!

As I approached Terry Semel's office at Warner Bros., I concentrated on calming and collecting my thoughts. It was 1986, and the fate of our next project, *Gorillas in the Mist,* would ride on the story I was about to tell Semel, then Warners' CEO. Our production company already had invested three years in the development of this true drama, which unfolded atop the Virunga Mountains in central Africa. Sigourney Weaver had agreed to star as renowned primatologist Dian Fossey, who studied, lived among, and ultimately died to protect the last surviving silverback mountain gorillas. Our director was Michael Apted, who just a few years earlier had directed the Oscar-winning *Coal Miner's Daughter,* and everything was in place to move into production. But the budget we'd just delivered to Warner Bros. called for more than $20 million, which in 1986 was an enormous sum, and although Semel had shown support for the project up to this point, now he'd gotten cold feet. Since Hollywood operates by the golden rule that he who has the gold makes the rules, this was a potentially lethal blow to our project.

Although I wasn't thinking in terms of purposeful narrative in those days, I instinctively understood that I had to move Semel emotionally if I was to change his mind. I'd gleaned from his colleagues that several years earlier Terry had greenlit a picture called *Greystoke,* a wildly over budget and commercially unsuccessful Tarzan movie in which men in monkey suits played gorillas. Except for the word "gorillas" in the script, our movie was an entirely different animal, but my inquiries told me that Terry had convinced himself our *Gorillas* could turn into another *Greystoke* fiasco. I had to tell him a story that would un-convince him by converting his fear into passion.

But before I could do that I knew from athletic experience that I needed to "get into state"—something I'd done before every sports competition. This meant ramping up my energy, dialing down any anxiety or confusion I was feeling, and acquiring a sudden case of attitudinal dyslexia that would read Terry's "no" as "on." I breathed deeply and slowly and focused on my intention for Semel to empathetically hear my story. Nested inside the story I planned to tell was the message that we weren't making a movie about men in monkey suits. That hopefully would assuage his economic anxiety. My story also would tell how our film would benefit him both financially and in terms of the way he was perceived, by making him a catalyst for saving one of the most important endangered species on the planet.

The door opened. No secrets. Terry knew I knew he was about to drop the ax on us. I reminded myself not to give the appearance of surrender. I stood tall and tried as I entered to convey the certainty and energy my mission required. I also quickly assessed Terry's state of mind. I'd been in meetings where my audience was so flustered and preoccupied that I was better off rescheduling. But this was not one of those times. Terry was ready for me, if only to deliver his condolences. It was now or never.

In an attempt to capture his attention and redirect his intention, I aimed my story straight for his heart, saying, "Someone's killing your relatives."

"What?" He shot me a look of alarm, but I'd corralled his attention and aroused his curiosity.

And so I began. "Your relatives are minding their own business, raising their families in the only home they've ever known, where their ancestors have lived for millennia. They're defenseless innocents, among the most beautiful creatures you'll ever see. These silverback gorillas, the lead characters in our film, are only two clicks away from us in the gene pool. But they are surrounded by enemies who want to steal their land and the source of their food. They're under attack by murderers who shoot them through the heart and then cut off their hands and feet as trophies."

I reached into my jacket and handed Semel an array of pictures that showed the gorillas and the atrocities I had just described. Among them were pictures of gorilla parts turned into souvenirs. "They're selling these on the streets of Rwanda," I told him. "It made me cry the last time I was there, and the only consolation was that our movie, while centered on the heroic tragedy of Dian Fossey, would spread the message that this is happening and bring new recruits to the silverbacks' cause."

Terry flinched at the picture of an ashtray made from a gorilla's paw. This image brought his full attention to the story I was telling. He was visibly repulsed as he put the photo down, but he couldn't take his eyes off it.

The key now for me was to show that I also understood and respected *his* problem, the financial risks this production would run, and his personal fear, that *Gorillas* would be another *Greystoke*. I had to reveal what was in my story for him.

I told Semel that his experience with *Greystoke* actually had taught us how *not* to make our film. No men overheating in gorilla suits on a soundstage this time. Our movie would tell the story of a real endangered species, not fictional characters. Our supporting cast consisted of the actual silverbacks in their real habitat. "And once audiences experience the gorillas' authenticity, their story will become a powerful viral marketing proposition."

Semel shook his head. "You plan to photograph live gorillas?"

I revealed my trump card. We already had shot many hours of footage in Africa. "Actually, the gorillas are writing this script. We're just adapting the dialog and the material to the stories the silverbacks have already acted out."

Terry rolled his eyes. "The gorillas wrote the script? You're nuts!"

I repeated calmly, "No men in gorilla suits."

"Ah," Terry said. Then he smiled, getting it. "Ha!" I could feel the mood shift in the room. Then, to prove my seriousness of purpose, I offered to post our fee against the plan. This was not insurance but assurance, for the financial risk was far greater than our fees, but it showed I meant to have skin in this game.

He ushered me toward the door. "Let me think about it. I have another meeting."

But the clock was against us. Now that I'd gotten this far, I didn't dare leave without an answer. It was time to drop my script and improvise.

Semel called for his secretary to send in his next visitor.

I lay down on the floor with my arms outstretched.

He frowned at me. "What's the matter?"

"I'm a wounded gorilla," I said. "If you're going say no, it's to them, too. Here and now."

This was risky business. I looked foolish and vulnerable. But as over-the-top as this move seemed, it also demonstrated how much I was willing to put on the line to achieve my goal. The risk of getting down on the floor didn't compare with the risk to the gorillas and our film if I left without a yes.

Also, this was a calculated risk. I was pressing Terry to become an active participant. I could not afford to just talk at him—I needed to draw him into the story so he could own it. Only then could I be certain he'd really heard my call to action.

Semel's new guest came in and sat staring down at me. Terry began talking as if I weren't there, but finally the guest interrupted and pointed at me. "What's his problem?"

"He's a gorilla." Semel tried to keep a straight face but burst out laughing. "He wants me to save him." Then his guest started laughing, and Semel said, "OK, we'll make our picture, but remember you've bet the farm."

In Hollywood, you've got to know when to stop auditioning. I leapt to my feet and, with a salute to Terry, sped off before he could change his mind. Two years later *Gorillas in the Mist* was nominated for five Academy Awards, including Best Actress (Sigourney Weaver) and Best Screenplay. It became a long-term creative and financial success. Most important, it succeeded in bringing global attention to the plight of the silverbacks that continues to this day. Twenty years later, though the mountain gorillas remain endangered, their habitat is protected and their numbers are increasing.

IT'S SHOWTIME!

My study of the art of the tell has taught me that every business requires a certain amount of show business. People in and out of the business world will pay closer attention, absorb more information, feel more engaged, and be far more likely to get your point if they feel like active participants, rather than passengers, in your story. How can they participate? By laughing, crying, getting excited, questioning old beliefs, embracing possibilities, answering questions, standing or moving their bodies, or handling your props. How the story is readied and set is critical, but equally important is the manner in which you actually deliver—or tell—your story, so that your audience can own it, act on it, and tell it forward.

All show business is interactive. So is the art of the tell. "No presenter's mouth can move as fast as the audience's eyes," Jerry Weissman told me when I asked why he stresses interactivity when coaching senior executives to prepare for their IPO road shows. Weissman is the founder of Power Presentations, whose client list includes the top brass at Microsoft, Yahoo!, Intel, Netflix, Cisco Systems, Sequoia Capital, and clients of Goldman Sachs, J.P. Morgan, Morgan Stanley, Citigroup, and Credit

Suisse. "As soon as the presenter becomes a one-way broadcaster," he explained to me, "there's no return feed. There's no loop; there's no synchronicity. When somebody has to pitch a VC for financing when a company goes public, they have to be interactive." Otherwise, he said, there's no communication and the presenter might as well save his or her breath.

Many of Weissman's clients come to him from the investment banking industry, where millions, even billions, of dollars can ride on the ability to communicate financial data to potential investor audiences. "PowerPoint has become the coin of the realm in this business," he told me. "They put the slides up and then they essentially read what's on the slide. I ask my clients, 'How do you feel when presenters read what's on the slide?' And they say, 'You could have mailed it to me.'" Then Weissman breaks the news that what's on the PowerPoint is not the story.

"You are the story," he tells them. "The presenter is the story." In other words, whatever your business, when it's time to tell your story, it's showtime!

GET INTO STATE

Athletes aren't the only ones who perform exercises to get themselves in state before going onto the game field. So do actors and performers, although their game field is the stage. And so do masters of the art of the tell, whose game field is wherever they tell their story. Getting in state isn't just a mental, emotional, or physical process; it's all three. It involves focusing your whole being on your intent to achieve your purpose. This state is vital to the art of the tell because your *intention* is actually what signals listeners to pay *attention* to you.

UCLA neuroscientist Dan Siegel has studied this process at length as part of his exploration of what he calls "mindsight," or human beings' innate ability to see into each other's mind. He explained to me that our mirror neurons only switch on when they sense another person is acting intentionally—with conscious and active purpose. As Siegel was talking, his arm moved by his side. I saw the motion but paid it no attention until he lifted that arm, pointed at the ceiling, and grinned. Siegel then explained that when I'd noticed his intentional act of pointing at the ceiling, my mirror neurons had responded, sending a signal to my brain to pay attention, and when he'd grinned, they accelerated that signal into empathy so that I imagined I, too, was pointing and grinning. But when his arm movement had seemed random and purposeless, my mirror neurons ignored it. "We sense the other person's intentions and imagine what an event means in his or her mind," Siegel told me. What this means for the art of the tell is that the teller's state of intention is key to making audiences listen.

Siegel's demonstration also showed that intention can speak louder than words. Humans begin reading each other's intentions as soon as they are physically close enough to see, hear, and smell each other. That means there are no secrets in the art of the tell—only unspoken words.

A childhood friend of mine, George E. Marcus, is now a professor of political science at Williams College and has written extensively about the role of unspoken communication in the success and failure of politicians. After reviewing the careers of modern political candidates in light of recent research in neuroscience, Marcus has concluded that, in fact, most communication between teller and audience is wordless, even unconscious, and leaders who ignore this basic truth tend to fail.

According to Marcus, "The brain knows in eighty milliseconds the gender of a person while we only 'see' the person at five hundred milliseconds." We receive this information through a system in the brain that functions as a constant surveillance system, scanning the environment for signs of potential trouble or danger. In addition to relaying gender, this ancient survival system tells us, as soon as we set eyes on another person, whether that individual is friend or foe, authentic or fake, trustworthy or dangerous. If we sense the other person is phony or distracted, we'll automatically put up our defenses, either by tuning out entirely or listening with suspicion. If we see a frown or can't meet the other person's gaze, our guard goes up and we feel anxiety, anticipating emotional attack or rejection. But if the other person smiles and looks directly into our eyes, we begin to relax and feel more trusting. Most of this signaling occurs without our even being aware of it. "Intuition," Marcus says, "is the brain knowing what consciousness later sees."

All this means that techniques to get in state need to be performed *before* you face your audience. Relax your body and control your breath, since this is the vehicle on which your story will ride. Review your story and goals. Focus on the emotions you intend to move in your audience. Also add a quick self-check to avoid inadvertent distractions or interruptions. You don't want a nervous falsetto, garlic on your breath, or an ink stain on your shirt to divert your audience from getting your story and its call to action! But above all, train both your body and mind on your clear intention to succeed. As leadership guru Warren Bennis explained at one of our story conclaves, the paramount reason to get in state is to concentrate energy on the desired outcome of your tell.

Bennis, who is distinguished professor of business administration and founding chairman of the Leadership Institute at the University of Southern California and was named by *BusinessWeek* in 2007 as one of the top ten thought leaders in business, told us, "The first leadership competency is the management of attention through a set of intentions or a vision, not in the mystical or religious sense, but in the sense of outcome, goal, or direction." Another leadership competency, he said, "is management of self—knowing one's skills and deploying them effectively." And getting in state helps marshal both these competencies.

To illustrate just how powerful one's state of intention can be, Bennis told me a story at lunch about the great aerialist Karl Wallenda, patriarch of the Flying Wallendas, who'd performed death-defying feats on the high wire for more than fifty years before tragically falling to his death at age seventy-one. Wallenda's capacity for concentration on his intention was so legendary that at first, no one could understand how this accident could have happened. However, Wallenda's wife later reflected that he'd been anxious that last day before taking the wire, a tightrope without a safety net in San Juan, Puerto Rico. For the first time in all the years she'd known him, he was concentrating before the show not on succeeding but on the risk of falling. He personally supervised the attachment of the guy wires, which he'd never done before. It was his fear of falling, more than likely, that made his fall come true. And just as likely, Bennis said, his concentration on success had acted as an equally self-fulfilling prophecy all the many times he'd triumphed on the high wire. A clear take-away from this story is that what you focus on grows.

EXPRESS AUTHENTIC, CONTAGIOUS ENERGY

Like intention, authenticity and energy cannot be faked. If you're telling a story you don't believe in, your audience will sense it instantly. They'll feel it and act on that feeling, even if they can't justify their feeling in words. The good news is that they will pick up just as instantly on your genuine enthusiasm and conviction. You don't need to stand on your head or shout or sing to show that your passion is real. You just need to let yourself feel it instead of suppressing it. Authentic energy is contagious. If your story truly excites you, and you let that excitement show, it will resonate with your audience.

How do you convey energy or enthusiasm for a product if the product's not so great, or if you're number three or four in the market? Unfortunately, for many businesspeople, that's reality. But it's not an insurmountable problem. The trick is to find something about the product or service that does excite you, even if it's something as small as the color of the item or the look of the service's website. Then focus on the aspect of your story that makes you feel genuinely enthusiastic.

One of the most high-octane advocates of telling to win that I know of in any business is Mark Burnett, who pioneered reality television. Since 2001 Burnett has been nominated for forty-eight Emmy Awards— for series such as *Survivor, The Apprentice, The Contender, Martha Stewart, Are You Smarter Than a 5th Grader?,* and *The MTV Awards*. Because Mark has turned personal enthusiasm into career rocket fuel, I wanted him to discuss this element of the tell with my UCLA grad students.

Burnett was even more emphatic than I'd expected in stressing the role of passion in the telling of business stories. "Our success or failure is determined by our level of energy," he said flatly. "I tell my people, 'Much more than our creativity, our level of energy inspires the people around us.'"

To explain how this works, he told the students the story he tells his employees. "The problem for successful businesspeople is really one of energy conservation. I put in a fourteen-, fifteen-, sixteen-hour day, and I need so much energy. Think of that figuratively as a bathtub full of water that you fill every morning to the brim. You crack that plug and let it drain, so by the time you come home the last drop has gone through the drain." Ideally, he emphasized, there's still some energy in the tub to get you home, but if you're confronted by "energy suckers," you'll be running on empty before noon.

By "energy suckers" Mark was talking about people who are focused only on themselves, who don't really care what they're offering, who have no passion, no zest, and whose affect, voice, and presentation drain energy from everyone around them. Energy is transmitted by the attitude of your body as well as your mind. If you slouch in your chair or lean on your podium, that tells your audience you're tired—maybe too tired to tell them a story of value. Standing or sitting up straight and looking your audience in the eye, on the other hand, tells them that you're alert, aware, and excited about the story you're about to tell. That energy transmits an unspoken promise that you can excite them, too.

The whole point of telling a purposeful story is to energize audiences around your mission or cause, and if your presentation sucks the energy out of them, then you've defeated your purpose. But does this mean that you can only tell an effective story when you're feeling upbeat and happy? Not at all! Energy takes many different emotional forms, and it's often most compelling when combined with vulnerability.

DEMONSTRATE VULNERABILITY

At one of our narrative conclaves, Keith Ferrazzi, an expert in professional relationship development and author of the best-selling books *Never Eat Alone* and *Who's Got Your Back,* said, "Vulnerability is one of the most underappreciated assets in business today. Everyone has something in common with every other person. And you won't find those similarities if you don't open up and expose your interests and concerns, allowing others to do likewise."

Keith's remark immediately took me back to February of 2008, when Steve Tisch became the only Academy Award winner ever to win the Vince Lombardi Trophy. As co-owner of the New York Giants, Tisch stood on the field after the Giants beat the Patriots in Super Bowl XLII, and received the trophy from Roger Goodell. He had an audience of 75,000 people in the stadium, and hundreds of millions more around the world via television, and as Tisch told the story of his father's love for the Giants and how strongly he felt his late father's spirit that night in Glendale, Arizona, tears welled up in Steve's eyes and his voice wobbled over the loudspeaker as he was overcome with a mixture of sadness and pride. The crowd cheered with empathy.

Watching Steve that night, I was touched and a little surprised by the vulnerability he revealed. I'd known Steve ever since he worked for me at Columbia Pictures, at the very start of his career, and it had always seemed to me that he'd made a point of charting his own course far from the shadow of his famous father, who not only co-owned the Giants but also had served as U.S. postmaster general and was chairman and co-owner, with Steve's uncles, of the Loews and Lorillard corporations. Steve had made his own light in Hollywood producing dozens of major movies, such as *Risky Business, The Long Kiss Goodnight,* and *Snatch,* and winning his Best Picture Oscar for *Forrest Gump*. I knew that his father had asked him on many occasions to return to New York to help him run the Giants, and Steve had always declined to ride the back of his father's success. Yet the tears Steve shed down there on the field spoke volumes about the emotional story behind Steve's ultimate decision to accept his father's mantle. Knowing that he was now leading the charge to build a new Giants stadium at a cost of more than $1 billion, I wondered how often he told his father's story to move this enterprise forward, and whether his vulnerability helped or hindered the telling.

When we met in New York and Steve answered my questions, his eyes welled up again. He brushed the tears away and acknowledged that this always happened when he told the story of how, when his father was diagnosed in 2004 with terminal brain cancer, Steve moved back to New York within forty-eight hours. "At first, the mission was to make sure that his medical care was the best available, but during the process my father once again asked, 'Now will you come work with me? I need a partner, a friend, a son.' It was time. There was that ticking clock, and I had to go from the on-deck circle to the batter's box literally in a matter of months. And we became partners. I became his best friend; I became his son." Eventually, as Bob Tisch got weaker, their roles reversed. "I became his father."

For Steve, the Giants represented this new family relationship. Not only did he assume his father's roles of chairman and co-owner of the New York Giants NFL franchise, but he began to see the team as his family's legacy and himself as the keeper of the flame.

One of his father's greatest dreams was to build a new Giants stadium, but he passed away before Steve got the green light from the state to go ahead. So Steve became the dream keeper, urging his partner John Mara, their architects, contractors, and city officials to move the stadium forward. "I told them the story of my journey with my father and its purpose," Steve said. "I told them I wanted to complete the journey in his memory, to embody his passion, to design a stadium that was symbolic of him as a New Yorker, as a football fan, as a generous, kind, powerful man. And while that may sound intangible, it's in every piece of cement, every steel beam, every seat."

I asked Steve how he handled his emotions when he told that story to different audiences. Did he show those deeper feelings to everyone?

"You can't help it," he said.

Plans for the new stadium moved steadily forward toward the anticipated opening in 2010, and for the most part Steve's willingness to show his vulnerability served him well. His transparency allowed audiences to connect with his story. There is a cautionary coda, however.

Late in 2008, after Tisch and Mara had imposed personal seat license fees on season ticket holders to help pay for the stadium, Tisch attempted to tell his father's story once again, but for a different purpose, before a halftime audience at Giants Stadium at the start of the next season, in front of eighty thousand angry fans who booed him off the podium. His goal that day was to raise funds in honor of his father for Stand Up to Cancer, a charity to fight cancer. He even had Christie Brinkley by his side to lend her support, but his audience was not interested in hearing his story. Because their driving emotions were anger and frustration at the price hike, his vulnerability didn't touch them. The moral of this coda is that no matter how authentic and vulnerable you may appear, if you ignore what interests your audience, don't expect to move them.

TURN "NO" TO "ON"

As I like to say, when great leaders hear the word "no," they often react as if dyslexic and interpret it to mean "on." Perseverance is as essential to the art of the tell as it is to leadership. What I've found, however, is that it's far easier to persevere when someone else tells you no than when you start telling *yourself* you can't or shouldn't keep going.

The trick to perseverance is not to eliminate fear, but to *use* it. Evolutionary neurologists tell us that our most primitive instincts give us three choices when we're afraid. We can fight, flee, or freeze. If you're retreating or paralyzed, obviously you're in no shape to tell your story. But the same adrenaline that primes you to fight can actually benefit your telling by ramping up your energy, heightening your passion, and intensifying your sense of urgency. The trick is to channel the adrenaline instead of resisting it.

I find that when I'm nervous before a meeting, it helps to remind myself that FEAR is simply *False Evidence Appearing Real*. False evidence can be beaten, and I know that most of the evidence causing worry is false. So, as I did with Terry Semel and *Gorillas in the Mist,* I'll mentally review my goals, story, the interests of my audience, and the reaction I intend to elicit, and by reassuring myself that I believe in the truth of the story I'm about to tell and the merit of my call to action, I can almost always convert my fear into momentum. That doesn't guarantee that every listener will heed my call to action as Terry ultimately did, but it does mean that I won't let fear of a *possible* no interfere with my telling.

Of course, that's easier said than done when you're telling a story that has already met with rejection or refusal from previous audiences. Those may simply have been the wrong audiences for your story, but how do you remain upbeat and determined under such circumstances? I put this question to my friend Mark Victor Hansen, the co-creator of the stratospherically popular *Chicken Soup for the Soul* series, because I knew he'd met serious resistance when trying to find a publisher for the first book in that series back in 1992. In fact, he and his partner Jack Canfield were turned down *144 times,* which is beyond mind-boggling when you think that the *Chicken Soup* series today has sold more than 112 million copies, with almost two hundred titles in print and translations into more than forty languages. I figured Mark must know some impressive tricks to have persevered in the face of so much rejection.

The first secret, Mark said, is to be absolutely clear in your story and your goal. He and Canfield had both built successful speaking careers by telling inspirational, motivational, uplifting, purposeful stories. They had proof of process that stories can change lives, and they wanted to tell this through a book of 101 powerful tales of ordinary people doing extraordinary things. Then, searching for a winning title, Canfield remembered how his grandmother claimed her chicken soup would cure anything. He and Mark were determined for their book to have the same healing powers, but for the soul. They knew instantly that *Chicken Soup for the Soul* was their title—and that they had a potential best seller.

The second secret, Mark suggested, is to heed the example of his books and use an inspiring story to remind you to keep turning "no" to "on." In his case, that story was told to him by billionaire and former presidential candidate Ross Perot when he asked Perot to write the foreword to their manuscript. Perot agreed and asked if they had a publisher. Hansen replied that they were still trying to decide how many publishers to approach. Perot laughed and said what mattered was "any," not "many." Then Perot told his own story about forming the data processing firm EDS with a $1,000 loan from his wife. He informed Hansen proudly that he was turned down seventy-seven times before winning his first contract, but that contract was worth $4 million. "He amortized those rejections along with the win," Hansen told me, "and it came out to $80,000 apiece." Perot would ultimately sell his stake in EDS for $2.4 billion.

The message of Perot's story was that you only need one to win, and Hansen got it loud and clear. "*Next* is the most powerful four-letter word in the English language," Hansen said.

But the third secret he shared was that perseverance doesn't mean just doing the same thing over and over again. Every rejection offers an opportunity to learn, refine, and improve your story and the way you tell it. He and Canfield didn't change their core story, but they always listened to criticism and used it to refine their tell and improve their offering. "Feedback is the breakfast of champions," Hansen told me.

Still, they kept coming up against the seemingly immovable object of mainstream publishers' insistence that "short story collections" never become the kind of best sellers Hansen and Canfield envisioned. Hansen kept telling them, "We're not selling short stories. We're changing the world, one story at a time." But he couldn't overcome the definitions and data sets they had in their heads. Finally, he and Canfield decided that the one publisher they needed to convince was, in fact, themselves.

They self-published *Chicken Soup for the Soul* in June 1993. Within sixteen months, it was on every major best-seller list in the United States and Canada. What drove the book was plain old word of mouth. Ordinary people bought it, loved it, and told the stories to their friends and neighbors. *Then* the media caught on, and Hansen appeared on just about every major media outlet in the country, including *The Oprah Winfrey Show,* the *Today* show, and *Larry King Live.* Over the next ten years, sales of branded *Chicken Soup for the Soul* merchandise reached $1.3 billion. There are now plans to expand the brand by working with TV networks on several shows and developing a major Internet presence.

Needless to say, all those publishers who'd turned Hansen and Canfield down changed their tune after the first books started flying off the shelves. New *Chicken Soup for the Soul* titles are distributed through Simon & Schuster. Meanwhile, *Time* magazine has dubbed Hansen "the publishing phenomenon of the decade."

"So all those rejections were just detours on the road to success?" I asked Hansen.

Hansen replied by quoting his agent, Jeff Herman. "No rejection is fatal until the writer walks away from the battle, leaving his dreams and goals behind."

HOLD 'EM OR FOLD 'EM

Just because you're prepared and in the right state to tell your story, that doesn't necessarily mean your audience is in any state to hear you. I have learned that it's wise, before saying word one, to assess "conditions on the ground" and make sure that you have a fighting chance of delivering your call to action. Will your audience listen? Will they be able to hear you? Or is there too much other physical or psychological noise for your story to penetrate? If your listener is in such a lousy mood that no story in the world is going to resonate, you'll be firing blanks no matter how great a tell you deliver.

This is not to say that conditions need to be perfect before you can tell your story. Most of the time, if you've readied and set a good story and gotten yourself in state, you can move your audience out of whatever state *they* are in. But sometimes you can tell walking in the door that you just don't stand a chance.

Such was the case in 1981 when I entered Ned Tanen's office at Universal Pictures, primed to win him over with a bold new story for our film version of *A Chorus Line*. At the time, I was chairman of PolyGram, a large company owned by the multinational giants Siemens and Philips, and Tanen was president of Universal, which had paid an ungodly fortune five years earlier for the rights to *Chorus Line,* then already a Broadway smash. Since Universal's initial development of the picture had stalled, we'd persuaded Tanen to relinquish the rights to us so that he could recover his capital investment. In return, Universal was to distribute and cofinance the picture that we developed and cast. Our problem was that the theatrical version of *Chorus Line* was *too* successful. The live touring company or smaller productions of the show had played in every high school, local theater, and tiny burgh in the country. Our film version needed to offer some new element to pique audience interest. So my team decided to change the framing of the story. We pulled together John Travolta, who'd been in *Saturday Night Fever* and *Grease,* and Mikhail Baryshnikov, the famed ballet artist who'd defected from Russia and who'd starred in *The Turning Point*. Both were at the height of their careers, and both expressed strong interest in co-starring in *A Chorus Line*. My job as producer and chairman of PolyGram was to get Ned Tanen aboard.

I knew that Tanen had giant mood swings. His language was often inflammatory and invariably confrontational. But he was head of Universal, and everything had to go through him. And if we couldn't give an answer to Travolta and Baryshnikov quickly, we'd lose this unique opportunity. I decided I couldn't do it on the telephone. I had to tell Tanen the story in person.

So I drove over the hill from West Los Angeles to Black Rock, the building where Ned Tanen shared a top floor with Lou Wasserman and Sid Sheinberg, the legendary heads of Universal. Their proximity would have been intimidating even without the financial weight that was riding on the story I had to tell. But as I entered Tanen's office, I focused my attention on him. He was clearly agitated, screaming at somebody on the phone. He yelled at his secretary to bring something to drink, then he literally growled at me, "What do you want?"

I had to present my proposition, but he was in no shape to hear it. I said, "Oh, I just came over to catch up with you."

Suddenly he jumped up. "Come on, I want to go for a ride. You got an hour?" I thought maybe it would be a good idea to get him out of the office and into a friendlier context where I could deliver my story successfully. And Ned loved race cars so much he collected them.

We got in the car and took off, his tongue now moving even faster than the wheels. Soon regretting my decision, I hung on for dear life as we ripped out into the desert.

Finally we reached a barren area far away from the city, and he told me to get out. I thought, *Now he's calming down, I'll be able to talk to him.* Then he opened up the trunk of the car and pulled out a shotgun.

I had one singular sensation, and it was not the story of *Chorus Line.*

Tanen started shooting cans and looking for jackrabbits to target. Despite the change in context, he was not in a happy place. I decided, on balance, that that gun in his hand could deliver a nastier "no" than any reaction I was likely to receive in his office. So I played along, shot the gun, humored him, and kept my mouth shut.

When I finally got back to my office, I groaned and faced the fact that I'd have to go again. Two days later I spoke to Tanen on the phone and sensed that he was in a good mood. I said, "Give me ten minutes." I jumped in the car, drove as fast as I could, and entered his office smiling.

"What's up?" he said, a totally different man than he'd been two days earlier.

I said, "You know the love story we're doing in *Chorus Line*?" He nodded. "Well, you know how wedding stories that end happily ever after always include something old, something new, something borrowed, something blue? I'm concerned that unless we add something new to the *Chorus Line* story the movie won't be successful, and the wedding here is between Travolta and Baryshnikov; they haven't committed yet, but they're interested, and with them I think we can get enough resources internationally to cofinance the picture." I took a deep breath.

"Fantastic. They'd be great," he said.

I paused a moment and added, "Literally, it's a wedding between Travolta and Baryshnikov. Travolta's playing the role Ann Reinking played on Broadway."

"That's funny."

I said, "I'm serious. I think it could be a total hit. *Chorus Line*'s core story's about the passions and tribulations of the dancers on the stage. That can't change. But by making its *secondary* story a romance between two guys, instead of between a man and a woman as it was in the original Broadway show, we might give the movie a more contemporary edge."

He gave me a long, scary look. "Well, that's adding the new—and maybe even the blue. You're insane. I could kill you for doing this."

Thank God I didn't try this story out in the desert, I thought.

And then Tanen said, "You think you're really going to pull this off?"

I said, "Look, I'm financing half the picture. My feet, my tongue, my heart, and my wallet—all are going in the same direction. So I'm in the same place as you. We're going to cry together or we're going to laugh together. Let's laugh together. It will be good."

He shrugged. "You think you can do it? Go for it." By knowing when to play 'em, I'd gotten my yes.

Alas, as it turned out, our German financing partners weren't interested in our new story. They were interested in hearing a story about lowering the picture's cost. And on that point, there was no good story to tell or sell. The picture never happened at Universal, and the rights ultimately were sold to another party, who followed the show's original story.

No matter how good your story is, no matter how good a story teller you are, and no matter what your business proposition, audience attitude matters. If they can't hear your story, they won't heed your call to action. So you've got to decide immediately coming in the door whether to hold 'em or fold 'em.

BE INTERACTIVE

When my two sons turned fourteen, they asked me to take them to mega-magician David Copperfield's show at the MGM Hotel in Las Vegas. They'd seen his extravaganza illusions on television and read in the *Guinness Book of World Records* about his feat of selling the most tickets ever worldwide to a magic show. They'd heard me talking about his twenty-one Emmys and ranking as the highest paid celebrity of the last ten years in *Forbes*. And because I knew him, they wanted to see him in person. I'd first met Copperfield when I was running Sony Pictures, and it occurred to me that one of his trademarks was the way he told compelling human stories to enhance his magic, so I decided not only to take my sons to the show but to meet with the master illusionist afterward to discuss his secrets for telling stories that moved people to believe in the impossible.

Watching his show through the lens of my interest in the art of the tell, I realized almost as soon as the stage curtains opened that Copperfield's skill at controlling audience reaction hinges almost entirely on his two-way interaction with the audience. And as the show unfolded, what stunned me even more than his sleight of hand was the simplicity of his interactive techniques. Though I'll never be able to fathom how he executes his illusions, I realized that any businessperson can hold an audience as spellbound as Copperfield does if that person masters these techniques.

David invited the audience not just to watch the show, but to participate both physically and emotionally. "What if," he asked, "you could do the impossible?" As he urged them to dare to dream, he chose folks to come up onstage with him and physically participate in the magic he performed within their reach and before their eyes.

Later I asked if he wasn't worried about getting a jerk or someone who didn't speak English. He told me that he prays for those surprises because they capture the audience's attention and prove that his act is spontaneous and authentic. "It's when you get to show your chops."

But Copperfield's most powerful technique for engaging his audience's attention is the emotional story he tells even as he moves, performs illusions, and prompts people's participation. In this show, Copperfield's true story centered on his grandfather, a crusty old man who dominated the lives of both David and his father but never gave them the approval they craved.

I noticed that, while the audience had been interested and enthusiastic during Copperfield's warm-up magic, as soon as he started telling the story about his family and his pain and desire, the quality of attention in the room palpably changed. Suddenly people were *inside* the story, utterly riveted as David spoke of his father's early dreams of becoming an actor, which he gave up under pressure from David's grandfather to open a store selling women's lingerie. Then David described his own discovery as a gawky young kid that performing magic could help him overcome his shyness, make friends, and connect with girls. But his grandfather dismissed that dream as well, despite David's knack for tricks. The old man predicted that David would be a complete failure if he pursued magic as a career, and he didn't want to ever watch him fail.

As David told that story on stage, you could feel his sadness resonating with every member of the audience as they recalled similar experiences and feelings in their own lives. We all empathized with his youthful frustration and longing to prove himself to his grandfather.

"My goal really is to have an emotional effect," Copperfield explained to me later. "The grandfather story begins with five minutes of me sitting on a stool talking. You wonder if the audience is going to go, *Where's the trick?* But I think if you're sincere, they think, *This guy really believes this,* and then they'll go with you."

Those five minutes concluded with David recalling a day when he was performing one of his first off-Broadway shows and looked up to see in the back row a man who resembled his grandfather. When he went back, the man was gone, so he thought he must have imagined or wished for him to be there. Then his grandfather died and David missed the chance to say good-bye.

A low moan rippled through the room. Everyone knew what it felt like to want a second chance with someone who's gone.

Now Copperfield employed another showman's technique for reinvigorating the audience's engagement. He changed tempo. He'd been talking slowly, but now he began moving very fast, inviting audience members up onstage, asking them questions. As they gave him random numbers, such as birth dates and phone numbers, to write on a large chalkboard, he told about his grandfather's lifelong dream of owning a 1949 Lincoln convertible. A picture of the car flashed on a screen behind him.

He also started to use more physical props, such as a box with nine locks that had been sitting onstage. Copperfield described how the family had cleaned out his grandfather's house after the old man died, and there in the back of a drawer was a ticket stub from the off-Broadway theater on the date when David had performed. A cry went up around the room. So his grandfather *was* there! David said he hoped that his grandfather was watching now. And with that, he opened the box to reveal a slip of paper on which was written the entire sequence of random numbers that the various people from the audience had marked on the board. He opened the locks with the combination of the numbers and pulled from inside the box a license plate with those same exact numbers!

This was the point where David's story and his magic merged. A silky curtain dropped over the stage, and two seconds later he pulled it away to reveal two tons of 1948 Lincoln convertible—his grandfather's dream car, bearing that same license—levitating ten feet off the ground!

The audience went crazy, clapping, cheering, ecstatic. We were wowed by the car—I was in the very first row and never saw it coming—but that wasn't the reason we felt so emotionally invested in this magic or why we all felt a lump in our throats. Even before I left the theater, I knew that, spectacular as the illusion had been, the story we were going to remember and tell forward about this show was David's simple human story about his grandfather.

Late that night David invited me to a showing of his own private museum, the largest magic collection in the world. But the address he gave me at midnight brought me to a storefront with corsets and bras. David touched one of the bras, and a hidden door opened up. This was a replica of his father's store, he told me, the very same father who, having given up acting, opened a lingerie business. I was still interacting with his story!

As we walked through the museum, with its posters of Houdini, Kellar, Mandolini; magic devices, statues, and ancient tricks, Copperfield described each legendary magician in detail—who he was, how he lived, and what he dreamed. "Houdini was successful because he was this schlubby-looking guy; he was kind of 'everyman' and he was able to escape from things. Everybody wanted to be released or freed. So, innately, his story connected them to his magic."

In other words, there was nothing accidental about Copperfield's emphasis on audience interaction through story. It wasn't just an artifice or window dressing. He viewed it as a fundamental tool of his trade, which he used not only to *attract* his audience's attention but also to suspend their disbelief and *distract* them from the mechanics of his illusions. How, I asked him, did he achieve that perfect balance of attention control?

"Magic in itself is this distanced thing," he replied. "You know that a car can't fly, and you know you're watching eye candy. The trick is to make people forget about the puzzle and forget about the disconnect, and go, *OK, take me.* Here I used the power of telling a story not to bring attention to the illusion, but to distract their eyes by engaging their heart. Name any great entertainment that touched you, and you'll find that exact same process. The visuals will be correct, the lighting will be correct, but unless your audience has been sideswiped by a story they connect to, that they care about, and that drives them to live in that excellent world of relatable wish-fulfillment, you'll never capture them."

And could he achieve this connection without the level of interaction that he incorporates into his shows? Copperfield shook his head no. "I get to visually break the fourth wall, and I can keep it fresh by watching them. I do lots of audience participation in the show because I get to ad-lib, as opposed to the same old thing. You feel like you're the master comedian, show business person."

One night years back, he told me, he was supposedly cut in two pieces and a guy in the back of the house screamed, "Move your feet!" The whole audience went dead silent thinking Copperfield had been caught. But actually this interaction made David ecstatic. "It's the greatest thing ever because the feet over there were real human feet. And I looked at the feet, and the feet do this thing, and the audience exploded. It was unbelievable. So every night after that, I had somebody in the back of the house scream, 'Move your feet!' It always got a good reaction."

Why was that kind of immediate and spontaneous interaction so effective? David explained that it makes the story feel real and sells the illusion. "The magic is much more powerful," he said, "if people feel like they are participating in it themselves, as if they are living their dream."

MOST OF US WON'T perform magic tricks when we tell business stories, but Copperfield's interactive techniques would make any business story more memorable, resonant, and actionable. Research has shown that most of us make decisions in an emotional manner and then find an intellectual alibi to justify them. If we don't feel that emotional what's-in-it-for-me, we're unlikely to go the next step. Our brains begin to make this call based on body language before the first word is even spoken. That's why, if you want your audience to make the decision to listen to your story, your body has to promise from the moment you enter the room what will be in your tell for each listener. Changing the rhythm of your voice, raising and lowering the volume, singling a person out for a dialog, or touching a listener on the shoulder doesn't require sleight of hand, but it can have a magical effect on your audience because it makes them feel as if they're engaged in a conversation, which makes them feel like part of your story, and that they have a stake in the outcome. Promise, through your posture, smile, and gestures, that the story you're about to tell not only won't hurt or bore them, but in fact is about to give them an emotional ride they'll enjoy and remember with pleasure. Then make sure your tell delivers on that promise from beginning to end, so that when you turn your story over to them, they are primed and eager to answer your call to action.

CAPTURE THEIR ATTENTION

When I became head of the studio at Columbia Pictures in the 1970s, the senior management team was at least thirty years older than me. They were suspicious of my youth and inexperience, and loath to accept me as their leader. I knew that I needed to do something dramatic to capture their attention and respect from the start. So the day of our first meeting after my promotion I entered the big conference room and plunked myself down as usual on a side chair, leaving the head of the conference table empty. Everyone noticed this seating choice immediately. Then I looked around, making eye contact with everyone in the room.

Without speaking, my actions were telling the story that I'd come with respect and humility. I was telling them I wanted to lead, but I understood I was young and that my authority had to be earned. Not until I felt I'd earned my leadership would I take the position at the head of their table.

This got their attention, and the mood in the room immediately calmed down.

Looking back, I try to imagine how my story would have played if I'd spoken it instead of acting it out, or if I'd said it and been sitting at the head of the table. I could have said it and meant it, but it wouldn't have sounded congruent or authentic. By violating their expectations, my unconventional seat selection captured my audience's attention and put those words in their mind as my words never could have. It interrupted the mental pattern of assumptions running around the room and helped mollify any unspoken resentment, anger, and uncertainty in my audience. The intention of this simple gesture was to tell them the story that we were all in this together.

The key to capturing your audience's attention is first to pay attention to *them*. Had I not known the mood of my audience and their expectations before entering the room, I probably would have blundered badly. But I anticipated their mind-set and planned a move that would immediately upset their negative expectations and bring us into a common zone.

Of course, if you're telling your story to a neutral or friendly audience, such strategic moves won't be needed to get their attention. But it's still important to interrupt the tumult of white noise running through their minds, so they can engage fully with you, and the best way to do that is through nonverbal signals such as I used when I entered the boardroom. Make eye contact. Smile to put your audience at ease. If appropriate, shake hands. Animate your voice, raising and lowering it as an actor might. Sometimes you can capture attention by lowering your voice so your audience is forced to lean in and listen harder. Sometimes a stretch of silence, especially after you've made an important point, will speak louder than words. But follow your listeners' signals. With rare exceptions, if you pay attention to them, they'll pay attention to you.

AROUSE YOUR LISTENERS' CURIOSITY

Back in 1983 producer Lynda Obst, then vice president of my production company, urged me to meet with her friend astrophysicist Carl Sagan to discuss the concept for his next book. At that time, Carl already was a well-known interdisciplinary phenomenon. His prize-winning thirteen-part documentary *Cosmos* had been the most widely watched public television series in history. An advisor to NASA, he directed the Laboratory for Planetary Studies at Cornell University. And he'd won a Pulitzer Prize for his 1977 book *The Dragons of Eden: Speculations on the Evolution of Human Intelligence*. Here was someone who could take a scientific premise and make it emotionally compelling and irresistibly exciting. I felt as if Merlin were coming to lunch at my modest West LA home.

We sat in the backyard for hours that spring afternoon as Carl told us of his passion for the SETI—Search for Extra Terrestrial Intelligence—program. He believed that if we were to make contact with another civilization it would come through listening to their conversation. But he didn't just narrate this story to me. He asked question after question to arouse my curiosity and involve me in the story.

"If you were to receive an interstellar greeting card from an extra-terrestrial force or life intelligence that said, 'Hello,' would you answer back?" he asked.

"Of course!" I answered.

"Why?" he parried.

"Because I'd want to find out what they knew. It might give me a tactical advantage. Plus, how could you not?"

Carl leaned closer and drilled into me with his kind but scary-smart gaze. "What if the 'Hello' were instructions? If they said, 'Build it'? You couldn't engage in dialog. Would you do as instructed?"

Now I was hooked. I felt danger, excitement, promise, wonder. His questions triggered my question, and we passed the story back and forth as a conversation.

I said, "What is 'it'?"

"Maybe you can't tell what it is. Maybe you're the President of the United States. Would you follow the instructions?"

I said, "I'd want to know what it does. Does it destroy my planet? Is it a Trojan horse that would invite the aliens in?"

He said, "Why would you be worried about inviting them in?"

"Well, every time a superior civilization in our history has met an inferior civilization, the inferior civilization was destroyed. So I'd think about that."

Ever the master story teller, he kept throwing out *What ifs*. "What if the plans were for a modern Noah's Ark? What if this ark were civilization's only hope of survival? What if you started building it, what would people think? What if you discovered the structure had a couple of seats in it? What if the instructions told you one of these seats was for you? Would you take a seat?"

I said, "I never much liked roller coasters. But I would see the people yelling and screaming, having a great time, and I'd see the coaster come back with everybody safe. In your scenario I have no evidence that this would be safe, or would ever come back. So probably my curiosity would be overwhelmed by my fear. I don't know. There would be a battle between those two emotions."

Carl leaned back and locked his hands behind his head. "Would you like to read the book about what happens and who takes the seat?"

"Absolutely!"

He said, "I'm going to write that book. Would you like to develop it into a movie?"

I said, "You got it. I'm in."

Carl had not taken me beyond the inciting incident of his story, yet he'd hooked and captured me. He'd even gotten me to narrate the reason why this project was so personally irresistible: because it was safe. I didn't have to take the actual interplanetary trip. I could travel in fantasy, sating my intellectual and emotional curiosity without having to risk my civilization or my life. He'd left me with the ultimate cliffhanger, and I could hardly wait to find out what happened next. Although that meant risking some money, by the time Carl was through with me, I felt as if that were chump change. I bought the rights to the book and with Lynda began the development of the screenplay for *Contact*. Although, sadly, Carl would not live to see the end result, the story he told that day eventually led to the Bob Zemeckis movie with Jodie Foster released by Warner Bros. in 1997.

As Carl well knew, questions are a story teller's friend. When your audience asks a question, it's not a sign that you're failing to tell your story well. It means you're telling it so well you've aroused their curiosity.

Excellent! Listen to the question and use it to reinforce your main points or open up new avenues that can strengthen your call to action. And lace questions of your own throughout your tell to enlist the audience's participation.

Some tellers balk at questions for fear of being drawn off track. Indeed, tangents can be perilous in the art of the tell, but as the teller, you always have the power to steer your story back in the right direction. If an irrelevant question pops up, promise to get back to it later (and make sure you do). If a question threatens to undermine or challenge your story, receive it respectfully, consider it, and try to understand where it's coming from. Then find some point of agreement with the questioner before resuming your telling. It's not always clear in the moment, but I find that unwanted questions often shed new and valuable light on my propositions.

ENGAGE THE SENSES

Scientists tell us that words account for only the smallest part of human communication. The majority is nonverbal, more than half based on what people see and more than a third transmitted through tone of voice. In other words, we do a lot of talking through our senses. The best tellers make a point of telling their stories through both verbal and nonverbal engagement because they know that the more the audience *feels* the story in their bodies, the better they will remember it. And I'm a believer because I was once told just such a physical story, which I still remember vividly thirty years later.

The teller was none other than World Heavyweight Champion Muhammad Ali. In the mid-1970s, when I was president of worldwide production for Columbia Pictures, Ali was consumed with the production of a film version of his autobiography, *The Greatest,* which we were to distribute. Although the picture wasn't even in production yet, he was concerned that the project get the support he felt it deserved. Howard

Bingham, his longtime compatriot, called me one day and asked if Ali could come and chat with a few of Columbia's mavens. A handful of us, including John Veitch, head of physical production, and Norman Levy, head of distribution, gathered in our CEO David Begelman's office. After we exchanged pleasantries, it quickly became apparent that Ali's exhortations were losing his audience. It was so early in the development process, and my colleagues didn't see the reason for his concern. They were looking out the window, fiddling with their pens, or just watching the champ blankly.

Suddenly Ali went silent. Changing tactics, he got up.

"You want to know how I beat Ken Norton after losing to him in 1973?"

That got their attention! A second later Ali had the executives standing in a boxing posture. He ordered us to keep our arms up and our bodies moving for thirty minutes, representing ten three-minute rounds. During these thirty minutes of nonstop activity, Ali engaged the execs with the story of both fights against Norton—the first of which Ali lost.

Norton had been a newcomer when the duo first fought at the Forum in Inglewood, Ali said. "I was in the worst shape of my career." He demonstrated how Norton had struck the blow that broke Ali's jaw. As the guys tried the jab, he said, "You gotta have a plan for every possibility."

Then he began to demonstrate how he'd trained for the second fight, which took place six months after losing the first. He got us all running in place as if our feet were on fire. "Always be moving." He mimicked jumping rope. He threw punches that we ducked or deflected. "Control, control, control," he said. "You got to get fit to win. On the morning of the rematch with Norton, I weighed in at two-twelve—my lightest for any fight during my comeback."

At the bell for round one, Ali said, he came out fast and was up on his toes circling to the left nonstop. He showed us how he'd worn Norton down by leaning on him or pushing on his neck, how he'd taunted him to throw harder punches, sapping his energy further. "I was ready to dance all night. During the first five rounds, I controlled that fight.

Norton couldn't touch me. Then I came down off my toes and Norton started to catch up, scoring to the body. But I fought him off." He demonstrated the blocks.

"In the twelfth round, I decided I had enough." Ali mimicked the flurry of punches that had stunned Norton; then paused and delivered the second set, which had finished him off. "I won 7–5 Ali." As he raised his fists in victory, his story's message was clear: The rematch against Norton had been as much a triumph of preparation as his movie would be—*if* everyone in that room worked as hard as Ali to make it happen.

At the end of that half hour we were all banging away, laughing, exhausted, and hugging one another. Ali's tell had brought us inside the experience of boxing and made us feel that winning takes more than just punching. The executives now understood just how much endurance and training and advance work it takes to go the distance in the ring. And that transformed their attitude about the film and the importance of strategizing for all ten rounds, from making it to selling the hell out of it.

Ali literally got us into mental shape for his marketing challenge. He then posed, squaring off with each of us, for photos that he autographed, knowing we'd hang those pictures in our offices. Those physical mementos would anchor our experience and remind us of our connection and commitment to Ali. For me, this story about preparation became a cornerstone for success. To this day, my picture with Ali is featured prominently in my office, and I frequently tell the story of its purposefulness.

This interactive approach paid great dividends for Ali. With the unconditional commitment of the marketing people as the cornermen of his campaign, *The Greatest* would help secure Ali's global appeal. That day The Greatest proved himself the champion of the art of the tell.

USE YOUR PROPS PROPERLY

Organizational story consultant Steve Denning uses the term "springboard story" to describe a story that can spring listeners to a new level of understanding and get them to action. Typically, he says, springboard stories are very short, true, and end on a positive note. They're told in minimalist fashion to leave plenty of space for the listener to create a version of the story that he or she can own and tell forward. When I paid a visit to the office of LASIK surgeon Dr. Robert Maloney, I realized that one of the most efficient and powerful ways to tell a springboard story is through props.

Maloney had performed a very successful LASIK surgery on my wife, who was so pleased with the results that she sent me in for a consultation. As it turned out, LASIK wouldn't correct my particular vision problem, but during the examination I became curious how Maloney managed to make his patients who do qualify—especially those who don't know anyone else who's had the surgery—believe that the radical benefit he promised was real.

Maloney pointed across the room and uttered one word—"See." There, between two chairs, stood a basket containing hundreds of discarded eyeglasses.

I was absolutely stunned by the brilliance of his use of props and the economy of this springboard story. One word. How elegant . . . *See.* As in "See the basket, and you will see." Those glasses were the perfect physical embodiment of one of the key benefits that other patients enjoyed and that awaited the nervous patient. No more burden of glasses! They told the whole miraculous story. It was like Lourdes!

I'VE ALSO FOUND PROPS to be useful in paving the way for story telling. In particular, props can help break the ice and bridge the gap with leaders in other fields or of higher stature. In 1992, for example, I was invited to lunch with former president Ronald Reagan and the former president of the Soviet Union, Mikhail Gorbachev. As CEO of Sony Entertainment, I saw this as an opportunity to open a conversation about bringing our Loews theater chain into Russia, a real emerging market. But how could I enlist Gorbachev in that effort? I had nothing in common with him. I needed to create a shared context in which my story would be heard.

I decided to bring a gift of distinction that would give all three of us something in common to talk about. At Tiffany's I bought three specially designed, engraved sterling silver Swiss Army knives—one for Gorbachev, one for Reagan, and one for myself. I'd heard that when Reagan was a boy, he used to play mumblety-peg, a game you play with a jackknife. My bet was that Gorbachev had played the same game when he was young. So this prop would prompt us to share stories of our youth and create an emotional connection. (This was long before the era of security checks, and it honestly did seem like an innocent gift—though you'd never get away with it today!)

As the two former presidents opened the Tiffany boxes and unfolded the knives, the Secret Service came running, but Reagan waved them away when I said, "Remember when you were kids, and you played mumblety-peg?" Not only did he remember mumblety-peg, but he stood up right there and then, and demonstrated by pantomiming the movements. Gorbachev had played the very same game in Russia as a boy, his translator said. And then I joined in, and Reagan's staff took our picture.

This prop created a common reference point that leveled the emotional playing field for all of us. The game playing diminished Gorbachev's formality and made him more open to the story I eventually told him about my vision for Loews in Russia. He not only directed me to the folks who could best serve our challenge, but he vouched for me when I approached them.

BUT PROPS DO NEED to be chosen with care, to insure that they accurately reflect the authenticity of the teller. As veteran campaign manager Susan Estrich told my UCLA students, politicians can suffer particularly negative consequences when they choose the wrong props.

Estrich, who is also a lawyer, a professor, an author, a feminist advocate, and a commentator for Fox News, became the first woman ever to manage a presidential campaign when she ran Michael Dukakis's 1998 bid for the White House. Today Dukakis is a visiting professor at the UCLA School of Public Affairs, and, by coincidence, the very day Estrich was to visit my course in 2008 I passed him walking across campus. As soon as I saw him, a memory from his campaign flew into my mind, of a little guy wearing an ill-fitting helmet riding around in a tank for a photo op. Unfortunately, that helmet hadn't told a good story for Dukakis. He'd come off as a little boy playing soldier—not an encouraging story for a man who would be President.

Later, talking to Susan Estrich in class, I asked her to tell us the backstory behind the helmet and the tank. She sighed at the memory. "Here was a guy who was not strong on defense. Michael Dukakis had a great education program. He had a great health insurance program. Had he gone to the health care factory and put on a little mask, with his nose sticking out, people would've said, 'He looks a little funny, but he's a health care nut, and he's fun.' Debate on your own terms, all right? We were never going to win if this was a fight about defense."

Unfortunately, Dukakis's other advisors insisted he show he was tough on defense—even though that story was untrue. "So Dukakis goes to a tank factory," Estrich recalled. "He gets on the tank. He puts the helmet on, and he fastens the strap. He thinks, *This is like riding a bike.* It's not like riding a bike! It's riding a tank. You're not supposed to have a good time on a tank!"

As soon as the first photograph was taken, it collided with his story that he'd make a strong commander in chief. The result was like a rocket-propelled boomerang. The disconnect between that one picture and the story he told helped scuttle Dukakis's campaign. After that it didn't matter what he claimed, Estrich said. Everybody looked at the picture and thought, *This guy is going to be commander in chief? No way. He doesn't belong on that tank.*

Now, the point is not that the artifact of the tank and that silly hat would have told a bad story for every candidate. It's just that this artifact was not congruent with Dukakis's oral story, so it tanked his campaign. Estrich pointed out that John McCain was always successful when he told his story through tanks, because defense was John McCain's story. He owned it. The stories Dukakis owned were nested in schools, hospitals, and job training centers. If he'd used those settings as props to prove that was what the election was about, Estrich said, he might have won.

LISTEN ACTIVELY

Purposeful tellers understand that the art of the tell is a dialogue, not a monologue. How you listen as a teller is as important to your success as the actual words you speak, but it's not just a matter of hearing the response of the other person. As a practitioner of the art of the tell, you must listen with all your senses, gauging your audience's emotions, attention, and interest—moment to moment. The more actively and empathetically you listen, the more you'll involve your audience in your tell. And the more engaged they feel in your story, the more likely they'll be to heed its call to action. Active listening is a powerful tool for you as the teller because it emotionally connects you to your audience and makes them feel valued. Tellers must pay close attention to what the audience— whether one or many—is experiencing, not just hearing. They must read their audience's eyes and every aspect of their body language to feel an empathetic connection that is continuous, strong, and unbroken. Tellers must have acute sensitivity to all of their audience's responses and adjust their story and its telling as needed to prevent confusion, impatience, or boredom. The goal of active listening for you, as teller, is to make your listeners feel that they are vital partners in your story experience.

Tony Robbins, a renowned life strategist, author, and turnaround expert, is also a longtime friend, and I can still remember the first time I attended one of his seminars, with an audience of nearly eight thousand diverse people. Tony's goal is to give individuals in his audience the opportunity to craft a new story to tell to themselves and others—one whose meaning can change their lives. After getting a volunteer to share his or her problem, thereby providing the "content," Tony in essence becomes the surrogate teller, using prompts and questions to help the person create a new story. In this role Tony listens "like a hawk," reading every aspect of the person's behavior and psyche. Also, while in this listening and "telling" mode, he watches the larger audience to ensure they get it too.

The day I attended Tony's seminar I was transfixed when a thirteen-year-old girl raised her hand and said she had tried to kill herself twice, once by hanging. For the next hour and a half the girl spilled out her story and then *retold* it in response to Tony's prompts. Later, explaining his method to me, Tony said, "My job with each person, through my questions and prompts and listening with acute sensitivity, is to lay the narrative bread crumbs, creating a trail they can pick up and follow to change their own story."

That day, we all joined in hearing, through Tony's method, this girl's story. As the words moved between them, you could have heard a pin drop. Tony's attention was so clear, active, and open that we all felt drawn into the story reshaping that was taking place. Each time Tony passed the story back to the girl, he seemed to open up and invite her—and thus, the larger audience—to interpret the last answer and anticipate the next question.

Tony's acute listening and laser-sharp questions, designed and delivered like a detective's, were, in fact, guiding the girl to tell herself a new, totally authentic story, yielding a new meaning. First, Tony asked why she tried to kill herself. She replied that her parents didn't understand her. That revealed her desire for her parents' understanding. Then Tony touched her hand to establish trust and asked what was going on with her parents when she started to feel this way. He didn't provide an answer or guess at her story but gave her time, not just to think about what the question was asking her, but to grasp what the question was telling her. She got it and told him they'd started having marital problems.

Then he leaned forward and narrowed his focus as if she were the only person in the room. "It sounds like you're afraid they're going to divorce," he said. And when she nodded, he asked, "What if they're not happy with their marriage?"

The girl said, "My mom knows they have problems, and she's tried to tell my dad. And my dad just does not want to hear it. And then sometimes I just feel torn, because my mom will try to pull me against my dad, and my dad tries to hold me against my mom."

Never taking his eyes off the girl, Tony prompted, "Had your parents ever been happy?" She said they had, in the beginning of their seventeen-year marriage—before she was born. He asked what she wanted most for her family.

"My family staying together."

At that point it became clear to the whole audience that the girl was probably attempting suicide as an unconscious way to unify her parents, to give them a bigger problem to face and solve together. But *she* didn't get her story's meaning yet, which was Tony's goal. He asked how she thought her parents felt when she attempted suicide. He asked how she thought her attempts influenced their decision to continue in an unhappy marriage.

The girl was now connecting to her own story the way we all were, trying objectively to figure out where its truth and meaning lay. And then she got it. She took charge of telling her authentic story. "My mom told me something. Before they were married, she got pregnant. And my dad really, really wanted to have kids, and my mom didn't, so they had an abortion. And I think he blames her for that; I think she blames herself for that too."

A gap had opened in the pain she felt from really "hearing" her old story, and in that gap we all could sense her desire to change the story. Through Tony's "telling" prompts and questions and his being an active listener, she took control of her story. Now she was authentic and congruent and was no longer telling the story as if she were the source of her family's problem. Her face lit with amazement as she acknowledged and owned the story she'd just told Tony. And, more important, as she acknowledged and owned its meaning. "My parents' unhappiness began before I was even born," she said. Tony then shared the takeaway that his "tell" had yielded: "The meanings we give our stories control our entire lives. Big problems start with little thoughts. And great achievements also start with little thoughts."

The girl looked as if she were waking from a state of deep concentration. Tony probed, trying to gauge her new story's impact. He asked if she'd ever try to take her life again. And she shook her head. "No," she said with surprise. "No. Because I'm not responsible for my parents' problems," she said. "I can't put all their blame on myself."

By the end of the seminar, everyone in the auditorium wanted to try Tony's method at home, and thousands made a beeline for the kiosk where his books and media products were sold. As I watched this eager human tide, I marveled at the realization that they were actually buying *Tony's* story, not the girl's. They were actually buying his call to action, his message that by changing their own stories they could directly change the experience and quality of their lives. The change that Tony's "telling" and active listening has facilitated is so compelling that more than 50 million people from more than one hundred countries have bought his best-selling books and multimedia products or attended his seminar engagements.

It occurred to me how completely transferable Tony's process of active listening was for business professionals. It simultaneously struck me how underutilized active listening was not only as an effective business tool, but also as a business imperative. Quite frankly, most businesspeople fail to listen actively and probe intelligently because they don't shut up long enough to do so. As a highly gregarious and outgoing person myself, I realized that, with all my talking, I was guilty on occasion of failing to listen and so missed out on chances to reshape my story for the better.

Here's the insight that I gleaned from Tony's interaction that has made a profound difference in my process: When I'm trying to either persuade someone or sell them something, the more time I spend getting them to do the talking—to tell me their story or, as it may be, their *problem*—the better able I am to reshape my story to address their specific challenge. The difference is being interested rather than trying to be interesting. This doesn't mean I don't prepare a story in advance. It means I stay in the moment, listening "like a hawk," and that what I then perceive shapes the telling of my stories. It's meant the difference between merely hitting the target and repeatedly hitting the bull's-eye.

BE PREPARED TO DROP YOUR SCRIPT

Have you ever been in the audience when a speaker who's lost his or her audience just keeps going with the prepared remarks? Do you remember how that made you feel as a listener? Bored? Annoyed? Anxious to escape? Whatever your reaction, it likely didn't help you absorb the speaker's message.

Tellers who stubbornly stay "on point" may be afraid to diverge from their script into uncharted waters. Or they may feel that too much time and money have gone into preparation to toss the plan aside. But neither excuse will bring back your listeners' attention, and unless you have their attention, why bother telling your story?

Fortunately, most audiences actually want to be reeled back in. If you're prepared to improvise, and you take advantage of whatever energy, signals, cues, or props are in the room, you can almost always salvage your tell. It may help to remember that you never have to memorize the truth. If you stay true to yourself, whatever "pops out" in that moment of spontaneity will be received by your listeners as authentic and will likely reinforce your connection to them in a way that "sticking to the script" does not allow. The other aspect of a great "tell," as I learned with the most unlikely of audiences some thirty years ago, is to trust in serendipity.

When I was CEO of PolyGram, we launched a television series called *Oceanquest*. This early reality show took a team of former Navy SEALS and expert divers and scientists led by Al Giddings around the world to film aquatic adventures in locations ranging from the Truk Lagoon in Micronesia to the waters under the ice of Antarctica. Our host was Miss

Universe Sean Wetherly, a novice who provided the emotional connection to the audience at home.

One critical segment was scripted to tell the story of the forbidden waters of Havana Harbor, where wrecks of galleons and pirate ships, which had carried treasure as far back as the sixteenth century, lay on the ocean floor. There was just one problem: it was the early 1980s, and neither the U.S. government nor the communist regime of Fidel Castro wanted a team of Americans filming there. By pleading that our mission was purely scientific and peaceful, I finally was able to get permission through the offices of former President Nixon. However, getting Cuban officials to sign off on our shoot in Havana Harbor was another matter. Millions of dollars and the success of the whole project hung in the balance, so after weeks of being stonewalled, we gambled that we could win approval more easily if we were physically on Cuban turf. We sailed ahead into Hemingway Marina and waited for Castro's response.

A local official finally turned up to say that Castro, himself a scuba diver, had taken an interest in our project and would be visiting the harbor to see our equipment. That ostensibly was his only interest. I asked if we could use this visit to request the president's permission to film under the harbor. The official shrugged. "El Jefe will be here ten minutes only. You are free to ask permission, but remember the rules—no autographs and no gifts."

Castro had already outlasted multiple American presidents, and whatever he said here was law, but I was determined to seize this opportunity. If he was interested in scuba diving, I would have Giddings tell him a ten-minute story about the nature of our equipment, which would compel him to give us permission.

We threw ourselves into readying and setting our story, with props consisting of the most sophisticated gear on the ship—underwater vehicles, diving suits, high-tech cameras, and other cool "equipment." All this was on display on the main deck when Castro arrived, entourage in tow.

Noticing the No Shoes sign affixed to the gangplank, El Jefe ordered his minions to unlace their boots before boarding our vessel. Then he strolled around the deck eyeing our toys. But nothing seemed to catch his attention. Realizing that our chance was slipping away, I began firing bullets—data about what we wanted to search for in Havana Harbor and reasons why we wanted to search for it. Castro glanced at his watch. The rest of his group, taking their cue, began to move toward the gangplank.

Suddenly Castro's demeanor changed. Sean Wetherly had appeared! And having just finished some shooting, she was still wearing her bathing costume. This piece of equipment stimulated more than El Jefe's national pride.

But then he noticed something else. Sean was holding a tooth as big as her hand, which had come from a 250-foot prehistoric great shark called a megalodon. This creature was some ten times larger than any shark living today, and its tooth clearly interested the president, so Sean handed it to him. I seized on this serendipity to reset my story into a tale of the megalodon.

As El Jefe fingered this enormous tooth, I told him how this gargantuan predator once prowled Havana's waters. I folded Cuba's ancient past into its present, tucking in anecdotes we'd unearthed about the famous and controversial incidents that had occurred in Havana Harbor during its centuries at the heart of world commerce, diplomacy, intrigue, and war. I closed my story with a call to action, saying we as filmmakers wanted to create an enduring record—an artifact, if you will—that told the world the story of Cuba's historic Havana Harbor.

The ten minutes we'd been promised stretched to four hours as Castro caught the story we'd told him and pitched it back with new and different suggestions for elements we might want to film. He gave us blanket permission to shoot anywhere in the harbor we wanted. My wife asked, and he willingly autographed virtually everything from T-shirts to dive equipment. And he later sent us a cache of lobsters and cigars—proof that successful stories don't always follow the script.

SURRENDER CONTROL

At one of our story conclaves, organizational story telling expert Steve Denning made an essential point. He said that the ultimate job of the teller is to let go. "The goal of story telling is to get the listener to take over your story," he said. "You want your story to become their story. Then they're going to create a new story from your story. It's going to be adapted, changed, adjusted." There's just one little catch: Once you have told your story, you have no control over what your audience does with it.

The hardest truth in the art of the tell is a simple human fact: You cannot control other people. What's more, no one likes to be commanded or bullied or manipulated. You'll face ferocious resistance each and every time you try. All you can control is your preparation, setting, and telling. What your listener does in response will depend on a multitude of factors, which may have nothing to do with you. However, the more your audience feels as if they own your story, the more likely they are to act on it. So once you've told your story, you need to intentionally surrender control of it to them.

It may help, instead of thinking about a story as "yours" or "mine," to consider it as "ours." When you tell a story as "ours," you invite your audience to step across the gap between teller and listener and engage in the story as a co-owner. If they do that, you can be sure the story is getting an empathetic hearing. And when they empathize, "our" story resonates.

You might think that the least likely person in any business to surrender control would be a film director. Actually, with few exceptions, the opposite is true. Films are such complex enterprises that most would never get made unless the director surrendered control to the writers, designers, producers, actors, and tech crews who bring movie ideas to life. But even as directors surrender control, they keep their vision intact by framing the story so that others can share it. For example, director Curtis Hanson explained to students in my UCLA graduate course Navigating a Narrative World that he told his team members the story of his vision for *L.A. Confidential* through a collage of images and artifacts from 1930s Los Angeles. Hanson personally selected these photographs to frame his unique concept for the look and feel of the movie, but in turning them over to the cast, costumers, set designers, lighting, camera, and sound people, he was entrusting every one of them to contribute his or her own talents and energy to the collective story. Hanson likened himself to a symphony conductor making sure the others "all were playing notes from the same page." But he needed them to play those notes using their own unique arts and skills. His goal was for their shared story to be richer than the one he originally told them. The strategy worked so well that *L.A. Confidential* received nine Academy Award nominations. Hanson won for Best Adapted Screenplay.

Every collaborative process involves this tension between the teller's singular vision and the need to surrender control to other participants. In running my own business, I try to frame the core vision for each of our enterprises, but I need every person who works on the project to view it as if he or she were the center of its universe. Kevin Plank told me he takes the same approach at Under Armour, where he encourages his employees to think, *Without me, the place would fall apart.* That sense of ownership is what keeps them showing up and performing with excitement and enthusiasm. But even as he surrenders control for the daily execution of his company's story, Kevin said, "My job is making sure that they see the shared vision, the goal."

That type of collaboration also informs major advertising campaigns, which typically begin with a story told person to person within a marketing team and then move outward. Key to these campaigns is a certain openness within the story, which invites listeners to make that story their own as they tell it forward. As media communications expert Bob Dickman told me, "In business there's often a compulsion to fill in every dot because we're rewarded for having the answer quickly. But actually, we need to create empty spaces and have more ambiguity. It's about knowing the essence rather than knowing everything." One major campaign that employed this principle began with a story told by a group of young marketing executives at JWT (J. Walter Thompson) and led to the most successful product launch in the century-plus history of De Beers, the world's largest diamond mining company.

ROB QUISH, COO OF JWT North America and CEO of JWT Inside, told me how this campaign unfolded when I was visiting his New York headquarters. First, he explained that JWT, the largest advertising agency brand in the U.S. and the fourth largest full-service marketing network in the world, has a marketing group inside the agency that is dedicated to De Beers. The problem that De Beers and the diamond industry faced was finding a way to sell very small diamonds. "The small ones have no value really in the diamond business," Rob told me. "How you put value into the small ones was the business challenge."

Enter the JWT team: Anne, Colby, Sarah, Ted, and David. They headed out across America to hear the stories of men and women in love—about the paths they had been on together and their hopes for the future. In Cleveland they explored couples' views on their future and uncovered a refreshing sense of hope and optimism. Couples believed that their relationship would strengthen over time, and that belief helped them get through the ups and downs of daily life together. The next morning, armed with a concept to play with, the JWT team boarded a plane to Austin, Texas, home to a dynamic community of creative thinkers whom the team felt could spark an idea for the product design.

The next night, the team and several Austin couples brainstormed design ideas in small groups. At the very end of the evening an idea emerged: "We thought about what is symbolic about life and the future. It starts with something small and gets larger," one man said. He held up a drawing of a bangle that featured seven round diamonds, going from small to large. "The diamonds getting larger represent how your love for each other grows as you go through life together. The stone at the end is largest because it represents that your love today is stronger than it's ever been. Here's a pendant with five diamonds dangling down; the diamonds get bigger as the design opens outward to a hopeful future." The man paused. "But we think it's not just about hope; it's about a promise of love growing stronger over time."

And at that moment everything fell into place. A design with diamonds graduated in size could be used to symbolize how a couple's love grows over time. This idea wasn't just about hope. It was a way for a couple to look back and celebrate how their love had grown, but also look forward, confident that the future would bring them closer as their shared experiences continued to strengthen their love.

Then they summed it up with the essence of the story: "With every step, love grows."

And with that, everyone in the room felt it and got it. The journey campaign would create a template through which each customer could tell and signify his or her unique love story!

But now JWT had to figure out how best to surrender that story to their customers, because the company couldn't just tell customers the stones represented their journey. Only when the story was personal would it become truly memorable, resonant, and actionable.

JWT needed to help people tell their stories. This meant fanning out across the country and engaging men and women in conversations. "The framing device of the story is *journey*," Quish said, "which implies transition and change." But having framed the story for their audience, the marketing team then stepped out of the teller's mode and assumed the role of personal story facilitators. They drew out tales of joy and hardship, commitment, desire, and passion that was sometimes impossible— especially for men—to express in words. "Every woman wants her husband to articulate his emotions," Quish said. "Fortunately, diamonds can help him do that. A diamond is a vehicle to tell a love story."

However, the stories JWT collected were not uniform. So they realized that the design of Journey jewelry had to come in a variety of shapes to represent the couple's particular path: an S curve, a circle, a heart, a zigzag. Perfect! These multi-diamond designs helped De Beers solve the industry's problem of how to use the non-keystone carat-weight diamonds that are so difficult to sell and also allowed manufacturers and retailers to participate in telling the Journey story by creating custom collections for their own customer base.

In late 2006 Journey Diamond Jewelry launched through a public relations, print, television, and online blitz. The goal at this stage was to put the words of the story into the mouths of jewelry salespeople so they could narrate it to customers. "We envisioned men entering a jewelry store, unsure and a bit overwhelmed," Quish told me. "He would tell the salesperson that he needed something for his wife to celebrate their twentieth anniversary. The salesperson would have to provide him with the story that he'd recognize as his own." So JWT would prompt the salespeople to say something like, "Journey Diamond Jewelry represents how your love for her grows over time. The graduated diamonds represent how your love keeps getting stronger through all your experiences, good times and bad, and how you'll keep loving each other more as time goes by." The idea was for the salesperson to surrender the story to the customer so that he could tell it forward—through the jewelry—to his wife.

In the first season of the campaign, the story of love's "journey" helped ramp up holiday sales of diamond jewelry by 9.4 percent. By the end of 2007, it had driven more than $2 billion in retail sales.

When I asked Quish why he thought this particular campaign had achieved such spectacular success, he answered, "Because it empowered salespeople to help consumers tell their own stories. In reality, the story isn't always perfect. It's real, emotional, challenging. This concept helped people communicate the imperfections of their lives and relationships while celebrating their strengths. Regardless of what they'd been through, regardless of the difficult times, their story would continue into the future. This is what people really want."

aHHa!

- Get yourself into state; it's about attitude, not aptitude.
- Bring high energy—the catalyst for great story telling.
- Your listeners may be one or many, but they're always an audience, and audiences expect experiences.
- Demonstrate vulnerability; it isn't a liability, it's an asset.
- Persist, persist, persist to turn "no" into "on."
- Be aware that your body is talking before your tongue moves.
- Capture your audience's attention first, fast, and foremost.
- Be interactive—engage your audience's senses early and often.
- Arouse your listener's curiosity.
- Choose carefully the props, tools, and resources that support your tell.
- Listen actively; it's a dialogue, not a monologue.
- Be ready and willing to drop your script when the situation calls for it—and it always calls for it.
- Surrender control and proprietorship of your story; your audience has to own it to tell it forward.

CHAPTER EIGHT

The Never-Ending Story

What makes a story endure for more than forty years? It was
Steven Spielberg who triggered that question for me when
I interviewed him in 2008 for my television show *Shootout*.
We were reminiscing about some of the movies we'd both
been involved with—*Close Encounters of the Third Kind* back in the 1970s,
Innerspace, Hook, and *The Color Purple*—when suddenly he turned to me
and said, "I don't know if you know this, but I used to go to your office at
Columbia when I was just starting." I did remember. Early in my career
at Columbia I used to invite lots of young creative movers and shakers to
my office, and even then Spielberg stood out. "You'd tutor us about how
to make movies," he recalled, "and you had an enormous chart on your
wall, with what every director in the world was planning, remember? You
had listed all their pictures in development and planned for production all
around town. And we'd just sit there in your office and listen to you talk
to us about how to manage the information of the business."

For forty years Spielberg had remembered my "board of directors"!
After his interview, I kept turning this thought over in my mind. Why had
that information display made such a strong impression on him? And

then it hit me that lots of other friends and colleagues also had referred to that gigantic corkboard chart over the years. In fact, the chart had been part of a never-ending story that helped to shape my career! But what made it so resonant and memorable for so long?

The story dated back to 1968, when I first arrived in Hollywood, having been recruited out of New York University Graduate School of Business, where I was pursuing an MBA degree. Vietnam was raging. Students were marching in the streets of Paris, New York, Rome, and Chicago. Dennis Hopper was in preproduction for *Easy Rider,* and Bob Dylan wasn't the only one to notice that times were a-changing. But at the same time, Barbra Streisand was finishing the distinctly non-revolutionary *Funny Girl* on a soundstage at Columbia, and across town at Paramount the pre–Dirty Harry Clint Eastwood was singing in the downright retro *Paint Your Wagon.* One of my first errands at the studio in "Gower Gulch," near the corner of Gower Street and Sunset Boulevard, was to deliver some documents to an executive session of Columbia Pictures' top brass, and as I looked around the conference table I realized that these dozen aging males still held the totality of power at this enormous studio. Since its founding under Harry Cohn in the 1920s, Columbia had made such classics as Frank Capra's *It Happened One Night;* Fred Zinneman's *From Here to Eternity;* Elia Kazan's *On the Waterfront;* Stanley Kubrick's *Dr. Strangelove;* and of course, David Lean's *Lawrence of Arabia.* Several of the men at that table had worked on the very first of those pictures, and they hadn't seemed to notice that the rest of the world was radically picking up the pace. Not only were these men becoming an anachronism, but so were the rules by which they ran their business. As the new kid in the room, I figured I might ease into one of their seats in fifteen or twenty years, but not without waiting them out. I didn't want to wait. That was my problem.

My so-called office at the time was a very long converted closet that might well have been used as a holding cell in a great escape movie. It wasn't long before I realized I had to make my own great escape.

I couldn't help but pay attention to the methods used by this old guard to make decisions. In business school I'd been trained that executives develop strict protocols to establish the optimal risk-benefit ratio. In law school I'd learned that case study provides vital lessons that can prevent faulty decisions in the future. Given that Columbia had recruited me from these institutions, I'd assumed the leaders of this great company, too, would apply a certain amount of intellectual heft to management decisions such as the selection of filmmakers for their high-budget movies. *Wrong!*

I'd been summoned to take notes at a production meeting in the office of Bob Weitman, who'd previously run MGM and was now the studio chief at Columbia. Several of his top cronies were throwing out names as possible directors for a film called *Fools' Parade,* a Depression-era convict movie starring Jimmy Stewart, who was the Tom Hanks of his era, and a very young Kurt Russell. Stewart had starred in so many landmark films—*Mr. Smith Goes to Washington, The Philadelphia Story, It's a Wonderful Life, Harvey, Rear Window,* and *Anatomy of a Murder*—that I just assumed these executives would want an equivalent giant to direct this superstar.

"Well," said Weitman, "I had a tuna sandwich with Andy McLaglen the other day. Maybe he'd be interested. I wonder if he's available."

At first I was merely puzzled. What does a tuna sandwich have to do with the skills needed to direct a major film with Jimmy Stewart? Trying to follow the logic, I wondered, what if he was having a steak sandwich? Or a salad? I smiled to myself. What if the director was a vegetarian? He'd never make the list.

Then Jonie Taps, a holdover from the Harry Cohn era, said, "You know, I think his agent is George Chasin. He's a good guy."

Billy Gordon, another Cohn holdover, who was now head of casting, piped up, "I bet Andy McLaglen doesn't have much on his plate. He could use the work."

"Great idea!" the others agreed.

I just sat there in a daze. When did being out of work qualify you to direct a major motion picture? Even I knew the director was the center of gravity in filmmaking. This is the person who interfaces with the heads of the studio and guides the production team, who develops and guides the story, has final authority on casting the picture, and controls the artistic execution of the project from preproduction through to the end of post-production. The director is the vision keeper. Could these studio chiefs possibly choose the right director on the basis of a tuna sandwich? If I could offer a better way to make this decision, maybe there was an opportunity for me to burnish my reputation and solve my career problem. A few weeks later I heard that Andy McLaglen had won what I now thought of as the tuna lottery and would direct *Fools' Parade*. I had nothing against Andy McLaglen, but I knew there had to be a better way to make this decision. So I went back down to my long, narrow nest and put white corkboard floor to ceiling on the entire back wall. I bought several boxes of colored pushpins—red, blue, orange, yellow, green—and a little Brother machine that pressed out adhesive labels. The World Wide Web wasn't even on the horizon in those days. This was the pre-information age, decades before the creation of the Internet Movie Database. We called adding machines "computers." Nevertheless, I had a sense that information was currency, and I wanted to organize the data about Holly-wood directors on my board so everyone in the decision-making process could add to it and take from it.

I listened up in the executive hallways to identify the types of information that would be most useful, and made categories on the board for each type of data. I posted the names of all active filmmakers. Then I linked them to their agency affiliations and color-coded them by the genres they specialized in—comedy, family, drama, action, musical, adventure, western, and science fiction. I divided the directors who were currently working from those who were between projects; sorted them by the size of budgets they'd managed and whether or not they came in on budget; and linked them to the stars they'd worked with. I sought out every bit of information I could find to update the board daily.

At first people stopping by my office thought I'd gone around the bend. Then they were amused. But as my "board of directors" took form, you could see in a flash which filmmakers were available across the entire spectrum of the industry, and what their strengths and weaknesses were. My visitors began to tell producers and other creative people in the building about it. They'd drop by to check the board out, and often they stayed longer than they'd expected to. As they corrected, added to, and revised my board of directors, it took on a life of its own, as if it were a living, breathing organism.

Without realizing it, I'd constructed a launchpad for my career by giving concrete form to the call to action of my tuna sandwich ahha! moment—the story I'd tell to every visitor who asked what I was doing with this giant board of directors. Everybody got that story, because they'd all seen decisions made for bizarre reasons due to lack of relevant and timely information. They'd made such decisions themselves. And in my office they not only heard the story of the problem, but they could also see and touch their one or many possible solutions.

Occasionally, if my visitor was allied with the old guard, my tuna story raised hackles. "Oh, so now you're the genius?" the incumbent would challenge.

"No," I'd say. "I'm not smart at all. I'm not making the decision. You're making the decision. You're in control. This is just what is going on in the business. If you're making a film, you want to know who's available and who's the best choice for your project and why. This information allows you to make your decision more effectively." Then I'd unwrap my tuna sandwich story, and a light would turn on.

Furthermore, I told them, my presentation was unbiased. "You go to the agencies, they're going to tell you about the names they represent. They're going to bias the data for their own benefit. I'm showing you the big picture, the entire canvas. You provide your own filter. You know what you're looking for. I'm just an advocate for organizing the information. You run it any way you want."

By surrendering control of the directors' board, I allowed my listeners to embrace and own it. One person told another, who told another, and my star steadily rose. Then, one day, guess who's coming to my office? Sidney Poitier pops in.

Sidney Poitier was then—and still is—one of my all-time heroes. Two years earlier he'd starred in Stanley Kramer's *Guess Who's Coming to Dinner*. He'd broken the Hollywood color barrier with leading roles in big-budget films ranging from *Porgy and Bess* and *A Raisin in the Sun* to *A Patch of Blue* and *In the Heat of the Night*. In 1959, the same year a black man named Mack Charles Parker was lynched by a mob in Mississippi, Sidney Poitier was nominated for an Oscar for his leading role in *The Defiant Ones,* and five years later he won Best Actor for his performance in *Lilies of the Field*. Now this young legend was standing in my office—information central.

"This is cool," he said as he surveyed the board. "I'm looking for someone who might be a good filmmaker for a project I'm considering." He spent more than an hour exploring the chart of directors. "How did you get the idea for this?" he asked at one point. I told him the story of the tuna sandwich. He just chuckled and kept following the pushpins.

"This sure does make life easier," Poitier said when he'd finished. He told me he'd made his pick. He thanked me. Then he went around and told everybody in town about the kid with the board of directors in the bowels of Columbia. He told the story of the tuna sandwich and my crazy innovation. And within a few weeks, people who didn't even work on the lot would find their way to 1438 North Gower Street. The board became a sought-after compass for many important decisions in Hollywood. Visitors would gather in and around my office and participate in my enterprise. Like tribal members correcting the chief story teller at a campfire, they'd say, "No, no, no, no, no, Lumet isn't doing that picture; he passed on it." Then they'd tell me to add a new up-and-coming director I'd never heard of, or to make note of someone who'd just gone flagrantly over budget. The board evolved like a primitive Wikipedia. As a result, I surrendered ownership of the outcome but kept gaining proprietorship of the idea.

The story spread, shining the light on me as an innovator, which distinguished me from the majority of other folks competing to climb the ladder. Before I created the board and began telling the story behind it,

I'd been stuck on the lowest rung. But when people in other companies began calling me for information or made a special trip to my closet, the senior people in my own studio couldn't help but notice. If information was currency, then I'd figured out a way to embed this currency in a story so that everyone who heard the story could spend it more wisely. And every time they did so, they told my professional story for me, and that propelled my career.

In retrospect I realize that the lesson of the "board of directors" is this: If you can find a way to activate your story so that it benefits others, they will go forth and tell your story for you. And a story that others tell virally on your behalf—especially if they feel they own it and have helped to shape and enliven it—is much more likely to become a never-ending story than one only you tell about or for yourself.

THE MULTIPLIER EFFECT

"Sometimes rejection can be a gift," Nancy Traversy was saying.

"Really!" I said. "How so?" Nancy is cofounder and CEO of Barefoot Books, which publishes my wife's children's books among their more than three hundred titles. We were visiting her home in southwest France to discuss marketing and distribution plans, but Nancy had been persuaded to tell us the story of how she'd grown what essentially was a cottage industry into a global brand.

"It was a pivotal moment," Nancy said. "By 2005 we'd been designing, producing, and marketing quality illustrated children's literature for more than twelve years. Our goal all along had been to establish ourselves as a kind of lifestyle brand that was all about the exciting emotional bond that occurs when parents read wonderful books to their kids, and now was our moment to break out the brand and position ourselves in a major way within the whole Borders book chain.

"In 2005 I met with the Borders marketing executives," Traversy recalled. "I said, 'You have to have a Barefoot Boutique in your children's section where parents can relax and tell stories to their kids. If you display our books together, you'll sell a lot more than if you scatter the books throughout the children's section. But the more important reason to have a Barefoot Boutique is to bring to life what Barefoot really stands for: parents connecting with their children through reading. Our brand embodies that connection, and we think Borders deserves to be part of that connection, too.'"

Then Traversy told the executives Barefoot's core story, which was actually Traversy and her partner Tessa Strickland's own personal story. "It's about two moms struggling to start a business, making children's books that place an equal emphasis on the quality of the words and the illustration. We were two women with seven kids between us. We weren't men in suits running this. We were real, and worked from home, and juggled family and school and kids. I remember my daughter traipsing up to the office, and she'd be stuffing envelopes, and I'd show her the art and say, 'Which one do you like better? Which one would you pick up?' We had illustrators arriving at breakfast and printers coming to sign off proofs of catalogs. So the kids grew up in a very entrepreneurial but creative way. There was never a separation between my work and who I was and who we were as a family. We could sum up our mission statement in the story of a barefoot child exploring her inner and outer worlds with her mom through our books. When people are barefoot, they're more in touch with themselves and the earth and their world. They're free and they're wild, connecting with the planet, connecting with others. We both told and lived this radical story through our company and our families right from the beginning." She sighed, remembering the response she'd gotten from the Borders execs. "They just looked at me and said, 'You can't brand a publisher. You're not a brand. There's no such thing as a lifestyle brand in publishing. You're crazy.'"

"You told your story to the wrong audience," I said.

"I sure did. They *were* the suits. They could not even begin to identify with our story. And that's when I said, 'I'm out of the chain. I can't deal with you guys anymore.'"

Traversy said everyone in publishing told her she'd committed commercial suicide. The big chains have traditionally ruled the distribution network for books, and conventional wisdom said that without their support, she might as well fold up shop.

"But actually it was the best thing that could have happened to us," she said. "We took a deep breath and looked for the essential elements within our story that could solve our problem. What we found was a whole new way to approach distribution and marketing."

The Barefoot story, Nancy emphasized, was not the story of any individual book in the line. It was about the women and children behind the whole line, including all the customers who read the books to their kids and talked about the books to other mothers, teachers, and librarians. That story of women and children telling and sharing stories was what gave the brand its authenticity and coherence. And that story also provided the solution to the company's distribution crisis after the rupture with Borders.

Traversy remembered, "We'd get e-mails and letters and handwritten notes and thank-you cards from moms saying, 'Thank God, someone out there is producing high-caliber books for children. You clearly care about me connecting with my kids through reading and sharing beauty, and not a lot of publishers do.' It occurred to us that all these women were echoing our story in their own ways. If we could harness that echo effect, we wouldn't need the chains to showcase our brand. These women could be our marketing and distribution network! That's when the whole 'living barefoot' idea came to me."

"Living barefoot," she explained, meant working from home with the right balance of a rewarding career and family. It was the essence of the story that she and Strickland had told and lived through Barefoot Books from the beginning, but now she saw a way to multiply that essence. "Living barefoot is different things to different people. But it's all centered around these values of connection, community, reading, sharing, creativity, awareness." By encouraging this network of women to tell and sell their own stories of Barefoot Books to their friends and neighbors, Traversy realized she could grow the brand in a fashion that was completely congruent with the core story of her company. Home selling actually was the most logical way to distribute a brand that had been conceived and produced at home from the very start.

When Traversy invited her customers to become Barefoot Ambassadors, "It instantly sparked a very viral grassroots word of mouth. They loved the fact that when they went out, the story they told was our story filtered through their own experience. That kept their excitement immediate and real, and inspired more and more people to get involved."

The essential element of the Barefoot story had always been connection, originally between parent and child as Barefoot partners. Now Traversy extended the meaning of connection to include all the Barefoot Ambassadors. Whether it was advice about mailing a catalog, managing a database, or selling through a personal Web page, she and Strickland had been there and done it, so they could support and guide these women through the vagaries of operating a small business. "The people that I'm talking to are not salesmen," she emphasized. "That's why we're so focused on our story and being very consistent and clear. They're people living this experience. None of them would sell anything else. They'd never sell Mary Kay cosmetics. They're people who live and breathe the lifestyle, but they do it in their own way through their own stories."

Traversy venerates the importance of connection by bringing Barefoot Books' top dozen sellers each year to the same beautiful home in Gascony, France, where we were visiting. But the reward is not simply a holiday. It's an opportunity to play a larger role in expanding the Barefoot story. "For three or four days we brainstorm about new product development, which they love. They really do care. And I think that homespun kind of close interaction is the essence of Barefoot Books."

Living Barefoot also seems to be the best revenge. In 2008, despite the economic downturn, Barefoot's North American sales shot up nearly 40 percent. Barefoot Books today are sold in the company's own flagship store in Boston and through other independent booksellers, and the chains are selling the brand again, too. However, the more than two thousand Barefoot Ambassadors account for more than 20 percent of the company's revenue. As the fastest-growing segment of the company, all these new tellers have turned Barefoot Books into a never-ending story.

THE KEY TO ESTABLISHING and sustaining a never-ending story is a constant proliferation of tellers who will preserve the essential elements of the original story even as they give that story their own personal thrust. If you want to turn your story into a never-ending story, then, the first priority is to identify the essential elements in your story. Keep your ears open for audiences who seem to be clearly echoing the essence of your story, and multiply that echo effect by encouraging these audiences to retell your story *in their own voice and through their own experience*. Whether the vehicle for this retelling is home selling, casual word of mouth, social networking, or viral technology, the bottom line is always the same: You want your story to live through its most enthusiastic audience.

ENDURE THROUGH ADVERSITY

You're not the master of the universe. If you can't adapt your story when circumstances change, it won't matter how viral its market is. Of course, not all adversity is equal. A politician whose story vaunts his family values is going to have a tough time continuing to tell that story if he's proved to be an adulterer. A company whose story is built on claims of safety and purity can't well sustain this story if the products start killing customers. But adversity that's no fault of the teller is a different matter.

Several years ago my wife gave me a T-shirt printed with a goofy hand-drawn image of "Jake," a character with a wide smile, dark glasses, and a beret, and the line LIFE IS GOOD beneath him. At the time I was complaining a lot about how tough business was, so she'd bought me this shirt to remind me that my life is indeed pretty good. After that, I began to notice LIFE IS GOOD clothing on other people, for example, a woman in a gym who had a prosthetic leg on full display as she walked on a treadmill. I stopped and pointed at her shirt and smiled. She nodded and said, "You better believe it." I looked up the figures on this optimistic clothing company and was stunned to learn that the brand sold in 4,500 independent retail outlets in the United States and in twenty-seven other countries. Moreover, since starting in 1994 the company had sold more than 20 million LIFE IS GOOD shirts and added more than nine hundred other items to their product line. Most incredibly of all, their growth rate of 30 percent a year had continued and even escalated after the disasters of 9/11, which you'd think would have tanked their feel-good story line. I decided to go to Boston and visit Bert and John Jacobs, the two iconoclastic brothers who founded this $100 million company, to ask how they'd kept their story alive.

Like Nancy Traversy, the Jacobs brothers told me that one key lay in identifying and honoring the essence of their core story. At Life is good, the resilient essence of the brothers' seminal story was an attitude of optimism and inclusivity.

"We'd always designed and drawn our own shirts," Bert said. "Between 1989 and 1994, in the pre–Life is good days, we'd go out for six weeks at a time to sell these shirts door to door at colleges. We came home from these road trips to our dive apartment above a sub shop and we'd throw a keg party so that we could tell everybody the stories of what happened on the road. We put all our artwork on the walls, and when our friends came over, it became a kind of focus group. In return for the beer and stories, we asked them to tell us what they liked and didn't like. We let them write on the walls. I'm sure our landlord loved it."

Despite all the fun, however, the brothers faced plenty of adversity right from the start. "One night we were down to our last seventy-eight dollars and considering giving up, when Johnny drew Jake [the character that would embody their story]. We got up the next day at noon—it was a great party—and stumbled out of bed into the living room, and there it was on the wall. One woman had written next to Jake, 'Is this guy single? I want him.' Guys wrote, 'What's he drinking? I have to get some.' Another girl wrote, 'This guy has life figured out.' The background to all these conversations was how screwed up the world had gotten. The six o'clock news had become the six o'clock violent murder report. So we wondered, could Jake tell the story that celebrates what's *right* in the world rather than what is wrong? We knew that a few companies had tried things like this, but none of them were *cool*. So John put shades on Jake. He put the beret on him to make him open-minded and creative and artistic. And the third thing was the smile. Unlike so many artists who are dark and angry, we were artistic *but happy*. Finally, we put about fifty phrases on the wall and the one that captured it all: 'Life is good.' One friend wrote, 'Three simple words . . . kind of says it all.' "

They printed forty-eight shirts and took them to a street fair in Central Square in Cambridge. "We sold all forty-eight shirts in forty-five minutes!" John said. "We'd never seen anything like it. The diversity of the people who bought the shirt was amazing: a little Mary Margaret schoolteacher, a big hulky Harley dude, a skateboard punk . . . all bought the same shirt!! We heard some of them say, 'Life *is* good.' "

Bert nodded. "And we said, 'We can get behind this.' "

And boy did they! Their business skyrocketed to about $3 million in 2000. Then 9/11 hit. This was a problem of an entirely new magnitude. The horror and scale of this tragedy created an existential crisis for the company.

"How do you sell *optimism* during a time like that?" John said. "We'd said our message was timeless and never ending. But this felt like the end."

But the seminal story of Life is good had been born out of adversity. It was a story about the power of friends to come together to raise one another's spirits and solve problems creatively and collectively. So the Jacobs brothers tapped the essential spirit of that story to help them solve this new crisis. Bert said, "We put a big poster of Jake on the wall and called a company-wide meeting. We said, 'We've told you many times that Jake is the one with the answers, not us. It's his story. So what would Jake do in this situation?'"

One young woman who hadn't been in the company very long raised her hand and said, "I think we should be part of the solution and have a fund-raiser for the families affected."

Bert grinned. "And we said, 'Hallelujah!! That feels like us!'"

They decided to sell a stylized LIFE IS GOOD American flag T-shirt for sixty days, nationwide, and give 100 percent of the profit to the United Way for the families of 9/11 victims. What that T-shirt told people was "Don't give up the story, life is good." It proactively morphed the message into the current environment, adapting the story to confront, rather than surrender to, the bad news. The company's core story shifted to face the light, and became that much more resonant and powerful and enduring.

"A lot of apparel companies did similar things," Bert said, "but they were offering 10 percent or 25 percent of profits to the cause. We did what felt right. We said *one hundred percent.*"

"Also," John reminded his brother, "there were people who said to us at the time, 'Don't do that, because everybody is going to buy that shirt and they won't buy your other stuff.' Well, first of all, that shirt raised $24,000 in the first four days! It was the most sales of one unit we'd ever done. And remember, at this time, commerce was stopped in its tracks. But the sales reps were excited because everybody wanted to do something to help. The retailers were doubling their orders. Our employees were working double shifts and not even asking to get paid for it. They just wanted to help. We'd set a goal of raising $20,000, and in sixty days, we raised hundreds of thousands of dollars for the families!"

Bert said, "The biggest lesson for John and me was, we didn't say, 'Oh, we're the owners of the company. This is the story, that's the way it is.' That's *not* the way it was! We had a meeting. We put up a poster of Jake. We stuck to our guns about our story having a place here. But we didn't tell our employees, 'You must do a fund-raiser.' Jake told the story of our future for us—to our employees, to our customers, and to the media, and that story endured through even the most difficult adversity!"

PLAYING THE STORY FORWARD

Which is the better choice? When a story has served its initial purpose, you can throw it away and start fresh, with all new bells and whistles; or you can preserve the essence of the original story but find new ways to tell it into the future, making it never ending. "My partners John Henry and Larry Lucchino and I confronted this problem," Tom Werner told me, "when we bought the Boston Red Sox in 2002."

Werner, now chairman of the Red Sox, was telling me this story in the owner's box at Fenway in 2008, so I knew he'd ultimately decided to stay and play, but he said it was anything but an easy decision. "This was the oldest club in the majors, and we played in the oldest stadium in the country—Fenway Park. There was immediate pressure that Fenway Park had outlived its usefulness and needed to be torn down. After all, it was built in 1912, it was cramped. We were going to meetings and people were saying, 'You have to tear down the park.' And of course, we're in business to make a profit, and we'd paid $380 million for this franchise."

Having grown up in Boston, I was a lifelong Red Sox fan and had spent a lot of my childhood in and around Fenway, so I well knew its history. In those days, I could only afford bleacher seats in the outfield. By contrast, this luxury suite behind home plate, with its open buffet, big plush couches, and bird's-eye view on this chilly May night, with the Red Sox playing down on the field against the Kansas City Royals, was like a fantasy world. I, for one, was glad he'd kept the park alive. And yet I myself bought teams and built stadiums, so from a sports business perspective I understood fully the merits of the proposition *Build it (new) and they will come.*

"The franchise assets included the Red Sox team, Fenway Park, their minor-league teams, NESN—a cable outlet—and branded merchandise,"

Tom said, "so building a new stadium that could hold tens of thousands more paying customers would mean vastly more revenue all around, not only through more tickets at higher ticket prices, but also more merchandise sales, more food sales, more advertising revenue, and more high-priced suites." And Tom hadn't even mentioned corporate naming rights, which might run as high as the $161 million deal that Coca-Cola had made with the Houston Astros for the right to name Minute Maid Park.

"Remember," Tom said, "the Boston Celtics' and Boston Bruins' antiquated old home, the Boston Garden, had been razed and replaced by the hugely successful Fleet Center in the heart of Boston."

"It must have been a hard call," I said.

"You can't imagine," Tom replied. "The pressure was compounded by the general trend among sports franchise owners to move major clubs out of aging urban stadiums and into state-of-the-art entertainment palaces."

"The Boston Patriots, who moved out of Boston to the new Gillette Stadium in Foxborough and declared themselves the New England Patriots, made a fortune," I pointed out.

"Right," Tom said. "The New England Red Sox—how does that sound?"

"Not too good. So how did you make your decision?"

"Very carefully!" Tom laughed, and I knew he was thinking about the debacle of his short-lived ownership of the San Diego Padres in the mid-1990s. The fans there called him "Hollywood Tom" because, as cofounder of the Carsey-Werner Company, he'd produced such hit series as *The Cosby Show* and *Roseanne*. When he tried to cross-pollinate his two interests by inviting Roseanne herself to sing the national anthem at a Padres game, she sang off-key, then grabbed her crotch and spat at home plate, trying to play it for laughs. Instead, she offended everyone in the stadium. In the four years Werner was an owner, Padres attendance fell 30 percent.

"My mistake in San Diego," he said now, "was not paying close enough attention to the interests of that audience before making changes. So when I came to Boston, my first priority was to do emotional due diligence."

As obvious a move as replacing Fenway might seem, it gave Tom pause when he heard the countless individual voices of generations of fans who warned that if he destroyed Fenway *he* would be destroying *their* story.

What is that story? Werner asked. Men very late in life told him about seeing Babe Ruth pitching in Fenway before Ruth's sale to the Yankees in 1919 triggered the legendary Curse of the Bambino, which according to local lore stopped the Red Sox from winning the World Series for the next eighty-plus years—a dry spell that was ongoing when Werner arrived. Tom heard stories of Jimmy Piersall climbing the center field wall and Ted Williams in the last inning at-bat of his last game, hitting a home run. Or the painful day when the ball rolled between Bill Buckner's legs, costing the Red Sox the 1986 World Series. Everyone said, "I was there"—the "there" being Fenway Park. They all carried the stories of Fenway out of the park and told them to friends, family, and colleagues, crossing generations and geography, making these stories never ending.

"I heard from people who'd moved far away who still considered Fenway their home field," Tom said.

"It's true," I said. "I'm one of them!" I thought back over all the stories I'd told and been told that were set at Fenway Park. I remembered telling people how as a kid I would stand outside the Green Monster, the thirty-seven-foot-high wall in left field, hoping to catch a fly ball coming over the top. I'd been viral marketing my story of Fenway my entire life!

"Maybe the proposition was not *Build it and they will come,* but rather *Tear it down and they* won't *come,*" I said.

"I learned that if we tore the stadium down," Werner continued, "the essence of our original story, which had endured for a hundred years, would die with it. We'd have to start all over, and the new story could never have the value, breadth, or depth of the old one. This ballpark is by far the most valuable element of the Red Sox story, because it alone will survive us all—as long as we tend it well. My job, I realized, was to protect and refuel the flame of Fenway to insure that our core story was never ending."

"The answer wasn't *Build it and they will come,*" I said.

"No, it was *Build it* up, *and they will* keep *coming!*" Tom stood up and beckoned for me to follow him out of the owner's box. It was in the fifth inning and I wasn't paying attention to the game anyway. I was much more curious about how my friend had dealt with his problem.

Tom told me as we walked that he'd realized the resolution was not to eviscerate the story, but rather to venerate it. "In Boston, Fenway Park is the enduring star. Managers and fans come and go, players get traded in and out, but this ballpark is like the flame that keeps the story alive." However, renovating the ballpark would take time and money. "I could not afford to let the flame falter during that process," Tom said. "So even before rebuilding got under way I searched for ways to shine the light on Fenway's enduring value, to ignite yet more stories. One of the things that binds people in Boston to Fenway are the stories retold of family experiences. My grandfather took me to my first game at Fenway Park, and my father and I went to games at Fenway Park. So we sought out ways to reignite the ballpark's stardom by renewing those bonds." For example, during the first season, Werner noticed that the team was going to be out of town on Father's Day, so he invited the fans to come to Fenway and throw catch with their sons and daughters. "We had to stop at 25,000 people! They had never been on the field at Fenway Park. They were so happy to just be on the field. They touched the Green Monster like it was the Wailing Wall! They picked up little pieces of sod and put them in their pockets as if it were moon dust! And that's when it hit me that Fenway was a true icon not just for the Red Sox but for all of Boston. It would have been a sacrilege to tear it down!"

I marveled at Tom's ingenuity. All those people who came to Fenway Park that Father's Day walked away with a new set of stories that they would tell to everyone they knew. *I was at Fenway. I touched the Green Wall. I pitched from the mound.* "That's how you spread your story," I said.

"Exactly," Tom agreed. "It wasn't just about nostalgia. It was about creating a destination, so that if the team lost"—he grinned—"which we do from time to time, then people would still feel like they had a special experience."

The physical renovation, too, was designed to heighten, not simply preserve, Fenway's destination appeal. And it was specifically staged so that fans could participate in the story of Fenway's serial transformation. "For the first time ever, we added seats above the Green Monster," Tom said, leading me out to experience them myself. And I could see why it had caused a sensation when this perch was added high above the famous left field wall. They were bar-style seats and there were only 250 of them, so in addition to having a vantage point that had never existed before, sitting in them you felt like you were part of a unique piece of the history of Fenway.

"The thing about baseball parks," Tom said as we walked back to the owner's box, "is that unlike football stadiums, they're all physically different. So you can play up your park's unique quirks and features to distinguish your story. In our second phase of renovation we created seats in right field with a deck where you can go to the game early and party. Next, we closed off the street in front of the ballpark two hours beforehand and created kind of a carnival atmosphere—Yawkey Way. Now people come to Fenway Park two hours earlier in anticipation of the next story, and not only is that great for their experience, but we're selling concessions to the fans two hours earlier."

Among the Red Sox concessions that Werner introduced was a T-shirt that read, EVERYONE CAN HAVE A BAD CENTURY. Then he began shopping for a new roster of star players who not only could win but also could stand up to the legacy of Babe Ruth in Fenway's never-ending story.

"People identify with heroes," Tom said, "so you've got to find people who are charismatic characters. We had a guy named Curt Schilling—we would say he's a horse one day and a horse's ass the rest of the week, but the one day of the week he pitched, he was phenomenal and so we put up with him. Then when we were playing in the 2004 Championship Series, he was injured in the earlier rounds and had an operation that would normally keep you out for three months. But he decided he had to give it one more try. During the game, fans could see his sock was bloody and he was fighting through it, and that was more than just pitching. That was a great story."

With players like Schilling, Pedro Martinez, and David Ortiz, the Red Sox won the World Series in 2004 for the first time since 1918. Then in 2007 they did it again. And by 2008 Fenway had sold out 388 consecutive home games—the second longest streak in baseball history—and reversed the Curse of the Bambino, which had haunted Fenway Park for nearly a century.

As we made our way back to the comfort of the owner's box, Werner continued, "The challenge of directing new iterations of the Fenway story is not that different from the challenge facing any teller of a large and well-established product or organizational story. We live at such a pace right now that even the strongest story has to change to endure." And the larger the enterprise, the more additional tellers this process of change has to involve. As the Native American saying goes, "It takes a thousand voices to tell a single story." Some of those voices will tell about the pain and some will tell about the glory, but every one of them will tell about the larger story's impact on that individual personally and emotionally at Fenway Park. Tom said his role, like that of any top management, was to protect his never-ending story's flame by keeping it stoked with new fuel that attracts new and old tellers alike. "You've got to protect the essential elements," he said, "while constantly adapting to change. That requires a sure touch, but also a light touch."

I chimed in with "Yeah, because if you hold the story too tight or too close, you'll lose the invaluable factor of serendipity."

Suddenly the crowd in the stadium below us roared. Tom pointed to the small, ancient scoreboard that had been operating unchanged for more than fifty years. A solid line of 0's stretched across the display. It was the seventh inning, and Jon Lester, who'd been pitching all night, was still on the mound after more than one hundred pitches. "You know," Werner said, leaning forward, "Jon was diagnosed with lymphoma year before last. We were afraid we'd lose him. Then he won the clinching game of the 2007 World Series for us."

"And tonight it looks like he's pitching a no-hitter!" I said. The twenty-four-year-old lefty's pitches had been coming faster and faster, speeding like bullets past one Royals batter after another.

"If he can pull this off," Tom said, "Lester will be the eighteenth pitcher in Red Sox history—and just the fifth left-hander—ever to throw a no-hitter."

Our attention fastened on the game as Lester kept firing balls at the mound. By the time Alberto Callaspo stepped up to the plate, those pitches were clocking in at ninety-four miles per hour, and the atmosphere in the stadium was so turbocharged, the Royals' last batter didn't stand a chance.

And then all hell broke loose as Lester made it happen with his 130th pitch of the night. He struck Callaspo out on a one-two pitch to complete the no-hitter, giving the Sox a 7–0 victory over the Royals. Sox backstop Jason Varitek came running out and lifted Lester off the ground, and a second later both of them were swallowed up in a mob of white jerseys. This was as good as winning the World Series!

With Lester as the reigning hero, the joy was off the charts. Everyone in Fenway Park was celebrating his victory, and I was no exception. After I finished yelling and hugging Werner, I did what everybody in that stadium was doing—I called my sons to tell them the story of what I'd just seen and heard and experienced.

I'd witnessed history being made anew in Fenway Park! *This,* I thought as I felt my heart race, *is the power of a never-ending story.*

aHHa!

- Empower your audience to tell your story forward.
- Create a multiplier effect. Find the core audience who can be apostles for your message and encourage them to tell your story through the power of their own words.

- In the face of adversity, be willing to recast your story through the lens of your listeners' new needs while remaining authentic to your story's core elements.
- Legacy stories are powerful and enduring. Abandon them at your peril.

CHAPTER NINE

The Beginning . . .

L et me take you back to the future of story telling.

When I was in New Guinea back at the beginning of my exploration of telling to win, it struck me that, since most of the tribes there had no written language, not one of their stories was written down. Yet some of those stories had endured for thousands of years! Moreover, the tribal culture depended on their ability to keep the vital details of their myths and legends intact from one generation to the next. How did they do that without the benefit of media like books or recordings?

High up Mount Hagen in the Upper Wahgi Valley, at the annual tribal sing-sing, I got my answer. Like companies at a trade show, hundreds of tribes had sent representatives to exhibit their latest regalia of masks, wigs, and tattoos, and to sing, dance, and tell stories. Clans that had been bent on slaughtering each other just a generation or two ago now demonstrated their prowess and power in mock battles. This, I thought with a laugh, was the Papuan equivalent of my experience at the Allen & Company's annual media mogul conference in Sun Valley, Idaho.

Then, in the midst of all this thumping and spear-rattling, I came upon a group of children listening with rapt attention to a man wearing nothing but a penis gourd. My guide informed me the man was a chief. "He's passing down the story of the rules and values that hold this tribe together."

"I wish I understood their language," I said. "I'd record this."

The guide pointed to a big wooden board standing upright next to the group. "You don't have to. If you offer a trade, the chief will give you that storyboard."

Storyboard? In Hollywood a storyboard is the schematic done in preproduction to visualize and detail the camera angles of scenes in a movie. This graphic map of the screenplay facilitates the story's translation into film. I thought storyboards were invented by the movie business! But these wooden boards, painted with rudimentary graphics describing this tribe's initiation ceremony, looked to predate the movies by centuries.

As I watched, the tribal elder occasionally checked what he was saying against the pictures on the board. Much like a director, he was making sure his version remained consistent with the approved plot! So in both our cultures, it seemed, storyboards addressed the same problem—that stories tend to vary from teller to teller.

Now, variety is a good thing, up to a point. In fact, it's a basic human craving. Anticipation of a new and different telling will arouse the audience's curiosity. However, if a teller changes the story too much, that can jeopardize the core message and intended impact. So the New Guinea tribes invented storyboards to safeguard the flame. This narrative aid reminded the teller of the story's essential elements and meaning so the important stuff didn't get lost through retelling.

In New Guinea as in Hollywood, the storyboards were intended as aids only. These boards *never* were used as replacements for the spoken story, any more than a director's storyboards—or the script, for that matter—replace the director's process of actually shooting the film. That's why the chief was willing to trade me one of his storyboards. In his mind, the true value lay within the story itself, and he carried that inside him.

The chief's Papuan storyboard now occupies a prominent place in my home, and the more deeply I've probed telling to win, the more clearly I've come to see that painted wood as an example of early technology that venerates the art of oral story telling. But if technology can venerate telling to win, could there emerge a technology that will some day replace it?

I posed this question to Bran Ferren when he came to one of my UCLA graduate courses. Ferren, the original magic man behind Disney's Imagineering brain trust, now heads the design and technical innovation company Applied Minds in partnership with mainframe computing pioneer Danny Hillis. Bran not only lives and breathes new media, he understands technology as a natural force throughout human history. Picking up on my description of the native storyboards as original media, Ferren said, "The story telling tradition was invented before we had the technology to record ideas. Then came graphics—pictograms. It took a long time to get to writing, because reading and writing are abstractions, but they were needed to make stories permanent and communicate them in a rich manner to people separated by time and space. Then it took a long time to get through the sequence of technological steps from writing to the book, which was the first distributable media. Today everybody acts like this whole computer revolution thing is gung ho, but just consider how long it took us to invent the book! We're only at the very dawn of the digital era. When it comes to how we'll communicate in the future, we're all dummies just learning to walk. It's far too early to predict exactly where this revolution will lead. However, just as writing did, it's bound to affect every aspect of human endeavor; including the way we tell and receive stories."

I asked Bran for an example of how this might happen.

"We have lots of physics and conceptual technology on the horizon that can communicate directly to a person's brain," he suggested. "Just like acoustic implants for helping people who are deaf, visual implants are now starting to happen. Imagine if I had a direct visual pathway into your visual cortex."

Ferren's suggestion was mind-boggling. Most of us are inspired by a fairly small number of people who are able to touch our hearts, and by extension open our minds, because they're great story tellers. What if those great story tellers could give anyone who clicked on their website the virtual experience not just of being in the same room, but of being fully inside the teller's mind? Could this be where virtual technology is heading? How might this change telling to win? I felt compelled to pursue this idea with other scientists and masters of new media.

In front of an audience of entrepreneurs and new media executives at the 2009 Twiistup digital conference in Los Angeles, I asked Brian Solis, one of the thought leaders who paved the way for social media, what he thought of Cisco's brilliant telepresence technology. "If you've ever sat in a room with telepresence," I said, "we're together virtually without being physically together. It looks and feels like we're in the same room face-to-face, so you're there without having to go there. A grand efficiency! If you're telling your story in telepresence, almost all of the elements of telling to win would be essential and deployable."

Solis is a digital analyst, sociologist, and futurist who now tracks the effects of emerging media on the convergence of marketing, communications, and publishing at BrianSolis.com. He wasn't quite as wowed by this cutting-edge technology as I was. "Telepresence is still missing the critical component that connects the heart and mind," he said. "There's a saying that the physical distance between the heart and mind is nine inches— meaning the two are linked and very close together. Videoconferencing, video on the Web, social media engagement in general are not catalysts for the kind of critical heart-mind energy that humans share when we're in the same room. And it's that immediate energy that tells us whether or not to form an interpersonal connection."

Chris Kemp, chief technology officer at NASA, told me this heartfelt connection depends on infinitesimal gestures and interpersonal nuances, which no current technology can capture or convey. "Low-resolution video hasn't taken off," Kemp said, "because it can't recreate the detailed signals of the eyes, face, smell, and sound. With someone face-to-face, you react in your gut—your enteric nervous system gives you a visceral read on the other person. It's a holdover from our primitive ancestors, who had to size up a stranger instantly to determine whether to trust him, fight him, or flee for their lives. You don't get this response with technology because your body knows you're talking to a screen. The tipping point will be if technology reproduces what it really feels like to interact with people."

Another scientist, Michael Wesch—the Kansas State University cultural anthropologist who's been dubbed "the explainer" by *Wired* magazine—expanded on this innate human response mechanism at an event at my home. Wesch pointed out that we're wired to constantly read one another's "microexpressions"—involuntary facial expressions that can occur as fast as one twenty-fifth of a second. These microscopic expressions signal the seven universal emotions—disgust, anger, fear, sadness, happiness, surprise, and contempt. Because they're encoded in our facial muscles, these signals are very difficult, if not impossible, to fake, and we rely on them heavily in high-stakes situations such as business negotiations.

"Micro-expressions are critical to creating empathy," Wesch said. "That's the way we're wired. The face makes more than four thousand different expressions, and they're subtle but critical because we subconsciously pick up on them and react to them. Both the mind and the heart recognize these signals, but current technology is not yet fully successful in conveying or duplicating them."

I'VE OFTEN HAD TO tell my business stories through Skype, voice mails, e-mails, text messages, blogs, and UPS overnight deck deliveries when I couldn't be in the room and face-to-face with my audience, and I've always found the tools in telling to win to be invaluable, whatever the media. But I know that distance inevitably puts me at a disadvantage. That's why, when it really matters, I walk, drive, or fly, if necessary, to be in the same room with my employees, shareholders, investors, customers, and business partners.

The micro-expressions Wesch described—the pauses, eye contact, body language, and gestures we make while in the room—invariably lose some or all of their impact when told from a distance using current media. While YouTube, for instance, offers the power to be expressive in a way that's not possible merely through text, YouTube still is several steps removed from the immediacy of meeting in person.

You want your audience to *feel* "I want to invest in you. I get your story." How do you make them feel good about you? By tapping into their empathy and engaging their interest. The best possible way to do that is in person.

You might think a champion of online blogging would disagree. So I asked Arianna Huffington for her take on state-of-the-heart versus state-of-the-art story telling. Arianna is cofounder and editor in chief of The Huffington Post, one of the web's most widely read, linked to, and frequently cited media brands. Ironically she doesn't believe online technology will ever replace direct human interaction. "The more time we spend in front of screens," she said when she visited one of my UCLA courses, "the more we crave human contact. I believe that intimate in-person interactions where we tell stories to realize our ambitions, goals, and dreams will only intensify as technology expands." And in business, she predicted, we'll come to rely more, rather than less, on direct human interaction—especially when it comes to gauging a prospective partner, client, or customer's character. "It doesn't mean we must be face-to-face to make all our decisions, but if there's something incredibly important on which everything depends, you always want to be in the room."

Phil McKinney, chief technology officer of Hewlett-Packard, apparently agrees. "Technology still can play only a supporting role," McKinney told me when we spoke together at the San Francisco Supernova conference. He said, "I'm a firm believer that the ability to see and feel the emotional response, to get that feedback mechanism when you're telling the story, is critically important. The technology just isn't there yet to get the same value online as you get in the room face-to-face."

Despite this, Bran Ferren emphatically believes that "the Internet represents the greatest story telling technology since the development of language. It will be far more important than reading and writing as a purposeful tool. Everything that is enabled by story telling will be enabled by the Internet."

I've known for a while that credibility and authenticity, seminal elements of telling to win, can definitely be enhanced through online engagement in the social graph, blogosphere, and message boards. But what I didn't fully realize until recently was how much digital currency we all accrue through the volume of status updates, posts, tweets, links, profiles, blogs, and websites associated with us. The social capital earned online is now migrating into the offline world, affecting how tellers and listeners interact and respond to one another. By quantifying your social capital through tools that measure your influence and connections online, your potential audiences can determine your authenticity before they even meet you. Your listeners may not even know you, but by liking you on Facebook or following you on Twitter, they can feel quite connected to you. On the other hand, if your listeners don't consider you sufficiently influential or connected online, they might doubt your credibility and be less inclined to listen to your story in person.

There are bound to be many more examples of such blurring at the intersection of the real and the virtual. As technology brings us closer together, our online experiences will increasingly impact our offline lives. The best strategy is to be ambidextrous, employing telling to win to live, play, learn, and succeed in both worlds. If history is a trustworthy guide, state-of-the-art technology won't ever replace state-of-the-heart technology. Simply put, telling to win is forever.

aHHa!

- Don't rely solely on sate-of-the-art technologies to connect. It's the state-of-the-*heart* technology that's the game changer when you tell your story in the room, face-to-face.
- Be ambidextrous—emotionally transport your listeners to your goal online and offline through the art of the tell.
- Tell to Win! Use it well. Use it purposefully. Use it to your greatest advantage.

ACKNOWLEDGMENTS

The authorship of this book is the shared inspiration and perspiration of the innumerable talents who told, harvested, shaped, and listened to the narratives that reveal the alchemy of its promise: that a purposeful story, well told, is the greatest tool for your success. To those who suffered through my ruminations and labors, my great gratitude for their talents, time, and energy: Rick Horgan; Aimee Liu; Hilary Tetenbaum; Nicole Young; Steve Hanselman; and of course, my wife, Tara, and our family.

Index

INDEX

INDEX

INDEX